Web Application Development with Yii and PHP

Second Edition

Learn the Yii application development framework by taking a step-by-step approach to building a Web-based project task tracking system from conception through production deployment

Jeffrey Winesett

BIRMINGHAM - MUMBAI

Web Application Development with Yii and PHP

Second Edition

First Edition: August 2010

Second Edition: November 2012

Production Reference: 1121112

Published by Packt Publishing Ltd.
Livery Place
35 Livery Street
Birmingham B3 2PB, UK.

ISBN 978-1-84951-872-7

www.packtpub.com

Cover Image by Asher Wishkerman (wishkerman@hotmail.com)

Credits

Author

Jeffrey Winesett

Reviewers

Wojciech Bancer

Carsten Brandt

Brett Gregson

Stephan Hohmann

Alexander Makarov

Acquisition Editor

Usha Iyer

Lead Technical Editors

Sonali Tharwani

Sweny M. Sukumaran

Technical Editor

Sharvari Baet

Copy Editors

Insiya Morbiwala

Laxmi Subramanian

Brandt D'Mello

Aditya Nair

Project Coordinator

Leena Purkait

Proofreader

Maria Gould

Indexers

Monica Ajmera Mehta

Tejal R. Soni

Rekha Nair

Production Coordinator

Arvindkumar Gupta

Cover Work

Arvindkumar Gupta

About the Author

Jeffrey Winesett has over ten years of experience building large-scale, web-based applications. He has been a strong proponent of using open source development frameworks when developing applications, and a champion of the Yii framework in particular since its initial alpha release. He frequently presents on, writes about, and develops with Yii as often as possible.

I would like to thank Qiang Xue for creating this amazing framework, and the entire Yii framework development team who continually improve and maintain it. I thank all of the technical reviewers, editors, and staff at Packt Publishing for their fantastic contributions, suggestions, and improvements.

I would also like to thank my family, who have provided encouragement and unconditional support, and to my many colleagues over the years for providing invaluable opportunities for me to explore new technologies, expand my knowledge, and shape my career.

About the Reviewers

Wojciech Bancer has a Master's Degree in Computer Science. He has over ten years of experience in web application development. In 2007, after passing the Zend exam, he gained a Zend Certified Engineer for PHP5 certificate. Wojciech started his career developing web applications in PHP4 and PHP5 as a freelancer. Later, he started working for a digital media agency in London, where he was introduced to various PHP frameworks and agile processes. Currently, he is a technical consultant for ORM London working on a range of web, mobile, and touch projects.

> To my wife and son, I wish them the best.

Carsten Brandt has been a freelance PHP developer for many years. He founded his own ISP company providing web development and hosting services in 2007. Together with his wife and little son, he is currently living in Berlin, Germany and studying Computer Science at Technische Universität Berlin.

He first started with Yii in 2010 and has contributed heavily to the yiiext extension repository `http://yiiext.github.com/` since then. After Yii moved to GitHub, he started contributing to the Yii framework code too, and since August 2012 he has been an active member of the Yii framework developer team.

> I would like to thank my beloved wife Mila for letting me do open source work in my free time, and not arguing too much when I stay late for doing work I don't get paid for.
>
> I would also like to thank Qiang Xue for creating this great framework, and Alexander Makarov, Maurizio Domba, and all other contributors for their active and valuable contributions, keeping Yii fast and solid.

Brett Gregson is a PHP/iOS software developer based in South Africa. His main area of expertise is user interface design and user experience. He is a big fan of the Yii framework and jQuery. He currently works at RAW Media Concepts in Johannesburg, South Africa.

Stephan Hohmann, having been raised in the reach of an 8086 IBM PC, had his career choice set in his early ages. After toying around with a plethora of programming languages and operating systems, Stephan has now settled mostly for Fedora Linux and web programming with PHP (for the time being). He is currently involved in making the Yii framework better and creating formidable applications with it.

Alexander Makarov is an experienced engineer from Russia, and a member of the Yii framework core team since 2010. He is the author of another book on the Yii framework called *Yii 1.1 Application Development Cookbook, Packt Publishing*.

Thanks to my family for being patient with me as I took up yet another project and spent less time with them.

Thanks to the Yii community for their encouragement and contributions. It would not have been possible to get free time if we were creating Yii without all these pull-requests at Github. You're the best!

www.PacktPub.com

Support files, eBooks, discount offers and more

You might want to visit www.PacktPub.com for support files and downloads related to your book.

Did you know that Packt offers eBook versions of every book published, with PDF and ePub files available? You can upgrade to the eBook version at www.PacktPub.com and as a print book customer, you are entitled to a discount on the eBook copy. Get in touch with us at service@packtpub.com for more details.

At www.PacktPub.com, you can also read a collection of free technical articles, sign up for a range of free newsletters and receive exclusive discounts and offers on Packt books and eBooks.

http://PacktLib.PacktPub.com

Do you need instant solutions to your IT questions? PacktLib is Packt's online digital book library. Here, you can access, read and search across Packt's entire library of books.

Why Subscribe?

- ▶ Fully searchable across every book published by Packt
- ▶ Copy and paste, print and bookmark content
- ▶ On demand and accessible via web browser

Free Access for Packt account holders

If you have an account with Packt at www.PacktPub.com, you can use this to access PacktLib today and view nine entirely free books. Simply use your login credentials for immediate access.

Table of Contents

Preface

This book is a step-by-step tutorial to developing a real-world application using the Yii web application development framework. The book attempts to mirror the environment of a software development team that is being tasked with building an online application, touching on each aspect of the software development lifecycle, as you build a project task management application from its conception to its production deployment.

After a brief, general introduction to the Yii framework, and going through the iconic "Hello World" example, the remaining chapters break down in the same way as software development iterations do in real-world projects. We begin with creating a working application with a valid, tested connection to a database.

We then move on to defining our main database entities and domain object model, and become familiar with Yii's **Object Relational Mapping (ORM)** layer *Active Record*. We learn how to lean on Yii's code generation tools to automatically build our create/read/update/delete (CRUD) functionality against our newly created models. We also focus on how Yii's form validation and submission model works. By the end of *Chapter 5, Managing Issues*, you will have a working application that allows you to manage the projects and issues (tasks) within those projects.

We then turn to the topic of user management. We learn about the built-in authentication model within Yii to assist with the application login and logout functionality. We take a deep dive into the authorization model, first taking advantage of Yii's simple access control model and then implementing the more sophisticated, **role-based access control (RBAC)** framework that Yii provides.

By the end of *Chapter 7, User Access Control,* all of the basics of a task-management application are in place. The next several chapters begin to focus on additional user features, user experience, and design. We add user comment functionality, introducing a reusable, content portlet architecture approach in the process. We add in an RSS web feed and demonstrate how easy it is to integrate other third-party tools and frameworks within a Yii application. We take advantage of Yii's theming structure to help streamline and design the application, and then introduce Yii's internationalization (I18N) features so that the application can be adapted to various languages and regions without engineering changes.

In the final chapter, we turn our focus to preparing the application for production deployment. We introduce ways to optimize performance and improve security, to prepare the application for a production environment.

What this book covers

Chapter 1, Meet Yii, provides you with a brief history of Yii, an introduction to the **Model View Controller** (**MVC**) application architecture, and you are introduced to the typical request life cycle as it makes its way from the end user through the application, and finally as a response back to the end user.

Chapter 2, Getting Started, is dedicated to downloading and installing the framework, creating a new Yii application shell, and introducing Gii, Yii's powerful and flexible code generation tool.

Chapter 3, The TrackStar Application, is where the TrackStar application is introduced. This is an online, project-management and issue-tracking application that you will be building throughout the remaining chapters. Here you learn how to connect a Yii application to an underlying database. You also learn how to run the interactive shell from the command line. The last part of this chapter is focused on providing an overview of unit and functional testing within a Yii application, and provides a concrete example of writing a unit test in Yii.

Chapter 4, Project CRUD, helps you to start interacting with the database, to begin adding features to the database-driven Yii application TrackStar. You learn how to use Yii Migrations for database change management, and we use the Gii tool to create model classes and also to build out create, read, update, and delete (CRUD) functionality using the model class. The reader is also introduced to configuring and performing form field validation in this chapter.

Chapter 5, Managing Issues, explains how additional related database tables are added to the TrackStar application, and how the reader is introduced to the relational Active Record in Yii. This chapter also covers using controller filters to tap into the application life cycle in order to provide pre-action and post-action processing. The official Yii extension library Zii is introduced, and we use Zii widgets to enhance the TrackStar application.

Chapter 6, User Management and Authentication, explains how to authenticate users in a Yii. While adding the ability to manage users in the TrackStar application, the reader learns to take advantage of *Behaviors* in Yii, which provide an extremely flexible approach to sharing common code and functionality across your Yii components. This chapter also covers the Yii authentication model in detail.

Chapter 7, User Access Control, is dedicated to Yii's authorization model. First we cover the simple access control features, which allow you to easily configure access rules for the controller actions that are based on several parameters. Then we look at how role-based access control (RBAC) is implemented in Yii, which allows a much more robust authorization model for complete access control based on hierarchical model of roles, operations, and tasks. Implementing role-based access control into the TrackStar application also introduced the reader to using the console command in Yii.

Chapter 8, Adding User Comments, helps demonstrate how to implement the feature for allowing users to leave comments on projects and issues in the TrackStar application; we introduce how to configure and use a statistical query relation, how to create highly reusable user interface components called *Widgets*, and how to define and use named scopes in Yii.

Chapter 9, Adding an RSS Web Feed, demonstrates how easy it is to use other third-party frameworks and libraries in Yii applications, and shows you how to use the URL management features of Yii to customize your applications' URL format and structure.

Chapter 10, Making It Look Good, helps you learn more about the views in Yii, and how to use layouts to manage markup and content shared across your application pages. *Theming* is also introduced, as we show how easy it is to give a Yii application a completely new look without having to alter any of the underlying engineering. We then take a look at internationalization (i18n) and localization (l10n) in Yii as language translation is added to our TrackStar application.

Chapter 11, Using Yii Modules, explains how to add administrative features to the TrackStar site by using a Yii module. Modules provide a very flexible approach to developing and managing the larger, self-contained sections of your application.

Chapter 12, Production Readiness, helps us prepare our TrackStar application for production. You learn about Yii's logging framework, caching techniques, and error-handling methods to help get your Yii applications production-ready.

What you need for this book

The following software are required for this book:

- Yii framework Version 1.1.12
- PHP 5.1 or above (5.3 or 5.4 recommended)
- MySQL 5.1 or above
- A web server capable of running PHP 5.1; the examples provided in the book were built and tested with the Apache HTTP server, on which Yii has been thoroughly tested within both Windows and Linux environments
- Zend Framework Version 1.1.12 or above (only needed for *Chapter 9, Adding an RSS Web Feed,* and the downloading and configuration of this library, which is covered in this chapter)

Who this book is for

If you are a PHP programmer with a knowledge of object-oriented programming and want to rapidly develop modern, sophisticated web applications, then this book is for you. No prior knowledge of Yii is required to read this book.

Conventions

In this book, you will find a number of styles of text that distinguish between different kinds of information. Here are some examples of these styles, and an explanation of their meaning.

Code words in text are shown as follows: "We can include other contexts through the use of the `include` directive."

A block of code is set as follows:

```
'components'=>array(
'db'=>array(
    'connectionString' => 'mysql:host=localhost;dbname=trackstar',
    'emulatePrepare' => true,
    'username' => '[YOUR-USERNAME]',
    'password' => '[YOUR-PASSWORD]',
    'charset' => 'utf8',
  ),
),
```

When we wish to draw your attention to a particular part of a code block, the relevant lines or items are set in bold:

```
'components'=>array(
'db'=>array(
    'connectionString' => 'mysql:host=localhost;dbname=trackstar',
    'emulatePrepare' => true,
    'username' => '[YOUR-USERNAME]',
    'password' => '[YOUR-PASSWORD]',
    'charset' => 'utf8',
  ),
),
```

Any command-line input or output is written as follows:

```
$ yiic migrate create <name>
%cd /WebRoot/trackstar/protected/tests
```

New terms and **important words** are shown in bold. Words that you see on the screen, in menus or dialog boxes for example, appear in the text like this: "clicking the **Next** button moves you to the next screen".

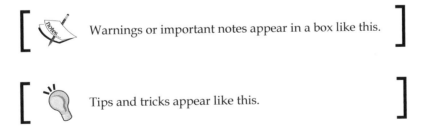

Warnings or important notes appear in a box like this.

Tips and tricks appear like this.

Reader feedback

Feedback from our readers is always welcome. Let us know what you think about this book—what you liked or may have disliked. Reader feedback is important for us to develop titles that you really get the most out of.

To send us general feedback, simply send an e-mail to feedback@packtpub.com, and mention the book title via the subject of your message.

If there is a topic that you have expertise in and you are interested in either writing or contributing to a book, see our author guide on www.packtpub.com/authors.

Customer support

Now that you are the proud owner of a Packt book, we have a number of things to help you to get the most from your purchase.

Downloading the example code

You can download the example code files for all Packt books you have purchased from your account at http://www.PacktPub.com. If you purchased this book elsewhere, you can visit http://www.PacktPub.com/support and register to have the files e-mailed directly to you.

Errata

Although we have taken every care to ensure the accuracy of our content, mistakes do happen. If you find a mistake in one of our books—maybe a mistake in the text or the code—we would be grateful if you would report this to us. By doing so, you can save other readers from frustration and help us improve subsequent versions of this book. If you find any errata, please report them by visiting http://www.packtpub.com/support, selecting your book, clicking on the **errata submission form** link, and entering the details of your errata. Once your errata are verified, your submission will be accepted and the errata will be uploaded on our website, or added to any list of existing errata, under the Errata section of that title. Any existing errata can be viewed by selecting your title from http://www.packtpub.com/support.

Piracy

Piracy of copyright material on the Internet is an ongoing problem across all media. At Packt, we take the protection of our copyright and licenses very seriously. If you come across any illegal copies of our works, in any form, on the Internet, please provide us with the location address or website name immediately so that we can pursue a remedy.

Please contact us at copyright@packtpub.com with a link to the suspected pirated material.

We appreciate your help in protecting our authors, and our ability to bring you valuable content.

Questions

You can contact us at questions@packtpub.com if you are having a problem with any aspect of the book, and we will do our best to address it.

1
Meet Yii

Web development frameworks help jump-start your application by immediately delivering the core foundation and plumbing needed to quickly turn your ideas scribbled on the whiteboard into functional, production-ready code. With all of the common features expected from web applications today, and available framework options that meet these expectations, there is little reason to code your next web application from scratch. A modern, flexible, and extensible framework is almost as essential a tool to today's web developer as the programming language itself. And when the two are particularly complementary, the results are an extremely powerful toolkit—Java and Spring, Ruby and Rails, C# and .NET, and PHP and Yii.

Yii is the brainchild of founder Qiang Xue, who started the development of this open source framework on January 1, 2008. Qiang had previously developed and maintained the PRADO framework for many years prior to starting this. The years of experience and user feedback cultivated from the PRADO project solidified the need for a much easier, more extensible, and more efficient PHP5-based framework, to meet the ever-growing needs of application developers. The initial alpha version of Yii was officially released to meet these needs in October of 2008. Its extremely impressive performance metrics when compared to other PHP-based frameworks immediately drew very positive attention. On December 3, 2008, Yii 1.0 was officially released, and as of Oct 1, 2012, the latest production-ready version is up to 1.1.12. It has a growing development team and continues to gain in popularity among PHP developers everyday.

The name **Yii** is an acronym for **Yes, it is**, and is pronounced as *Yee* or (*ji:*). Yii is a high-performance, component-based, web application framework written in PHP5. The name is also representative of the adjectives most used to describe it, such as easy, efficient, and extensible. Let's take a quick look at each of these characteristics of Yii, turn by turn.

Easy

To run a Yii version 1.x-powered web application, all you need are the core framework files and a web server supporting PHP 5.1.0 or higher. To develop with Yii, you only need to know PHP and object-oriented programming. You are not required to learn any new configuration or templating language. Building a Yii application mainly involves writing and maintaining your own custom PHP classes, some of which will extend from the core, Yii framework component classes.

Yii incorporates many of the great ideas and work from other well-known web programming frameworks and applications. So if you are coming to Yii from using other web development frameworks, it is likely that you will find it familiar and easy to navigate.

Yii also embraces a *convention over configuration* philosophy, which contributes to its ease of use. This means that Yii has sensible defaults for almost all the aspects that are used for configuring your application. Following the prescribed conventions, you can write less code and spend less time developing your application. However, Yii does not force your hand. It allows you to customize all of its defaults and makes it easy to override all of these conventions. We will be covering some of these defaults and conventions later in this chapter and throughout the book.

Efficient

Yii is a high-performance, component-based framework that can be used for developing web applications on any scale. It encourages maximum code reuse in web programming and can significantly accelerate the development process. As mentioned previously, if you stick with Yii's built-in conventions, you can get your application up and running with little or no manual configuration.

Yii is also designed to help you with *DRY* development. **DRY** stands for **Don't Repeat Yourself**, a key concept of agile application development. All Yii applications are built using the **Model-View-Controller (MVC)** architecture. Yii enforces this development pattern by providing a place to keep each piece of your MVC code. This minimizes duplication and helps promote code reuse and ease of maintainability. The less code you need to write, the less time it takes to get your application to market. The easier it is to maintain your application, the longer it will stay on the market.

Of course, the framework is not just efficient to use, it is remarkably fast and performance optimized. Yii has been developed with performance optimization in mind from the very beginning, and the result is one of the most efficient PHP frameworks around. So any additional overhead that Yii adds to applications written on top of it is extremely negligible.

Extensible

Yii has been carefully designed to allow nearly every piece of its code to be extended and customized to meet any project requirement. In fact, it is difficult not to take advantage of Yii's ease of extensibility, since a primary activity when developing a Yii application is extending the core framework classes. And if you want to turn your extended code into useful tools for other developers, Yii provides easy-to-follow steps and guidelines to help you create such third-party extensions. This allows you to contribute to Yii's ever-growing list of features and actively participate in extending Yii itself.

Remarkably, this ease-of-use, superior performance, and depth of extensibility does not come at the cost of sacrificing its features. Yii is packed with features to help you meet those high demands placed on today's web applications. AJAX-enabled widgets, RESTful and SOAP Web services integration, enforcement of an MVC architecture, DAO and relational ActiveRecord database layer, sophisticated caching, hierarchical role-based access control, theming, internationalization (I18N), and localization (L10N) are just the tip of the Yii iceberg. As of version 1.1, the core framework is now packaged with an official extension library called *Zii*. These extensions are developed and maintained by the core framework team members, and continue to extend Yii's core feature set. And with a deep community of users who are also contributing by writing Yii extensions, the overall feature set available to a Yii-powered application is growing daily. A list of available, user-contributed extensions on the Yii framework website can be found at `http://www.yiiframework.com/extensions`. There is also an *unofficial* extension repository of great extensions that can be found at `http://yiiext.github.com/`, which really demonstrates the strength of the community and the extensibility of this framework.

MVC architecture

As mentioned earlier, Yii is an MVC framework and provides an explicit directory structure for each piece of model, view, and controller code. Before we get started with building our first Yii application, we need to define a few key terms and look at how Yii implements and enforces this MVC architecture.

Model

Typically in an MVC architecture, the *model* is responsible for maintaining the state, and should encapsulate the business rules that apply to the data that defines this state. A model in Yii is any instance of the framework class CModel or its child class. A model class is typically comprised of data attributes that can have separate labels (something user friendly for the purpose of display), and can be validated against a set of rules defined in the model. The data that makes up the attributes in the model class could come from a row of a database table or from the fields in a user input form.

Yii implements two kinds of models, namely the form model (a CFormModel class) and active record (a CActiveRecord class). They both extend from the same base class CModel. The class CFormModel represents a data model that collects HTML form inputs. It encapsulates all the logic for form field validation, and any other business logic that may need to be applied to the form field data. It can then store this data in memory or, with the help of an active record model, store data in a database.

Active Record (AR) is a design pattern used to abstract database access in an object-oriented fashion. Each AR object in Yii is an instance of CActiveRecord or its child class, which wraps a single row in a database table or view, that encapsulates all the logic and details around database access, and houses much of the business logic that is required to be applied to that data. The data field values for each column in the table row are represented as properties of the active record object. Active Record is described in more detail a little later.

View

Typically the *view* is responsible for rendering the user interface, often based on the data in the model. A view in Yii is a PHP script that contains user interface-related elements, often built using HTML, but can also contain PHP statements. Usually, any PHP statements within the view are very simple, conditional or looping statements, or refer to other Yii UI-related elements such as HTML helper class methods or prebuilt widgets. More sophisticated logic should be separated from the view and placed appropriately in either the model, if dealing directly with the data, or the controller, for more general business logic.

Controller

The *controller* is our main director of a routed request, and is responsible for taking user input, interacting with the model, and instructing the view to update and display appropriately. A controller in Yii is an instance of CController or a child class thereof. When a controller runs, it performs the requested action, which then interacts with the necessary models, and renders an appropriate view. An action, in its simplest form, is a controller class method whose name starts with the word *action*.

Stitching these together: Yii request routing

In MVC implementations, a web request typically has the following life cycle:

- The browser sends a request to the server hosting the MVC application
- A controller action is invoked to handle the request
- The controller interacts with the model
- The controller invokes the view
- The view renders the data (often as HTML) and returns it to the browser for display

Yii's MVC implementation is no exception. In a Yii application, incoming requests from the browser are first received by a router. The router analyzes the request to decide where in the application it should be sent for further processing. In most cases, the router identifies a specific action method within a controller class to which the request is passed. This action method will look at the incoming request data, possibly interact with the model, and perform other needed business logic. Eventually, this action method will prepare the response data and send it to the view. The view will then format this data to conform to the desired layout and design, and return it for the browser to display.

Blog posting example

To help all of this make more sense, let's look at a fictitious example. Let's pretend that we have used Yii to build ourselves a new blog site http://yourblog.com. This site is like most typical blog sites out there. The home page displays a list of recently posted blog posts. The names of each of these blog postings are hyperlinks that take the user to the page that displays the full article. The following diagram illustrates how Yii handles an incoming request sent from clicking on one of these hypothetical blog post links:

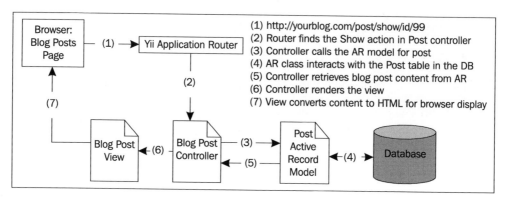

The figure traces the request that is made from a user clicking on the link:

http://yourblog.com/post/show/id/99

First the request is sent to the router. The router parses the request, to decide where to send it. The structure of the URL is key to the decision that the router will make. By default, Yii recognizes URLs with the following format:

http://hostname/index.php?r=ControllerID/ActionID

The r querystring variable refers to the route that is analyzed by the Yii router. It will parse this route to determine the appropriate controller and action method, to further handle the request. Now you may have immediately noticed that our example URL above does not follow this default format. It is a very simple matter of configuring the application to recognize the URLs in the following format:

http://hostname/ControllerID/ActionID

We will continue to use this simplified format for the purposes of this example. The `ControllerID` name in the URL refers to the name of the controller. By default this is the first part of the controller class name, up to the word `Controller`. So for example, if your controller class name is `TestController`, the `ControllerID` name would be *test*. `ActionID` similarly refers to the name of the action that is defined by the controller. If the action is a simple method defined within the controller, this will be whatever follows the word `action` in the method name. For example, if your action method is named `actionCreate()`, the `ActionID` name is `create`.

> If the `ActionID` is omitted, the controller will take the default action, which by convention is a method in the controller called `actionIndex()`. If the `ControllerID` is also omitted, the application will use the default controller. The Yii default controller is called `SiteController`.

Turning back to the example, the router will analyze the URL, `http://yourblog.com/post/show/id/99`, and take the first part of the URL path `post` to be the `ControllerID` and the second part `show` to be the `ActionID`. This will translate to routing the request to the `actionShow()` method within the `PostController` class. The last part of the URL, the `id/99` part, is a *name/value* querystring parameter that will be available to the method during processing. In this example, the number `99` represents the unique internal ID for the selected blog post.

In our fictitious blog application, the `actionShow()` method handles requests for specific blog post entries. It uses the querystring variable `id` to determine which specific post is being requested. It asks the model to retrieve information about blog post entry number 99. The model AR class interacts with the database to retrieve the requested data. After retrieving the data from the model, our controller further prepares it for display by making it available to the view. The view is then responsible for handling the data layout and providing a response back to the browser for user display.

This MVC architecture allows us to separate our data presentation from our data manipulation, validation, and other application business logic. This makes it very easy for developers to change aspects of the application without affecting the UI, and for UI designers to freely make changes without affecting the model or business logic. This separation also makes it very easy to provide multiple presentations of the same model code. For example, you could use the same model code that drives the HTML layout of `http://yourblog.com` to drive an RIA presentation, a mobile application, web services, or a command-line interface. In the end, following these set conventions and separating the functionality will result in an application that is much easier to extend and maintain.

Yii does a lot more to help you enforce this separation, than simply providing some naming conventions and suggestions for where your code should be placed. It helps to take care of all the lower-level, "glue" code needed to stitch all the pieces together. This allows you to reap the benefits of a strict MVC designed application without having to spend all the time in coding the details yourself. Let's take a look at some of these lower-level details.

Object-relational mapping and Active Record

For the most part, the web applications we build house their data in a relational database. The blog posting application we used in the previous example holds blog post content in database tables. However, web applications need the data that is held in the persistent database storage to be mapped to in-memory class properties that define the domain objects. **Object-relational mapping (ORM)** libraries provide this mapping of database tables to domain object classes.

Much of the code that deals with ORM is about describing how fields in the database correspond to properties in our in-memory objects, and is tedious and repetitive to write. Luckily, Yii comes to the rescue and saves us from this repetition and tedium by providing an ORM layer in the form of the Active Record (AR) pattern.

Active Record

As previously mentioned, AR is a design pattern used to abstract database access in an object-oriented fashion. It maps tables to classes, rows to objects, and columns to class properties. In other words, each instance of an Active Record class represents a single row in a database table. However, an AR class is more than just a set of attributes that are mapped to columns in a database table. It also houses the necessary business logic to be applied to that data. The end result is a class that defines everything about how it should be written to and read from the database.

By relying on convention and sticking with reasonable defaults, Yii's implementation of AR will save the developer a ton of time that might otherwise be spent in configuration, or in writing the tedious and repetitive SQL statements required to create, read, update, and delete data. It also allows the developer to access data stored in the database in an object-oriented manner. To illustrate this, let's take our fictitious blog example once again. The following is some example code that uses AR to operate on a specific blog posting, whose internal ID, which is also used as the table's primary key, is 99. It first retrieves the posting by using the primary key. It then changes the title and updates the database to save the changes:

```
$post=Post::model()->findByPk(99);
$post->title='Some new title';
$post->save();
```

Active Record completely relieves us of the tedium of having to write any SQL code or to otherwise deal with the underlying database.

In fact, active record in Yii does even more than this. It integrates seamlessly with many other aspects of the Yii framework. There are many "active" HTML helper input form fields that tie directly to their respective AR class attributes. In this way, AR extracts the input form field values directly into the model. It also supports sophisticated, automated data validation, and if the validation fails, the Yii view classes easily display the validation errors to the end user. We will be revisiting AR and providing concrete examples many times throughout this book.

The view and controller

The view and the controller are very close cousins. The controller makes available the data for display to the view, and the view generates pages that trigger events that send data to the controller.

In Yii, a view file belongs to the controller class that rendered it. In this way, we can access the controller instance by simply referring to $this inside a view script. This implementation makes the view and controller very intimate indeed.

When it comes to Yii controllers, there is a lot more to the story than just calling the model and rendering views. Controllers can manage services to provide sophisticated pre and postprocessing on requests, implement basic access control rules to limit access to certain actions, manage application-wide layout and nested layout file rendering, manage pagination of data, and many other behind-the-scenes services. Again, we have Yii to thank for not having to get our hands dirty with these messy details.

There is a lot to Yii. The best way to explore all its beauty is to start using it. Now that we have some of the very basic ideas and terminology under our belt, we are in a great position to do just that.

Summary

In this chapter, we were introduced at a very high-level to the Yii PHP Web application framework. We also covered a number of software design concepts embraced by Yii. Don't worry if the abstract nature of this initial discussion was a tad lost on you. It will all make sense once we dive into specific examples. But to recap, we specifically covered:

- The importance and utility of application development frameworks
- What Yii is and the characteristics of Yii that make it incredibly powerful and useful
- MVC application architecture and the implementation of this architecture in Yii
- A typical Yii web request life cycle and URL structure
- Object-relational mapping and Active Record in Yii

In the next chapter, we will go through the simple Yii installation process and start building a working application to better illustrate all of these ideas.

2
Getting Started

The real pleasures and benefits of Yii are quickly revealed simply by using it. In this chapter, we will see how the concepts introduced in the previous chapter are manifested in an example Yii application. In the spirit of Yii's philosophy of convention over configuration, we will follow a standard convention and begin by writing a "Hello, World!" program in Yii.

In this chapter we will cover:

- Yii framework installation
- Creating a new application
- Creating controllers and views
- Adding dynamic content to view files
- Yii request routing and linking pages together

Our first step is to install the framework. Let's do that now.

Installing Yii

Prior to installing Yii, you must configure your application development environment as a web server capable of supporting PHP 5.1.0 or above. Yii has been thoroughly tested with the Apache HTTP server on Windows and Linux operating systems. It may also run on other web servers and platforms that support PHP 5. We assume that the reader has previously engaged in PHP development, and has access to or otherwise has knowledge of how to set up such an environment. We will leave the installation of a web server and PHP itself, as an exercise to the reader.

Some popular installation packages include:
- `http://www.apachefriends.org/en/xampp.html`
- `http://www.mamp.info/en/index.html (mac only)`

The basic Yii installation is almost trivial. There are really only two necessary steps:

1. Download the Yii framework from `http://www.yiiframework.com/download/`.

2. Unpack the downloaded file to a web-accessible directory. There are several versions of Yii to choose from when downloading the framework. We will be using version 1.1.12 for the purpose of this book, which is the latest stable version as of the time of writing. Though most of the example code should work with any 1.1.x version of Yii, there may be some subtle differences if you are using a different version. Please attempt to use 1.1.12 if you are following along with the examples.

After you have downloaded the framework files and unpacked them in a web-accessible directory, list the contents. You should see the following high-level directories and files:

- CHANGELOG
- LICENSE
- README
- UPGRADE
- demos/
- framework/
- requirements/

Now that we have our framework unpacked in a web-accessible directory, it is advised that you verify that your server satisfies all of the requirements of using Yii, to ensure that the installation was a success. Luckily, doing so is very easy. Yii comes with a simple requirements checking tool. To use the tool and have it verify the requirements for your installation, simply point your browser to the `index.php` entry script under the `requirements/` directory that came with the downloaded files. For example, assuming that the name of the directory containing all of the framework files is simply called `yii`, the URL to access the requirements checker might look like:

`http://localhost/yii/requirements/index.php`

The following screenshot shows the results that we see for our configuration:

Yii Requirement Checker

Description

This script checks if your server configuration meets the requirements for running Yii Web applications. It checks if the server is running the right version of PHP, if appropriate PHP extensions have been loaded, and if php.ini file settings are correct.

Conclusion

Your server configuration satisfies the minimum requirements by Yii. Please pay attention to the warnings listed below if your application will use the corresponding features.

Details

Name	Result	Required By	Memo
PHP version	Passed	Yii Framework	PHP 5.1.0 or higher is required.
$_SERVER variable	Passed	Yii Framework	
Reflection extension	Passed	Yii Framework	
PCRE extension	Passed	Yii Framework	
SPL extension	Passed	Yii Framework	
DOM extension	Passed	CWsdlGenerator	
PDO extension	Passed	All DB-related classes	
PDO SQLite extension	Warning	All DB-related classes	This is required if you are using SQLite database.
PDO MySQL extension	Passed	All DB-related classes	This is required if you are using MySQL database.
PDO PostgreSQL extension	Warning	All DB-related classes	This is required if you are using PostgreSQL database.
Memcache extension	Warning	CMemCache	
APC extension	Passed	CApcCache	
Mcrypt extension	Passed	CSecurityManager	This is required by encrypt and decrypt methods.
SOAP extension	Passed	CWebService, CWebServiceAction	
GD extension	Passed	CCaptchaAction	

☐ passed ☐ failed ☐ warning

Using the requirements checker is not, in itself, a requirement for installation. But it is certainly recommended to ensure proper installation. As you can see, not all of our results under the details section received a **Passed** status, as some display a **Warning** result. Of course, your configuration will most likely be slightly different from ours, and consequently your results may be slightly different as well. That is okay. It is not necessary that all of the checks under the **Details** section pass, but it is necessary to receive the following message under the **Conclusion** section: **Your server configuration satisfies the minimum requirements by Yii**.

The Yii framework files do not need to be, and it is recommended they not be, placed in a publicly accessible web directory. We did this here simply to quickly take advantage of the requirements checker in our browser. A Yii application has a one entry script, which is usually the only file that needs to be placed in the webroot (by webroot, we mean the directory containing the index.php entry script). Other PHP scripts, including all of the Yii framework files, should be protected from outside user access to avoid security issues. Simply reference the directory containing the Yii framework files in the entry script and place these files outside of the webroot.

Installing a database

Throughout this book, we will be using a database to support many of our examples and the application that we will be writing. In order to properly follow along with this book, it is recommended you install a database server. Though you can use any database that is supported by PHP with Yii, if you want to use some of the built-in database abstraction layers and tools within Yii, as we will be using, you will need to use one that is supported by the framework. As of version 1.1 those are:

- MySQL 4.1 or later
- PostgresSQL 7.3 or later
- SQLite 2 and 3
- Microsoft SQL Server 2000 or later
- Oracle

While you may follow along with all of the examples in this book by using any of the supported database servers, we will be using MySQL (5.1 to be more specific) as our database server throughout all the examples. It is recommended that you also use MySQL, version 5 or greater, to ensure that the examples provided work without having to make adjustments. We won't need a database for our simple "Hello, World!" application seen in this chapter.

Now that we have installed the framework and have verified that we have met the minimum requirements, let's move on to creating a brand new Yii web application.

Creating a new application

To create a new application, we are going to use a little powerhouse of a tool that comes packaged with the framework, called *yiic*. This is a command-line tool that you can use to quickly bootstrap a brand new Yii application. It is not mandatory to use this tool, but it saves time and guarantees that a proper directory and file structure is in place for the application.

To use this tool, open up your command line, and navigate to a place in your filesystem where you will want to create your application's directory structure. For the purpose of this demo application, we will assume the following:

- YiiRoot is the name of the directory where you have installed the Yii framework files
- WebRoot is configured as a document root of your web server

From your command line, change to your WebRoot directory and execute the yiic command:

```
% cd WebRoot
% YiiRoot/framework/yiic webapp helloworld

    Create a Web application under '/Webroot/helloworld'? [Yes|No]
    Yes
          mkdir /WebRoot/helloworld
          mkdir /WebRoot/helloworld/assets
          mkdir /WebRoot/helloworld/css
       generate css/bg.gif
       generate css/form.css
       generate css/main.css


    Your application has been created successfully under /Webroot/
    helloworld.
```

The yiic command may not work for you as expected, especially if you are attempting to use it in a Windows environment. The yiic file is an executable that runs using your command-line version of PHP. It invokes the yiic.php script. You may need to fully qualify by using php in front, as in $ php yiic or $ php yiic.php. You may also need to specify the PHP executable to be used, such as C:\PHP5\php.exe yiic.php. There is also the yiic.bat file, which executes the yiic.php file, that may be more suitable for Windows users. You may need to ensure that your PHP executable location is accessible in your %PATH% variable. Please try these variations to find a suitable solution for your computer configuration. I will continue to simply refer to this command as yiic.

The `yiic webapp` command is used to create a brand new Yii web application. It takes just a single argument to specify either the absolute or relative path to the directory in which the application should be created. The result is the generation of all the necessary directories and files that are used to provide a skeleton of the default Yii web application.

Let's list the contents of our new application to see what was created for us:

```
assets/     images/     index.php   themes/
css/        index-test.php   protected/
```

The following is a description of these high-level items that were automatically created:

- `index.php`: Web application entry script file
- `index-test.php`: Entry script file for loading a test configuration
- `assets/`: Contains published resource files
- `css/`: Contains CSS files
- `images/`: Contains image files
- `themes/`: Contains application themes
- `protected/`: Contains protected (non-public) application files

With the execution of one simple command from the command line, we have created all the directory structure and files needed to immediately take advantage of Yii's sensible default configuration. All of these directories and files, along with the subdirectories and files that they contain, can look a little daunting at first glance. However, we can ignore most of them as we are getting started. What is important to note is that all of these directories and files are actually a working web application. The `yiic` command has populated the application with enough code to establish a simple home page, a typical contact-us page to provide an example of a web form, and a login page to demonstrate basic authorization and authentication in Yii. If your web server supports the GD2 graphics library extension, you will also see a CAPTCHA widget on the contact-us form, and the application will have the corresponding validation for this form field.

As long as your web server is running, you should be able to open up your browser and navigate to `http://localhost/helloworld/index.php`. Here you will be presented with a **My Web Application** home page along with the friendly greeting **Welcome To My Web Application**, followed by some helpful next steps information. The following screenshot shows this example home page:

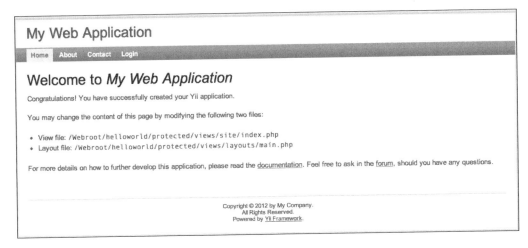

 You will need to ensure that both the `assets/` and `protected/` `runtime/` directories are writable by your web server process, otherwise you may see an error rather than the working application.

You'll notice that there is a working application navigation bar along the top of the page. From left to right there is **Home**, **About**, **Contact**, and **Login**. Click around and explore. Clicking on the **About** link provides a simple example of a static page. The **Contact** link will take you to the contact us form that was mentioned before, along with the CAPTCHA input field in the form. (Again, you will only see the CAPTCHA field if you have the gd graphics extension as part of your PHP configuration.)

The **Login** link will take you to a page displaying a login form. This is working code with form validations, as well as username and password credential validation and authentication. Using either *demo/demo* or *admin/admin* as the username/password combination will get you logged onto the site. Try it out! You can try a login that will fail (any combination other than demo/demo or admin/admin) and see the error validation messages get displayed. After successfully logging in, the **Login** link in the header changes to a **Logout** link (username), where the username is either demo or admin depending on the username that you used to log in. It is amazing that so much has been accomplished without having to do any coding.

"Hello, World!"

All of this generated code will start to make more sense once we walk through a simple example. To try out this new system, let's build that "Hello, World!" program we promised at the start of this chapter. A "Hello, World!" program in Yii will be a simple web page application that sends this very important message to our browser.

As discussed in *Chapter 1, Meet Yii*, Yii is a Model-View-Controller framework. A typical Yii web application takes in an incoming request from a user, processes information in that request in order to create a controller, and then calls an action within that controller. The controller can then invoke a particular view to render and return a response to the user. If dealing with data, the controller may also interact with a model to handle all the **CRUD (Create, Read, Update, Delete)** operations on that data. In our simple "Hello, World!" application, all we will require is the code for a controller and a view. We are not dealing with any data, so a model will not be needed. Let's begin our example by creating our controller.

Creating the controller

Previously, we used the `yiic webapp` command to help us generate a new Yii web application. To create a new controller for our "Hello, World!" application, we'll use another utility tool provided by Yii. This tool is called Gii. **Gii** is a highly customizable and extensible, web-based, code-generating platform.

Configuring Gii

Before we can use Gii, we have to configure it within our application. We do this in our main application configuration file located at `protected/config/main.php`. To configure Gii, open up this file and uncomment the `gii` module. Our autogenerated code already added the `gii` configuration, but it is commented out. So all we need to do is uncomment and then also add our own password, as shown in the following snippet:

```
return array(
  'basePath'=>dirname(__FILE__).DIRECTORY_SEPARATOR.'..',
  'name'=>'My Web Application',

  // preloading 'log' component
  'preload'=>array('log'),

  // autoloading model and component classes
  'import'=>array(
    'application.models.*',
    'application.components.*',
```

```
        ),

    'modules'=>array(
                // uncomment the following to enable the Gii tool
                /*
                'gii'=>array(
                        'class'=>'system.gii.GiiModule',
                        'password'=>'Enter Your Password Here',
                        // If removed, Gii defaults to localhost only.
    Edit carefully to taste.
                        'ipFilters'=>array('127.0.0.1','::1'),
                ),
                */
        ),
```

Once uncommented, Gii is configured as an application module. We will cover Yii *modules* in detail, later in the book. The important thing at this point is to make sure this is added to the configuration file and that you provide your password. With this in place, navigate to the tool via `http://localhost/helloworld/index.php?r=gii`.

> Actually, you can specify the password value as `false` then the module will not require a password. Since the ipFilters property is specified to only allow access to the localhost machine, it is safe to set the password to `false` for you local development environment.

Okay, after a successful entry of your password (unless you specified that a password should not be used), you are presented with the menu page listing Gii's main features:

Gii has several code generation options listed in the left-hand side menu. We want to create a new controller, so click on the **Controller Generator** menu item.

Doing so will bring us to a form that allows us to fill out the relevant details to create a new Yii controller class. In the following screenshot, we have already filled out the **Controller ID** value to be message, and we have added an **Action ID** value that we are calling hello. The following screenshot also reflects that we have clicked on the **Preview** button. This is showing us all of the files that will be generated along with our controller class:

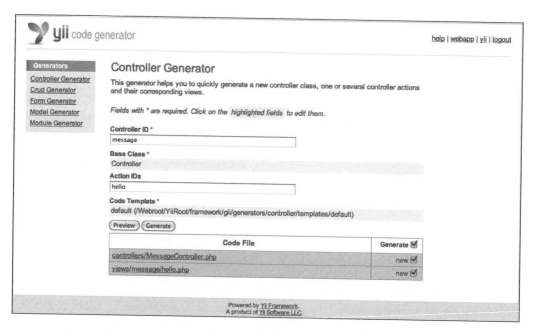

We can see that in addition to our MessageController class, Gii is also going to create a view file for each of the Action IDs that we specified. You may recall from *Chapter 1, Meet Yii*, that if message is the **Controller ID**, our corresponding class file is named MessageController. Similarly if we provide an **Action ID** value of hello, we would expect there to be a method name in the controller called actionHello.

You can also click on the links provided in the **Preview** option to see the code that will be generated for each file. Go ahead and check them out. Once you are happy with what is going to be generated, go ahead and click on the **Generate** button. You should receive a message telling you that the controller was successfully created, with a link to try it now. If instead you received an error message, make sure that the controllers/ and views/ directories are writable by your web server process.

Clicking on the **try it now** link will actually take us to a *404 page not found* error page. The reason for this is that we did not specify the default actionID index when we created our new controller. We decided to call ours hello instead. All we need to do in order to make the request route to our actionHello() method is to add the actionID to the URL. This is shown in the following screenshot:

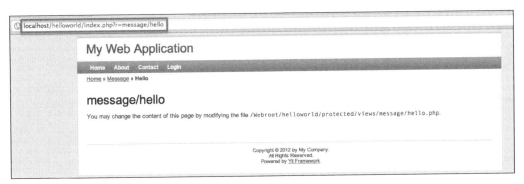

Now we have it displaying the result of calling the MessageController::actionHello() method.

This is great. With a little help from Gii, we have generated a new controller PHP file called MessageController.php, and it was placed properly under the default controllers' directory protected/controllers/. The generated MessageController class extends an application base class Controller located at protected/components/Controller.php, and this class in turn extends the base framework class CController. Since we specified the actionID hello, a simple action was also created within MessageController called actionHello(). Gii also assumed that this action, like most actions defined by a controller, will need to render a view. So it added the code to this method to render a view file by the same name, hello.php, and placed it in the default directory protected/views/message/ for view files associated with this controller. Here is the uncommented part of the code that was generated for the MessageController class:

```php
<?php
class MessageController extends Controller
{
        public function actionHello()
        {
                $this->render('hello');
        }
}
```

As we can see, since we did not specify 'index' as one of the actionIDs when creating this controller with Gii, there is no `actionIndex()` method. As was discussed in *Chapter 1, Meet Yii*, by convention, a request that specifies a message as the controllerID, but does not specify an action, will be routed to the `actionIndex()` method for further processing. This is why we initially saw the 404 error, because the request was not specifying an actionID.

Let's take a second and fix this. As we have mentioned, Yii favors convention over configuration and has sensible defaults for almost everything. At the same time, almost everything is also configurable, and the default action for a controller is no exception. With a simple, single line at the top of our `MessageController`, we can define our `actionHello()` method as the default action. Add the following line to the top of the `MessageController` class:

```php
<?php

class MessageController extends Controller
{
    public $defaultAction = 'hello';
```

Try it out by navigating to http://localhost/helloworld/index.php?r=message. You should still see the `hello action` page being displayed and no longer see the error page.

One final step

To turn this into a "Hello, World!" application, all we need to do is customize our `hello.php` view to display "Hello, World!". Doing so is simple. Edit the file `protected/views/message/hello.php` so that it contains just the following code:

```php
<?php
<h1>Hello World!</h1>
```

Save it, and view it again in your browser: http://localhost/helloworld/index.php?r=message.

It now displays our introductory greeting, as shown in the following screenshot:

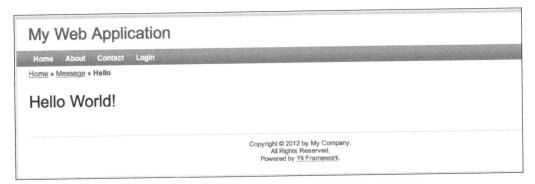

We have our simple application working with stunningly minimal code. All we have added is one line of HTML to our `hello.php` view file.

> You may be wondering where/how all of the other HTML is being generated. Our basic `hello.php` view file only contains a single line with an `<h1>` tag. When we call `render()` in our controller, there is also a layout view file being applied. No need to worry too much about this now, as we will be covering layouts in greater detail later. But if curious, you can take a look at the `protected/views/layouts/` directory to see the layout files that have been defined and to help shine a little light on where the rest of the HTML is defined.

Reviewing our request routing

Let's review how Yii analyzes our request within the context of this example application:

1. Navigate to the "Hello, World!" page by pointing your browser at the URL `http://localhost/helloworld/index.php?r=message` (or you can use the equivalent URL `http://localhost/helloworld/index.php?r=message/hello`).

2. Yii analyzes the URL. The **r** (route) querystring variable indicates that the controllerID is `message`. This tells Yii to route the request to the message controller class, which it finds in `protected/controllers/MessageController.php`.

3. Yii also discovers that the actionID specified is `hello`. (Or if no actionID is specified, it routes to the controller's default action.) So the action method `actionHello()` is invoked within the `MessageController`.

4. The `actionHello()` method renders the `hello.php` view file located at `protected/views/message/hello.php`. And we altered this view file to simply display our introductory greeting, which is then returned to the browser.

This all came together with very little effort. By following Yii's default conventions, the entire application request routing has been seamlessly stitched together for us. Of course, Yii gives us every opportunity to override this default workflow if needed, but the more you stick with the conventions, the less time you will spend in tweaking configuration code.

Adding dynamic content

The simplest way to add dynamic content to our view template is to embed PHP code into the template itself. View files are rendered by our simple application to result in HTML, and any basic text in these files is passed through without being changed. However, any content between `<?php` and `?>` is interpreted and executed as PHP code. This is a typical way that PHP code is embedded within HTML files and is probably familiar to you.

Adding the date and time

To spice up our page with dynamic content, let's display the date and time:

1. Open up the hello view again and add the following line below the greeting text:

   ```
   <h3><?php echo date("D M j G:i:s T Y"); ?></h3>
   ```

2. Save and view: `http://localhost/helloworld/index.php?r=message/hello`.

Presto! We have added dynamic content to our application. With each page refresh, we can see the displayed content changing.

Admittedly this is not terribly exciting, but it does show you how to embed simple PHP code into our view templates.

A different approach for adding the date and time

Although this approach of embedding PHP code directly into the view file does allow for any PHP code of any amount or complexity, it is strongly recommended that these statements do not alter data models and remain simple, display-oriented statements. This will help keep our business logic separate from our presentation code, which is part of the benefit of using the MVC architecture.

Moving the data creation to the controller

Let's move the logic that creates the time back to the controller and have the view do nothing more than display the time. We'll move the determination of the time into our `actionHello()` method within the controller and set the value in an instance variable called `$time`.

First let's alter the controller action. Currently our action in our `MessageController`, `actionHello()`, simply makes a call to render our hello view by executing the following code:

```
$this->render('hello');
```

Before we render the view, let's add the call to determine the time and then store it in a local variable called `$theTime`. Let's then alter our call to `render()` by adding a second parameter, which includes this variable:

```
$theTime = date("D M j G:i:s T Y");
$this->render('hello',array('time'=>$theTime));
```

When calling `render()` with a second parameter containing array data, it will extract the values of the array into PHP variables and make those variables available to the view script. The keys in the array will be the names of the variables made available to our view file. So in this example, our array key 'time', whose value is `$theTime`, will be extracted into a variable named `$time`, which will be made available in the view. This is one way to pass data from the controller to the view.

This assumes you are using the default view renderer with Yii. As has been mentioned many times previously, Yii allows you to customize nearly everything, and you can specify different view rendering implementations if you so desire. Other view renders may not behave in exactly the same way.

Now let's alter the view to use this $time variable rather than calling the date function itself:

1. Open up the HelloWorld view file again, and replace the line that we previously added to echo the time with the following:

```
<h3><?php echo $time; ?></h3>
```

2. Save and view the results again: http://localhost/helloworld/index. php?r=message/hello

Once again we see the time displaying just as before, so the end result is no different with the two approaches.

We have demonstrated the two approaches to adding PHP-generated content to the view template files. The first approach puts the data creation logic directly into the view file itself. The second approach houses this logic in the controller class, and feeds the information to the view file by using variables. The end result is the same; the time is displayed in our rendered HTML, but the second approach takes a small step forward in keeping the data acquisition and manipulation, that is business-logic, separate from our presentation code. This separation is exactly what a Model-View-Controller architecture strives to provide, and Yii's explicit directory structure and sensible defaults make this a snap to implement.

Have you been paying attention?

It was mentioned in *Chapter 1, Meet Yii*, that the view and controller are indeed very close cousins. So much so that $this within a view file refers to the Controller class that rendered the view.

In the previous example, we explicitly fed the time to the view file from the controller by using the second argument in the render method. This second argument explicitly sets the variables that are immediately available to the view file. But there is another approach you can try out for yourself.

Alter the previous example by defining a public class property on MessageController, rather than a locally scoped variable whose value is the current date time. Then display the time in the view file by accessing this class property via $this.

 The downloadable codebase has the solution to this "do-it-yourself" exercise included.

Linking pages together

Typical web applications have more than one page within them for users to experience, and our simple application should be no exception. Let's add another page that displays a response from the World, "Goodbye, Yii developer!", and link to this page from our "Hello, World!" page, and vice versa.

Normally, each rendered HTML page within a Yii web application will correspond to a separate view (though this does not always have to be the case). So we will create a new view and use a separate action method to render this view. When adding a new page like this, we also need to consider whether or not to use a separate controller. Since our Hello and Goodbye pages are related and very similar, there is no compelling reason to delegate the application logic to a separate controller class at the moment.

Linking to a new page

Let's have the URL for our new page be of the form `http://localhost/ helloworld/index.php?r=message/goodbye`.

Sticking with Yii conventions, this decision defines the name of our action method, which we need in the controller, as well as the name of our view. So open up `MessageController` and add an `actionGoodbye()` method just below our `actionHello()` action:

```
class MessageController extends Controller
{

  ...


  public function actionGoodbye()
  {
    $this->render('goodbye');
  }


    ...

}
```

Next, we have to create our view file in the `/protected/views/message/` directory. This should be called `goodbye.php` as it should be the same as the actionID that we chose.

 Please keep in mind that this is just a recommended convention. The view does not, by any means, have to have the same name as the action. The view file name just has to match the first argument of `render()`.

Create an empty file in that directory, and add the single line:

```
<h1>Goodbye, Yii developer!</h1>
```

Saving and viewing `http://localhost/helloworld/index.php?r=message/goodbye` again will display the goodbye message.

Now we need to add the links to connect the two pages. To add a link on the Hello screen to the Goodbye page, we could add an `<a>` tag directly to the `hello.php` view file and hardcode the URL structure as follows:

```
<a href="/helloworld/index.php?r=message/goodbye">Goodbye!</a>
```

And this would work, but it tightly couples the view code implementation to a specific URL structure, which might change at some point. If the URL structure were to change, these links would become invalid.

 Remember in *Chapter 1, Meet Yii,* when we went through the blog posting application example? We used URLs that were of a different, more SEO-friendly format than the Yii default format, namely:

`http://yourhostname/controllerID/actionID`

It is a simple matter of configuring a Yii Web application to use this "path" format, as opposed to the querystring format we are using in this example. Being able to easily change the URL format can be important to web applications. As long as we avoid hardcoding them throughout our application, changing them will remain a simple matter of altering the application configuration file.

Getting a little help from Yii CHtml

Luckily, Yii comes to the rescue here. Yii comes with myriad helper methods that can be used in view templates. These methods exist in the static HTML helper framework class CHtml. In this case, we want to employ the helper method "link" that takes in a *controllerID/actionID* pair and creates the appropriate hyperlink for you, based on how the URL structure is configured for the application. Since all these helper methods are static, we can call them directly without the need to create an explicit instance of the CHtml class. Using this link helper, we can add a link in our hello.php view just below where we echoed the time, as follows:

```
<p><?php echo CHtml::link('Goodbye'array('message/goodbye')); ?></p>
```

Save and view the "Hello, World!" page: http://localhost/helloworld/index.php?r=message/hello

You should see the hyperlink, and clicking on it should take you to the goodbye page. The first parameter in the call to the link method is the text that will be displayed in the hyperlink. The second parameter is an array that holds the value for our *controllerID/actionID* pair.

We can follow the same approach to place a reciprocal link in our Goodbye view:

```
<h1>Goodbye, Yii developer!</h1>
<p><?php echo CHtml::link('Hello',array('message/hello')); ?></p>
```

Save and view the goodbye page:

http://localhost/helloworld/index.php?r=message/goodbye

You should now see an active link back to the "Hello, World!" page, from the goodbye page.

So we now know a couple of ways to link web pages together in our simple application. One approach added an HTML <a> tag directly to the view file and hardcoded the URL structure. The other, preferred approach, made use of Yii's CHtml helper class to help construct the URLs based on the *controllerID/actionID* pairs, so that the resulting format will always conform to the application configuration. In this way, we can easily alter the URL format throughout the application, without having to go back and change every view file that happens to have internal links.

Our simple "Hello, World!" application really reaps the benefits of Yii's convention over configuration philosophy. By applying certain default behavior and following the recommended conventions, the building of this simple application and our entire request routing process just fell together in a very easy and convenient way.

Summary

In this chapter, we constructed an extremely simple application in order to cover many topics. First we installed the framework. We then used the `yiic` console command to bootstrap the creation of a new Yii application. We then introduced an incredibly powerful code generation tool called Gii. We used this to create a new controller within our simple application.

Once our application was in place, we could see first hand how Yii handles the request and routing to controllers and actions. We then moved on to creating and displaying very simple dynamic content. And finally, we looked at how to link the pages in a Yii application together.

While this incredibly simple application has provided concrete examples to help us better understand the use of the Yii framework, it is far too simplistic to demonstrate Yii's ability to ease the building of our real-world applications. In order to demonstrate this, we need to build a real-world web application. We are going to do just that. In the next chapter, we will introduce you to the project task and issue tracking application that we will be building throughout the remainder of this book.

3
The TrackStar Application

We could continue to keep adding to our simple "Hello, World!" application to provide examples of Yii's features, but that won't really help to understand the framework in the context of a real-world application. In order to do that, we need to build towards something that will more closely resemble the types of applications web developers actually have to build. That is exactly what we are going to be doing throughout the rest of this book.

In this chapter, we will introduce the project task-tracking application called **TrackStar**. There are many other project management and issue-tracking applications out there in the world, and the basic functionality of ours will not be any different from many of these. So why build it, you ask? It turns out that this type of user-based application has many features that are common to many web applications. This will allow us to achieve two primary goals:

- Showcase Yii's incredible utility and feature set as we build useful functionality and conquer real-world web application challenges
- Provide real-world examples and approaches that will immediately be applicable to your next web application project

Introducing TrackStar

TrackStar is a **software development life cycle (SDLC)** issue-management application. Its main goal is to help keep track of the many issues that arise throughout the course of building software applications. It is a user-based application that allows the creation of user accounts and grants access to the application features once a user has been authenticated and authorized. It allows a user to add and manage projects.

Projects can have users associated with them (typically the team members working on the project) as well as issues. The project issues will be things such as development tasks and application bugs. The issues can be assigned to members of the project and will have a status such as *not yet started*, *started*, and *finished*. In this way, the tracking tool can give an accurate depiction of the projects with regard to what has been accomplished, what is currently in progress, and what is yet to be started.

Creating user stories

Simple user stories are a great way to identify the necessary feature functionality of an application. User stories, in their simplest form, state what a user can do with a piece of software. They should start simple, and grow in complexity as you dive into more and more of the details around each feature. Our goal here is to start with just enough complexity to allow us to get started. If necessary, we'll add more detail later.

We briefly touched on the three main entities that play a large role in this application, namely *users*, *projects*, and *issues*. These are our primary domain objects and are extremely important items in this application. So let's start with them.

Users

TrackStar is a user-based web application. At a high level, the user can be in one of two user states:

- Anonymous
- Authenticated

An **anonymous** user is any user of the application that has not been authenticated through the login process. Anonymous users will only have access to register for a new account or login. All other functionality will be restricted to authenticated users.

An **authenticated** user is any user that has provided valid authentication credentials through the login process. In other words, authenticated users are users that have logged in. Authenticated users will have access to the main feature functionality of the application, such as creating and managing projects, and project issues.

Projects

Managing the project is the primary purpose of the TrackStar application. A project represents a general, high-level goal to be achieved by one or more users of the application. The project is typically broken down into more granular tasks, or issues, that represent the smaller steps that need to be taken to achieve the overall goal.

As an example, let's take what we are going to be doing throughout this book, that is, building a project and issue-tracking management application. Unfortunately, we can't use our yet-to-be-created application as a tool to help us track its own development, but if we could, we might create a project named "Build The TrackStar Project/Issue Management Tool". This project would be broken down into more granular project issues, for example, "Create the login screen", "Design database schema for issues", and so on.

Authenticated users can create new projects. The creator of the project within an account will have a special role within that project called the **project owner**. Project owners have the ability to edit and delete these projects as well as add new members to the project. Other users associated with the project, besides the project owner, are referred to simply as **project members**. Project members will have the ability to add new issues as well as edit existing ones.

Issues

Project issues will be classified into one of three categories:

- **Features**: Items that represent real features to be added to the application. For example, implementation of the login functionality.

- **Tasks**: Items that represent work that needs to be done, but are not an actual feature of the software. For example, setting up the build and integration server.

- **Bugs**: Items that represent application behaviors that are not working as expected. For example, the account registration form does not validate the format of an input e-mail address.

And issues can be in one of the following three status states:

- Not yet started
- Started
- Finished

Project members can add new issues to a project as well as edit and delete them. They can assign issues to themselves or other project members.

For now, this is enough information on these three main entities to allow us to move forward. We could go into a lot more detail about "what exactly does account registration entail?" or "how exactly does one add a new task to a project?", but we have outlined enough specifications to begin on these basic features. We'll nail down the more granular details as we proceed with the implementation.

However before we start, we should jot down some basic navigation and application workflow. This will help everyone to better understand the general layout and flow of the application we are building.

Navigation and page flow

It is always good to outline the main pages within an application and see how they fit together. This will help us quickly identify some needed Yii controllers, actions, and views, as well as help to set everyone's expectations on what we'll be building towards at the onset of our development.

The following diagram shows the basic application flow, from logging in through to the project details listing:

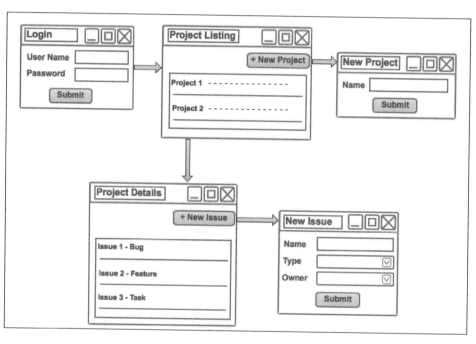

When a user first comes to the application, they must log in and authenticate themselves prior to proceeding to any functionality. Once successfully logged in, they will be presented with a list of their current projects along with the ability to create a new project. Choosing a specific project will take them to the project details page. The project details page will present a list of the issues by type. There will also be the ability to add a new issue as well as edit any of the listed issues.

This is all pretty basic functionality, but the figure gives us a little more information on how the application is stitched together and allows us to start identifying our needed models, views, and controllers better. It also allows something visual to be shared with others so that everyone involved has the same *picture* of what we are working towards. In my experience, almost everyone prefers pictures over written specifications when first thinking through a new application.

Data relationships

We still need to think a little more about the data we will be working with as we begin to build toward these specifications. If we pick out all the main nouns from our system, we may end up with a pretty good list of domain objects and, by extension of using active record, the data we want to model. Our previously outlined user stories identify the following:

- A User
- A Project
- An Issue

Based on this and the other details provided in the user stories and application workflow diagram, a first attempt at the necessary data model is shown in the following diagram:

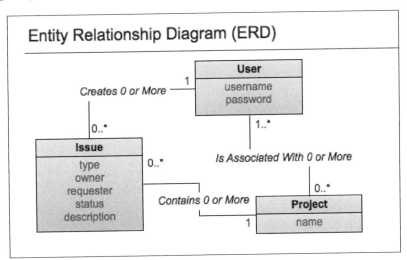

This is a very basic object model that outlines our primary data entities, their respective attributes, and some of the relationships between them. The 1..* and 0..* on either side of the line between the project and user objects represents that there is a many-to-many relationship between them. A user can be associated with zero or more projects, and a project has one or more users. Similarly, we have represented the fact that a project can have 0 or more issues associated with it, whereas an issue belongs to just one specific project. Also, a user can be the owner of (or requestor of) many issues, but an issue just has one owner (also just one requestor).

We have kept the attributes as simple as possible at this stage. A user is going to need a username and a password in order to get past the login screen. The project has only a name attribute.

An issue has the most associated information based on what we currently know about them. As discussed briefly in the previously defined user stories, issues will have a type attribute to distinguish the general category (bug, feature, or task). They will also have a status attribute to indicate the progress of the issue being worked on. There will be a logged in user who initially creates the issue; this is the requestor. And once a user in the system has been assigned to work on the issue, they will be the owner of the issue. We have also defined the description attribute to allow for some descriptive text of the issue to be entered.

Note that we have not been explicitly talking about schemas or databases yet. The fact is that until we think through what is really needed from a data perspective, we won't know the right tool to use to house this data. Would flat files on the filesystem work just as well as a relational database? Do we need to persist data at all?

The answers to these questions are not always necessary at this early planning stage. It is better to focus more on the features we want and the type of data needed to support these features. We can turn to the explicit technology implementation details after we have had a chance to discuss these ideas with other project stakeholders, to ensure we are on the right track. Other project stakeholders include anyone and everyone involved in this development project. This can include the client, if you are building an application for someone else, as well as other development team members, product/project managers, and so on. It is always a good idea to get some feedback from "the team" to help validate the approach and any assumptions being made.

In our case, there is really no one else involved in this development effort. So, we can quickly draw some conclusions to answer our data-related questions and move forward with our application development.

Since this is a web-based application, and given the nature of the information we need to store, retrieve, and manipulate, we can conclude that it would be best to persist the data in this application. Also, based on the relationships that exist between the types of data we want to capture and manage, a good approach to storing this data would be in a relational database. Based on its ease of use, excellent price point, its general popularity among PHP application developers, and its compatibility with the Yii framework, we will be using MySQL as the specific database server.

Now that we know enough about what we are going to start building and how we are going to start building it, let's get started.

Creating the new application

First things first, let's get the initial Yii web application created. We have already seen how easy this is to accomplish in *Chapter 2, Getting Started*. As we did there, we will assume the following:

- `YiiRoot` is the directory where you have installed Yii
- `WebRoot` is configured as the document root of your web server (that is, to where `http://localhost/` resolves)

So from the command line, change to your `WebRoot` directory and execute the following:

```
% YiiRoot/framework/yiic webapp trackstar
Create a Web application under '/Webroot/trackstar'? [Yes|No] Yes
```

This provides us with our skeleton directory structure and our out-of-the-box working application. You should be able to view the home page of this new application by navigating to `http://localhost/trackstar/index.php?r=site/index`.

 Because our default controller is SiteController and the default action within that controller is `actionIndex()`, we could also navigate to the same page without specifying the route.

Connecting to the database

Now that we have our skeleton application up and running, let's work on getting it properly connected to a database. In fact, the skeleton application was autoconfigured to use a database. A by-product of using the yiic tool is that our new application is configured to use a SQLite database. If you take a peek in the main application configuration file, located at `protected/config/main.php`, you will see the following declaration about halfway down:

```
'db'=>array('connectionString' => 'sqlite:'.dirname(__FILE__).'/../
data/testdrive.db',
    ),
```

And you can also verify the existence of `protected/data/testdrive.db`, which is the SQLite database it is configured to use.

Since we have already made the decision to use MySQL, we'll need to make some configuration changes. However, before we change the configuration to use a MySQL database server, let's briefly talk about Yii and databases more generally.

Yii and databases

Yii provides great support for database programming. Yii's **Data Access Objects (DAO)** are built on top of the **PHP Data Objects (PDO)** extension (`http://php.net/pdo`). This is a database abstraction layer that enables the application to interact with the database through a database-independent interface. All the supported **database management systems (DBMS)** are encapsulated behind a single uniform interface. In this way, the code can remain database independent and the applications developed using Yii DAO can easily be switched to use a different DBMS without the need for modification.

To establish a connection with a supported DBMS, you can simply create a new `CDbConnection` instance:

```
$connection=new CDbConnection($dsn,$username,$password);
```

Here the format of the `$dsn` variable depends on the specific PDO database driver being used. Some common formats include:

- SQLite: `sqlite:/path/to/dbfile`
- MySQL: `mysql:host=localhost;dbname=testdb`
- PostgreSQL: `pgsql:host=localhost;port=5432;dbname=testdb`
- SQL Server: `mssql:host=localhost;dbname=testdb`
- Oracle: `oci:dbname=//localhost:1521/testdb`

`CDbConnection` also extends from `CApplicationComponent`, which allows it to be configured as an application component. This means that we can add it to the components property of the application, and customize the class and property values in the main configuration file. This is our preferred approach, which we will detail next.

Adding a db connection as an application component

Let's take a quick step back. When we created the initial application, we specified the application type to be a web application. Remember we specified `webapp` on the command line. Doing so specified that the application singleton class that is created upon each request be of the type `CWebApplication`. This Yii application singleton is the execution context within which all request processing is run. Its main task is to resolve the user request and route it to an appropriate controller for further processing. This was represented as the Yii Application Router back in the diagrams used in *Chapter 1, Meet Yii*, when we covered the request routing. It also serves as the central place for keeping application-level configuration values.

To customize our application configuration, we normally provide a configuration file to initialize its property values when the application instance is being created. The main application configuration file is located in `/protected/config/main.php`. This is a PHP file containing an array of key-value pairs. Each key represents the name of a property of the application instance, and each value is the corresponding property's initial value. If you open up this file, you will see that several settings have already been configured for us.

Adding an application component to the configuration is easy. Open up the file (`/protected/config/main.php`) and locate the components property.

We can see that there are entries already specifying a `log` and `user` application component. These will be covered in the subsequent chapters. We can also see (and as we noted previously) that there is a `db` component there as well, configured to use a SQLite connection to a SQLite database located at `protected/data/testdrive.db`. There is also a commented out section that defines this `db` component to use a MySQL database. All we need to do is remove the SQLite `db` component definition, uncomment the section that defines the MySQL component, and then make the appropriate changes to match your database name, username, and password so the connection can be made. The following code shows this change:

```
// application components
  'components'=>array(

    ...
      //comment out or remove the reference to the sqlite db
/*
'db'=>array(
```

```
            'connectionString' => 'sqlite:'.dirname(__FILE__).'/../data/
      testdrive.db',
          ),
      */
          // uncomment the following to use a MySQL database
              'db'=>array(
            'connectionString' => 'mysql:host=localhost;dbname=trackstar',
            'emulatePrepare' => true,
            'username' => '[your-db-username]',
            'password' => '[your-db-password]',
            'charset' => 'utf8',
          ),
```

This assumes that a MySQL database has been created called `trackstar` and is available to connect using the localhost. Depending on your environment, you may need to specify the localhost IP of `127.0.0.1` rather than `localhost`. One of the great benefits of making this an application component is that now, anywhere throughout our application, we can reference the database connection simply as a property of the main Yii application `Yii::app()->db`. Similarly, we can use this as a reference for any of the other components defined in the `config` file.

The `charset` property when set to `'utf8'` sets the character set used for the database connection. This property is only used for MySQL and PostgreSQL databases. It will default to null, which means that it will use the default charset. We are setting it here to ensure proper `utf8` unicode character support for our PHP application.

The `emulatePrepare => true` configuration sets a PDO attribute (PDO::ATTR_EMULATE_PREPARES) to `true`, which is recommended if you are using PHP 5.1.3 or higher. This was added to PHP 5.1.3, and when used, causes the PDO native query parser to be used rather than the native prepared statements APIs in the MySQL client. The native prepared statements in the MySQL client cannot take advantage of the query cache, and as such have been known to result in poor performance. The PDO native query parser can use the query cache, and so it is recommended to use this option if available (PHP 5.1.3 or higher).

So, we have specified a MySQL database called `trackstar` as well as the username and password needed to connect to this database. We did not show you how to create such a database in MySQL. We assume you understand how to set up a MySQL database and how to use it. Please refer to your specific database documentation if you are unsure of how to create a new database, called `trackstar`, and configure a username and password for connectivity.

Testing the database connection

Before we move on, we should ensure that our database connection is actually working. There are a few ways we could do this. We'll look at two approaches. In the first approach, we'll use the `yiic` command-line tool to start an interactive shell for our application and ensure that there are no errors when we attempt to reference the application `db` component. Then we'll provide a second approach that will introduce us to unit testing in Yii with PHPUnit.

Using the interactive shell

We'll start off with a simple test using the Yii interactive shell. As you recall, we used the `webapp` command along with the `yiic` command-line utility to create our new application. Another command to use with this utility is `shell`. This allows you to run PHP commands within the context of the Yii application, directly from the command line.

To start the shell, navigate to the root directory of the application, that is the directory that contains the `index.php` entry script `Webroot/trackstar/`. Then run the `yiic` utility, passing in `shell` as the command (refer to the following screenshot).

```
$./protected/yiic shell
Yii Interactive Tool v1.1 (based on Yii v1.1.12)
Please type 'help' for help. Type 'exit' to quit.
>>
```

This starts the shell and allows you to enter the commands directly after the >> prompt.

What we want to do to test our connection is ensure that our database connection application component is accessible. We can simply `echo` out the connection string and verify that it returns what we set it to in our configuration. So from the shell prompt type the following:

```
>> echo Yii::app()->db->connectionString;
```

It should echo something similar to the following:

mysql:host=localhost;dbname=trackstar

This demonstrates that the `db` application component is configured correctly and available for use in our application.

Automated testing – unit and functional tests

Gathering feedback is of fundamental importance to application development; feedback from the users of the application and other project stakeholders, feedback from the development team members, and feedback directly from the software itself. Developing software in a manner that will allow it to tell you when something is broken can turn the fear associated with integrating and deploying applications into boredom. The method by which you can empower your software with this feedback mechanism is writing automated unit and functional tests, and then executing them repeatedly and often.

Unit and functional testing

Unit tests are written to provide the developer with verification that the code is doing the right things. Functional tests are written to provide the developer, as well as other project stakeholders, with verification that the application as a whole is doing things the right way.

Unit tests

Unit tests are the tests that focus on the smallest units within a software application. In an object-oriented application, such as a Yii web application, the smallest units are the public methods that make up the interfaces to the classes. Unit tests should focus on one single class and not require other classes or objects to run it. Their purpose is to validate that a single unit of code is working as expected.

Functional tests

Functional tests focus on testing the end-to-end feature functionality of the application. These tests exist at a higher level than the unit tests and typically require multiple classes or objects to run. Their purpose is to validate that a given feature of the application is working as expected.

Benefits of testing

There are many benefits to writing unit and functional tests. For one, they are a great way to provide documentation. Unit tests can quickly tell the exact story of why a block of code exists. Similarly, the functional tests document what features are implemented within an application. If you stay diligent in writing these tests, then the documentation continues to evolve naturally as the application evolves.

They are also invaluable as a feedback mechanism to constantly reassure the developer and other project stakeholders that the code and application is working as expected. You run your tests every time you make changes to the code and get immediate feedback on whether or not something that you altered inadvertently changed the expected behavior of the system. You can then address these issues immediately. This really increases the confidence that developers have with the application and translates to less bugs and more successful projects.

This immediate feedback also helps to facilitate change and improve the design of the code. A developer is more likely to make improvements to existing code, if a suite of tests are in place to immediately provide feedback as to whether the changes made altered the application behavior. The confidence provided by a suite of unit and functional tests allows developers to write better software, release more stable applications, and ship quality products.

Testing in Yii

As of version 1.1, Yii is tightly integrated with the PHPUnit (`http://www.phpunit.de/`) and Selenium Remote Control (`http://seleniumhq.org/projects/remote-control/`) testing frameworks. You may certainly test Yii PHP code with any of the testing frameworks available. However, the tight integration of Yii with the two previously mentioned frameworks makes things even easier. And making things easy is one of our primary goals here.

When we used the `yiic webapp` console command to create our new web application, we noticed that many files and directories were automatically created for us. The ones among these that are relevant to writing and executing automated tests are the following:

File/directory	Contains/stores
`trackstar/`	Contains all the files listed in the file/directory column
`protected/`	Protected application files
`tests/`	Tests for the application
`fixtures/`	Database fixtures
`functional/`	Functional tests
`unit/`	Unit tests
`report/`	Coverage reports
`bootstrap.php`	The script executed at the very beginning of the tests
`phpunit.xml`	The PHPUnit configuration file
`WebTestCase.php`	The base class for web-based functional tests

You can place your test files into three main directories, namely `fixtures`, `functional`, and `unit`. The `report` directory is used to store the generated code coverage reports.

 The PHP extension, XDebug, must be installed in order to generate reports. For details on this installation, see `http://xdebug.org/docs/install`. This extension is not required for the following example.

Unit tests

A unit test in Yii is written as a PHP class that extends from the framework class `CTestCase`. The conventions prescribe it to be named `AbcTest`, where `Abc` is replaced by the name of the class being tested. For example, if we were to test the `MessageController` class in our "Hello, World!" application from *Chapter 2, Getting Started*, we would name the test class `MessageControllerTest`. This class is saved in a file called `MessageControllerTest.php` under the directory `protected/tests/unit/`.

The test class primarily has a set of test methods named `testXyz`, where `Xyz` is often the same as the method name for which you are writing the test.

Continuing with the `MessageController` example, if we were testing our `actionHelloworld()` method, we would name the corresponding test method `testActionHelloworld()` in our `MessageControllerTest` class.

Installing PHPUnit

As of version 1.1, Yii is tightly integrated with the PHPUnit (`http://www.phpunit.de/`) testing framework.

In order to follow through with this example, you will need to install PHPUnit. This should be done using the Pear Installer. (For more information on Pear, see `http://pear.php.net/`.) Please visit the following URL for more information on how to install PHPUnit based on your environment configuration:

`https://github.com/sebastianbergmann/phpunit/`

 It is certainly beyond the scope of this book to specifically cover PHPUnit's testing features. It is recommended that you take some time to go through the documentation to get a feel for the jargon and for writing basic unit tests: `https://github.com/sebastianbergmann/phpunit/`

Testing the connection

Assuming you have successfully installed PHPUnit, we can add a test for our database connection under `protected/tests/unit/`. Let's create a simple database connectivity test file under this directory called `DbTest.php`. Add this new file with the following contents:

```php
<?php
class DbTest extends CTestCase
{
    public function testConnection()
    {
        $this->assertTrue(true);
    }
}
```

Here we have added a fairly trivial test. The `assertTrue()` method, which is a part of PHPUnit, is an assertion that will pass if the argument passed to it is `true`, and it will fail if it is `false`. In this case, it is testing if `true` is `true`. So this test will certainly pass. We are doing this to make sure that our new application is working as expected, for testing with PHPUnit. Navigate to the tests folder and execute this new test:

%cd /WebRoot/trackstar/protected/tests

%phpunit unit/DbTest.php

```
...
Time: 0 seconds, Memory: 10.00Mb

OK (1 test, 1 assertion)
```

 If for some reason this test failed on your system, you may need to change `protected/tests/bootstrap.php` so that the variable `$yiit` properly points to your `/YiiRoot/yiit.php` file.

Confident that our testing framework is working as expected within our newly created TrackStar application, we can use this to write a test for the db connection.

Change the `assertEquals(true)` statement in the `testConnection()` test method to:

```php
$this->assertNotNull(Yii::app()->db->connectionString);
```

And rerun the test:

```
%phpunit unit/DbTest.php

    ...
    Time: 0 seconds, Memory: 10.00Mb

    OK (1 test, 1 assertion)
```

As you recall, since we configured our database connection as an application component named db, Yii::app()->db should return an instance of the CDbConnection class. If the application failed to establish a database connection, this test would return an error. Since the test still passes, we can move forward with the confidence that the database connection is set up properly.

Summary

This chapter introduced the task-tracking application, TrackStar, which we will be developing throughout the rest of this book. We talked about what the application is and what it does, and provided some high-level requirements for the application in the form of informal user stories. We then identified some of the main domain objects we will need to create, as well as worked through some of the data we will need to be able to house and manage.

We then took our first step towards building our TrackStar application. We created a new application with all of the working functionality that comes "for free" from the autogenerated code. We also configured our application to be connected to a MySQL database and demonstrated two approaches to test that connection. One approach demonstrated Yii's integration with PHPUnit and how to write automated tests for your Yii application.

In the next chapter, we will get to finally sink our teeth into more sophisticated features. We will begin to do some actual coding as we implement the needed functionality to manage our project entities within the application.

4
Project CRUD

Now that we have a basic application in place and configured to communicate with our database, we can begin to work on some real features of our application. We know that the "project" is one of the most fundamental components in our application. A user cannot do anything useful with the TrackStar application without first either creating or choosing an existing project within which to add tasks and other issues. For this reason, we want to first turn our focus to getting some project functionality into the application.

Feature planning

At the end of our efforts in this chapter, our application should allow users to create new projects, select from a list of existing projects, update/edit existing projects, and delete existing projects.

In order to achieve this goal, we should identify the more granular tasks on which to focus. The list below identifies a list of tasks we aim to accomplish within this chapter:

- Design the database schema to support projects
- Build the necessary tables and all other database objects identified in the schema
- Create the Yii AR model classes needed to allow the application to easily interact with the created database table(s)
- Create the Yii controller class(es) that will house the functionality to do the following:
    - Create new projects
    - Retrieve a list of existing projects for display
    - Update the data associated with existing projects
    - Delete existing projects

- Create the Yii view files and presentation tier logic that will:
  - Display the form to allow for new project creation
  - Display a listing of all the existing projects
  - Display the form to allow for a user to edit an existing project
  - Add a delete button to the project listing to allow for project deletion

This is certainly enough to get us started.

Creating the project table

Back in *Chapter 3, The TrackStar Application*, we talked about the basic data that represents a project, and we decided that we would use a MySQL relational database to build the persistence layer of this application. Now we need to design and build the table that will persist our project data.

We know projects need to have a name and a description. We are also going to keep some basic table auditing information on each table by tracking the time a record was created and updated, as well as who created and updated the record.

Based on these properties, the following is how the project table will look:

```
CREATE TABLE tbl_`project` (
`id` INTEGER NOT NULL auto_increment,
`name` varchar(255) NOT NULL,
`description` text NOT NULL,
`create_time` DATETIME default NULL,
`create_user_id` INTEGER default NULL,
`update_time` DATETIME default NULL,
`update_user_id` INTEGER default NULL,
PRIMARY KEY  (`id`)
) ENGINE = InnoDB
;
```

Now, before we jump right in and just use our favorite MySQL database editor to create this table, we need to talk about how we can use Yii to manage the changes that will take place in our database schema as we build our TrackStar application.

Yii database migrations

We know it is a good practice to track version changes of our application source code. As you are following along in building our TrackStar application, it would be wise to use version control software such as SVN or GIT to help manage all the changes we make to our codebase along the way. If our codebase changes get out of sync with our database changes, it is likely that our entire application will break. So, it would also be really great to manage the structural changes we will be making to our database along the way.

Yii helps us out in this regard. Yii provides a database migration tool that keeps track of database migration history and allows us to apply new migrations as well as revert existing migrations to allow us to restore the database structure to a previous state.

The Yii migration utility is a console command that we use with the `yiic` command-line tool. As a console command, it uses a configuration file specific to console commands, which, by default, is `protected/config/console.php`. We need to properly configure our database component in this file. Just as we did in our `main.php config` file, we need to define our `db` component to use our MySQL database. If you open up the `protected/config/console.php` configuration file, you'll see that it already has a MySQL configuration defined, but it is commented out. Let's remove the SQLite configuration and uncomment the MySQL configuration, changing the username and password as appropriate for your database settings:

```
'components'=>array(
'db'=>array(
    'connectionString' => 'mysql:host=localhost;dbname=trackstar',
    'emulatePrepare' => true,
    'username' => '[YOUR-USERNAME]',
    'password' => '[YOUR-PASSWORD]',
    'charset' => 'utf8',
  ),
),
```

Now that we have our configuration change in place, we can proceed to create the migration. To do so, we use the `yiic` command-line utility tool with the `migrate` command. Creating a migration takes the general form of:

```
$ yiic migrate create <name>
```

Here, the required `name` parameter allows us to specify a brief description of the database change we are making. The `name` parameter is used as part of the migration filename and PHP class name. Therefore, it should only contain letters, digits, or underscore characters. Yii takes the input name parameter, and appends a UTC timestamp (in the format of *yymmdd_hhmmss*), with the letter *m* for migration, to use as both the filename and the PHP class name. Let's go ahead and create a new migration for our project table, and this naming convention will be made clearer. From the command line, navigate to the application `protected/` directory and then issue the command to create a new migration using the name `create_project_table`:

```
$cd /Webroot/trackstar/protected/
$./yiic migrate create create_project_table

Yii Migration Tool v1.0 (based on Yii v1.1.12)

Create new migration '/Webroot/trackstar/protected/migrations
/m121108_195611_create_project_table.php'? (yes|no) [no]:yes
New migration created successfully.
```

This creates the file `/Webroot/trackstar/protected/migrations/` `m121108_195611_create_project_table.php` with the following content:

```php
class m121108_195611_create_project_table extends CDbMigration
{
  public function up()
  {
  }

  public function down()
  {
    echo "m121108_195611_create_project_table does not support
    migration down.\n";
    return false;
  }

  /*
  // Use safeUp/safeDown to do migration with transaction
  public function safeUp()
  {
  }

  public function safeDown()
  {
  }
  */
}
```

Of course, we'll have to make some changes to this file in order to have it create our new table. We implement the up() method to apply our desired database changes and we implement the down() method to revert these changes, which will allow us to revert to a previous version of our database structure. The safeUp() and safeDown() methods are similar, but they will execute the changes within a database transaction in order to treat the entire migration as an atomic unit to be executed in an all-or-nothing manner. In this case, the change we want to apply is to create a new table, and we can revert this change by dropping the table. These changes are as follows:

```
public function up()
{
  $this->createTable('tbl_project', array(
    'id' => 'pk',
     'name' => 'string NOT NULL',
    'description' => 'text NOT NULL',
    'create_time' => 'datetime DEFAULT NULL',
    'create_user_id' => 'int(11) DEFAULT NULL',
    'update_time' => 'datetime DEFAULT NULL',
    'update_user_id' => 'int(11) DEFAULT NULL',
  ), 'ENGINE=InnoDB');
}

public function down()
{
  $this->dropTable('tbl_project');
}
```

After saving our changes, we can execute the migration. From still within the protected/ directory, execute the migration as such:

```
$./yiic migrate

Yii Migration Tool v1.0 (based on Yii v1.1.12)

Total 1 new migration to be applied:
    m121108_195611_create_project_table

Apply the above migration? (yes|no) [no]:yes
*** applying m121108_195611_create_project_table
    > create table tbl_project ... done (time: 0.068s)
*** applied m121108_195611_create_project_table (time: 0.071s)


Migrated up successfully.
```

Using the migrate command with no arguments will result in migrating up (that is executing the `up()` method) for every migration that has not yet been applied. And, since this is the first time we have run a migration, Yii is going to create a new migration history table, `tbl_migration`, for us automatically. Yii uses this table to keep track of what migrations have already been applied. If we specify *down* as a command-line argument to the migrate command, the last applied migration will be reverted by running the `down()` method of that migration.

Now that we have applied our migration, our new `tbl_project` table has now been created and is ready for us to use.

> We'll be using Yii migrations throughout the book as we develop our TrackStar application, so we'll continue to learn more about them as we use them. For more detailed information on Yii migrations, see:
>
> `http://www.yiiframework.com/doc/guide/1.1/en/`
> `database.migration`

Naming conventions

You may have noticed that we defined our database table as well as all of the column names in lowercase. Throughout our development, we will use lowercase for all table names and column names. This is primarily because different DBMSs handle case sensitivity differently. As one example, **PostgreSQL** treats column names as case insensitive by default, and we must quote a column in a query condition if the column contains mixed-case letters. Using lowercase would help eliminate this problem.

You may have also noticed that we used a `tbl_` prefix in naming our projects table. As of version 1.1.0, Yii provides integrated support for using a table prefix. A table prefix is a string that is prepended to the names of the tables. It is often used in shared hosting environments where multiple applications share a single database and use different table prefixes to differentiate from each other; a sort of name-spacing for your database objects. For example, one application could use `tbl_` as a prefix while another could use `yii_`. Also, some database administrators use this as a naming convention to prefix database objects with an identifier as to what type of entity they are or otherwise going to use. They use a prefix to help organize objects into similar groups. Using table prefixes is a matter of preference and certainly not required.

In order to take full advantage of the integrated table prefix support in Yii, one must appropriately set the `CDbConnection::tablePrefix` property to be the desired table prefix. Then, in SQL statements used throughout the application, one can use `{{TableName}}` to refer to table names, where `TableName` is the name of the table, but without the prefix. For example, if we were to make this configuration change, we could use the following code to query all projects:

```
$sql='SELECT * FROM {{project}}';
$projects=Yii::app()->db->createCommand($sql)->queryAll();
```

But this is getting a little ahead of ourselves. Let's leave our configuration as it is for now, and revisit this topic when we get into database querying a little later in our application development.

Creating the AR model class

Now that we have the `tbl_project` table created, we need to create the Yii model class to allow us to easily manage the data in that table. We introduced Yii's ORM layer, **Active Record** (AR), back in *Chapter 1, Meet Yii*. Now we will see a concrete example of that in the context of this application.

Configuring Gii

Back in *Chapter 2, Getting Started* when we were building our simple "Hello, World!" Yii application, we introduced the code generation tool, **Gii**. If you recall, before we could begin using Gii, we had to configure it for use within our application. We need to do so again in our new TrackStar application. As a reminder, to configure Gii for use, open up `protected/config/main.php` and the Gii module is defined as follows:

```
return array(
   ...

   ...
   'modules'=>array(
'gii'=>array(
      'class'=>'system.gii.GiiModule',
      'password'=>false,
      // If removed, Gii defaults to localhost only. Edit carefully
to taste.
      'ipFilters'=>array('127.0.0.1','::1'),
    ),
     ...
   ),
```

This configures Gii as an application module. We will cover Yii *modules* in detail later in the book. The important thing at this point is to make sure this is added to the configuration file and that you provide your password (or set the password to `false` for development environments to avoid being prompted with the login screen). Now, navigate to the tool by going to `http://localhost/trackstar/index.php?r=gii`.

Using Gii to create our Project AR class

The main menu page for Gii looks like the following:

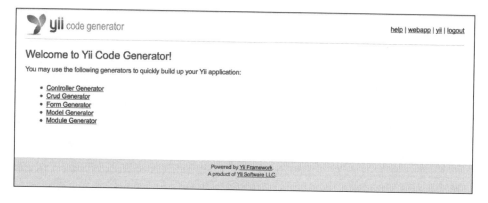

Since we want to create a new model class for our `tbl_project` table, the **Model Generator** option seems like the right choice. Clicking on that link takes us to the following page:

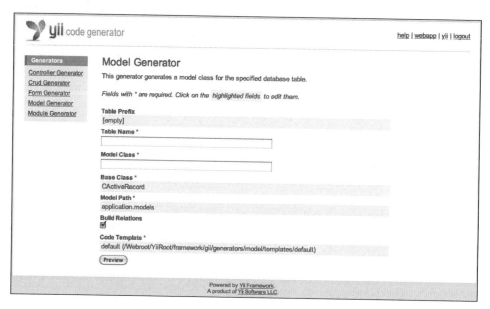

The **Table Prefix** field is primarily used to help Gii determine how to name the AR class we are generating. If you are using a prefix, you can add this here. This way, it won't use that prefix when naming the new class. In our case, we are using the tbl_ prefix, so we should specify that here. Specifying this value will mean that our new generated AR class will be named Project, rather than Tbl_project.

The next two fields are asking for our table name and the name of the class file we want it to generate. Type in the name of our table tbl_project in the **Table Name** field, and watch as the **Model Class** name autopopulates. The convention for the **Model Class** name is the name of the table, minus the prefix, and starts with an uppercase letter. So, it will assume a name of Project for our model class name, but you can of course customize this.

The next few fields allow for further customization. The **Base Class** field is used to specify the class from which our model class will extend. This will need to be CActiveRecord or a child class thereof. The **Model Path** field lets us specify where in the application directory structure to output the new file. The default is protected/ models/ (alias application.models). The **Build Relations** checkbox allows you to decide whether or not to have Gii automatically define relationships between AR objects by using the relationships defined between MySQL database tables. It is checked by default. The last field allows us to specify a template on which the code generation is based. We can customize the default one to meet any specific needs we have that might be common to all such class files. For now, the default values for these fields meet our needs just fine.

Proceed by clicking on the **Preview** button. This will result in the following table displaying along the bottom of the page:

Preview Generate	
Code File	**Generate**
models/Project.php	new ☑

This link allows you to preview the code that will be generated. Before you hit **Generate,** click on the models/Project.php link. The following screenshot displays what this preview will look like:

It provides a scrollable pop up so that we can preview the file that will be generated.

Okay, close this pop up and go ahead and click on the **Generate** button. Assuming all went well, you should see something like the following screenshot displayed towards the bottom of the page:

The code has been generated successfully.

Ensure that the path to which Gii is attempting to create the new file, `protected/models/` (or if you changed the location, whatever directory path you specified in the **Model Path** form field), is writable by your web server process prior to attempting to generate your new model class. Otherwise, you will receive a write permissions error.

Gii has created a new Yii active record model class for us and named it `Project.php` as we instructed. It has also placed it, as we instructed, in the default Yii location for model classes, `protected/models/`. This class is a wrapper class for our `tbl_project` database table. All of the columns in the `tbl_project` table are accessible as properties of the `Project` AR class.

Enabling CRUD operations for projects

We now have a new AR model class, but now what? Typically in an MVC architecture, we need a controller and a view to go with our model to complete the picture. In our case, we need to be able to manage our projects in the application. We need to be able to create new projects, retrieve information about existing projects, update the information on existing projects, and delete existing projects. We need to add a controller class that will handle these CRUD (Create, Read, Update, Delete) operations on our model class, as well as a view file to provide a GUI to allow the user to do this in the browser. One approach we could take is to open our favorite code editor and create a new controller and view classes. But, luckily, we don't have to.

Creating CRUD scaffolding for projects

Once again, the Gii tool is going to rescue us from having to write common, tedious, and often time-consuming code. CRUD operations are such a common need on database tables created for applications that the developers of Yii decided to provide this for us. If coming from other frameworks, you may know this by the term **scaffolding**. Let's see how to take advantage of this in Yii.

Navigate back to the main Gii menu located at `http://localhost/trackstar/index.php?r=gii` and select the **Crud Generator** link. You will be presented with the following screen:

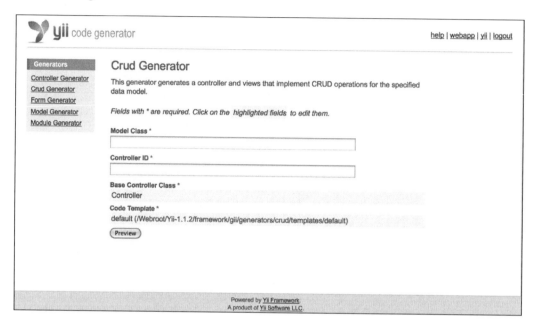

Here we are presented with two input form fields. The first one is asking for us to specify the **Model Class** against which we would like all of the CRUD operations to be generated. In our case, this is the `Project` AR class we created earlier. So we'll type in **Project** in this field. As we do this, we notice that the **Controller ID** field is autopopulated with the name **project**. This is Yii's naming convention. Of course, you can change this to be another name if you prefer, but we'll stick with this default for now. We'll also use the default base controller class, `Controller`, which was created for us when we initially created our application, as well as the default code template file from which to generate the class file.

With all of these fields filled in, clicking on the **Preview** button results in the following table being displayed at the bottom of the page:

Code File	Generate ☐
controllers/ProjectController.php	new ☑
views/project/_form.php	new ☑
views/project/_search.php	new ☑
views/project/_view.php	new ☑
views/project/admin.php	new ☑
views/project/create.php	new ☑
views/project/index.php	new ☑
views/project/update.php	new ☑
views/project/view.php	new ☑

Powered by Yii Framework.
A product of Yii Software LLC.

We can see that quite a few files are going to be generated. A new `ProjectController` controller class that will house all of the CRUD action methods is at the top of the list. The rest of the list represents all of the many separate view files that are also going to be created. There is a separate view file for each of the operations as well as one that will provide the ability to search project records. You can, of course, choose not to generate some of these by changing the checkboxes in the corresponding **Generate** column in the table. However, for our purposes, we would like Gii to create all of these for us.

Go ahead and click on the **Generate** button. You should see the following success message at the bottom of the page:

The controller has been generated successfully. You may try it now.

You may need to ensure that both /protected/controllers as well as /protected/views under the root application directory are both writable by the web server process. Otherwise, you will receive permission errors, rather than this success result.

We can now click on the **try it now** link to take our new functionality for a test drive.

Doing so takes you to a project listing page. This is the page that displays all of the projects currently in the system. In our case, we have not created any yet, so the page gives us a **No results found** message. Let's change this by creating a new project.

Creating a new project

On the project listing page (`http://localhost/trackstar/index.php?r=project`) there is a little navigation area on the right-hand side of the page. Click on the **Create Project** link. You'll discover this actually takes us to the login page, rather than a form to create a new project. The reason for this is that the code Gii has generated applies a rule that stipulates only properly authenticated users (that is logged in users) can create new projects. Any anonymous user that attempts to access the functionality to create a new project will be redirected to the login page. We'll cover authentication and authorization in detail later. For now, go ahead and log in using the credentials username as `demo` and password as `demo`.

A successful login should redirect you to the following URL:

`http://localhost/trackstar/index.php?r=project/create`

This page displays an input form for adding a new project, as shown in the following screenshot:

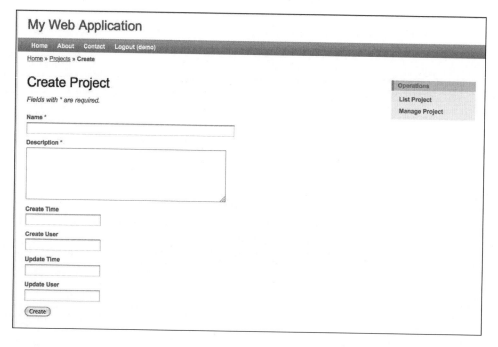

Let's quickly fill out this form to create a new project. The form indicates there are two required fields, **Name** and **Description**. The Gii code generator was smart enough to know that since we defined the `tbl_project.name` and `tbl_project.description` columns in our database table as `NOT NULL`, this should translate to required form fields when creating a new project. Pretty cool, right?

So, we'll need to at least fill out these two fields. Give it the name, `Test Project`, and give the description as `Test project description`. Clicking on the **Create** button will post the form data back to the server and attempt to add a new project record. If there are any validation errors, a simple error message will display that highlights each field in error. A successful save will redirect to the specific listing for the newly created project. Ours was successful and we were redirected to the page `http://localhost/trackstar/index.php?r=project/view&id=1`, as shown in the following screenshot:

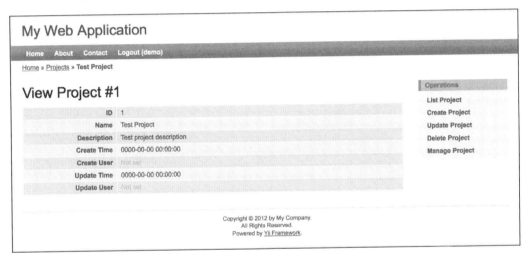

As we briefly mentioned previously, one thing we notice about our new project creation form is that both the name and the description fields were marked as being required. This is due to the fact that we defined the name and description columns in our database table to not allow for null values. Let's take a look at how these required fields work in Yii.

Form field validation

When working with AR model classes within forms in Yii, setting validation rules around form fields is a snap. This is done by specifying values in an array defined in the `rules()` method within AR model classes.

If you take a look at the code in the `Project` model class, (`/protected/models/Project.php`) you'll discover that the `rules()` public function has already been defined for us, and that there are already a few rules in there:

```
/**
 * @return array validation rules for model attributes.
 */
public function rules()
{
    // NOTE: you should only define rules for those attributes that
    // will receive user inputs.
    return array(
        array('name, description', 'required'),
        array('create_user_id, update_user_id', 'numerical',
'integerOnly'=>true),
        array('name', 'length', 'max'=>255),
        array('create_time, update_time', 'safe'),
        // The following rule is used by search().
        // Please remove those attributes that should not be searched.
        array('id, name, description, create_time, create_user_id,
update_time, update_user_id', 'safe', 'on'=>'search'),
    );
}
```

The `rules()` method returns an array of rules. Each rule is of the following general format:

```
Array('Attribute List', 'Validator', 'on'=>'Scenario List', …
additional options);
```

The `Attribute List` is a string of comma separated class property names to be validated according to the `Validator`. The `Validator` specifies what kind of rule should be enforced. The `on` parameter specifies a list of scenarios in which the rule should be applied. For example, if we were to specify that a validation should be applied in an `insert` scenario context, this would indicate that the rule should only be applied during an insert of a new record.

If a specific scenario is not defined, the validation rule is applied in all scenarios whenever validation is performed on the model data.

 As of Version 1.1.11 of Yii, you can also specify an `except` parameter, which allows you to exclude validations for certain scenarios. The syntax is the same as for the `on` parameter.

Finally, you can also specify additional options as `name=>value pairs`, which are used to initialize the validator's properties. These additional options will vary depending on the properties of the validator being specified.

The validator can either be a method in the model class, or a separate validator class. If defined as a model class method, it must have the following signature:

```
/**
 * @param string the name of the attribute to be validated
 * @param array options specified in the validation rule
 */
public function validatorName($attribute,$params)
{
...
}
```

If using a separate class to define the validator, that class must extend from `CValidator`.

There are actually three ways to specify a validator:

- Specify a method name in the model class itself
- Specify a separate class that is of a validator type (that is a class that extends `CValidator`)
- Specify a predefined alias to an existing validator class in the Yii framework

Yii provides many predefined validator classes for you and also provides aliases with which to reference these when defining rules. The complete list of predefined validator class aliases as of Yii Version 1.1.12 is as follows:

- **boolean**: Alias of `CBooleanValidator`, validates the attribute that contains either `true` or `false`
- **captcha**: Alias of `CCaptchaValidator`, validates the attribute value that is same as the verification code displayed in a CAPTCHA
- **compare**: Alias of `CCompareValidator`, compares two attributes and validates they are equal
- **email**: Alias of `CEmailValidator`, validates the attribute value that is a valid e-mail address
- **date**: Alias of `CDateValidator`, validates the attribute value that is a valid date, time, or date-time value
- **default**: Alias of `CDefaultValueValidator`, assigns a default value to the attributes specified

- **exist**: Alias of CExistValidator, validates the attribute value against a specified table column in a database

- **file**: Alias of CFileValidator, validates the attribute value that contains the name of an uploaded file

- **filter**: Alias of CFilterValidator, transforms the attribute value with a specified filter

- **in**: Alias of CRangeValidator, validates if the data is within a prespecified range of values, or exists within a specified list of values

- **length**: Alias of CStringValidator, validates whether the length of the attribute value is within a specified range

- **match**: Alias of CRegularExpressionValidator, uses a regular expression to validate the attribute value

- **numerical**: Alias of CNumberValidator, validates whether the attribute value is a valid number

- **required**: Alias of CRequiredValidator, validates whether the attribute value is empty or not

- **type**: alias of CTypeValidator, validates whether the attribute value is of a specific data type

- **unique**: Alias of CUniqueValidator, validates that the attribute value is unique, and is compared against a database table column

- **url**: Alias of CUrlValidator, validates whether the attribute value is a valid URL

We see that in our rules() function, there is a rule defined that specifies the name and description attributes and uses the Yii alias required to specify the validator:

```
array('name, description', 'required'),
```

It is the declaration of this validation rule that is responsible for the little red asterisks next to the **Name** and **Description** fields on the new project form. This indicates that this field is now required. If we go back to our new project creation form (http://localhost/trackstar/index.php?r=project/create) and attempt to submit the form without specifying either the **Name** or **Description**, we'll get a nicely formatted error message telling us that we cannot submit the form with blank values for these fields, as shown in the following screenshot:

Create Project

*Fields with * are required.*

> Please fix the following input errors:
> * Name cannot be blank.
> * Description cannot be blank.

Name *

Name cannot be blank.

Description *

Description cannot be blank.

Create Time

 As we previously mentioned, the Gii code generation tool will automatically add validation rules to the AR class based on the definitions of the columns in the underlying table. We saw this for the **Name** and **Description** columns defined with NOT NULL constraints that had associated required validators defined. As another example, columns that have length restrictions, like our name column being defined as `varchar(255)`, will have character limit rules automatically applied. We notice by taking another look at our `rules()` method in the `Project` AR class that Gii autocreated the rule `array('name', 'length', 'max'=>255)` for us based on its column definition. For more information about validators see `http://www.yiiframework.com/doc/guide/1.1/en/form.model#declaring-validation-rules`.

Reading the project

We have actually already seen this in action when we were taken to the project details page after successfully saving a new project `http://localhost/trackstar/index.php?r=project/view&id=1`. This page demonstrates the *R* in CRUD. However, to view the entire listing, we can click on the **List Project** link in the right-hand side column. This takes us back to where we started, except now we have our newly created project in the project list. So, we have the ability to retrieve a listing of all of the projects in the application, as well as view the details of each project individually.

Updating and deleting projects

Navigating back to a project details page can be done by clicking on the little project **ID** link on any of the projects in the listing. Let's do this for our newly created project, which is **ID: 1** in our case. Clicking on this link takes us to the project details page for this project. This page has a number of action operations in its right-hand side column that are shown in following screenshot:

We can see both of the **Update Project** and **Delete Project** links, which provide us with the *U* and *D* in our CRUD operations respectively. We'll leave it up to you to verify that these links work as expected.

The delete functionality is restricted to admin users; that is, you have to be logged in using the username/password combination of `admin/admin`. So, if you are verifying the delete functionality and receive a 403 error, ensure you are logged in as an administrator. This is discussed in more detail later, and we cover authentication and authorization in great detail in a later chapter.

Managing projects in Admin mode

The last link that we have not covered in the previous screenshot depicting our project operations is the **Manage Project** link. Go ahead and click on this link. It will most likely result in an authorization error as shown in the following screenshot:

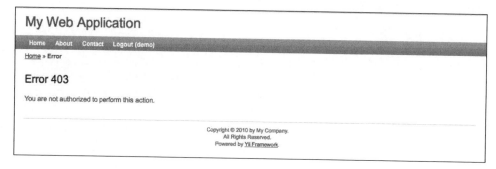

The reason for this error is that this functionality invokes a simple access control feature in Yii, and restricts access to *admin* users only. If you recall, when we logged into the application in order to create a new project, we used demo/demo as our username/password combination. This demo user does not have the authorization to access this admin page. The code generated by Gii restricts the access to this functionality.

An **administrator** in this context is simply someone who has logged in with the username/password combination of admin/admin. Go ahead and log out of the application by clicking on **Logout (demo)** present in the main navigation bar. Then log in again, but this time, use these administrator credentials. Once successfully logged in as admin you should notice the top navigation logout link change to **Logout (admin)**. Then navigate back to a specific project listing page, for example, http://localhost/trackstar/index.php?r=project/view&id=1, and try the **Manage Project** link again. You should now see what is shown in the following screenshot:

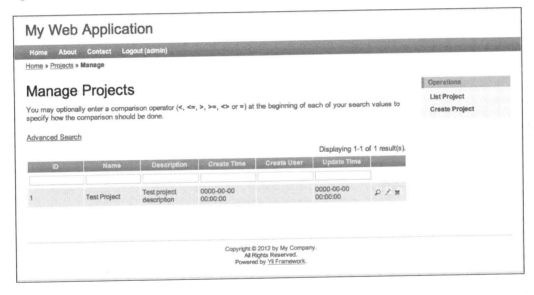

What we now see is a highly interactive version of our project listing page. It displays all the projects in an interactive data table. Each row has inline links to view, update, and delete each project. Clicking on any of the column header links sorts the project list by that column value. And the little input boxes in the second row allow you to search this project list by keywords within those individual column values. The advanced search link exposes an entire search form providing the ability to specify multiple search criteria to submit against one search. The following screenshot displays this advanced search form:

We have basically implemented all of the functionality we set out to achieve in this iteration, and haven't really had to code much of anything. In fact, with the help of Gii, not only did we create all of the CRUD functionality, we have also implemented basic project searching functionality that we were not expecting to achieve. Though very basic, we have a fully functioning application, with features specific to a project task tracking application, and have made very little effort to achieve it.

Of course we still have a lot of work to complete on our TrackStar application. All of this scaffolding code is not intended to fully replace application development. It provides us with an excellent starting point and foundation on which to continue to build our application. As we work through all the details and nuances of how the project functionality should work, we can rely on this autogenerated code to keep things moving forward at a rapid pace.

Summary

Even though we did not do much coding in this chapter, we accomplished quite a lot. We created a new database table, which allowed us to see Yii Active Record (AR) in action. We used the Gii tool to first create an AR model class to wrap our `tbl_project` database table. We then demonstrated how to use the Gii code generation tool to generate actual CRUD functionality in the web application. This amazing tool quickly created the functionality we needed, and even took it a step further by providing us with an administrative dashboard allowing us to search and sort our projects based on different criteria. We also demonstrated how to implement model data validation and how this translates to form field validation in Yii.

In the next chapter, we will build on what we have learned here and dive more deeply into Active Record in Yii as we introduce related entities in our data model.

5
Managing Issues

In the previous chapter, we delivered the basic functionality around the project entity. The project is at the foundation of the TrackStar application. However, projects by themselves are not terribly useful. Projects are the basic containers of the issues we want this application to manage. Since managing project issues is the main purpose of this application, we want to start adding in some basic issue-management functionality.

Feature planning

We already have the ability to create and list projects, but there is no way to manage the issues related to the projects. At the end of this chapter, we want the application to expose all CRUD operations on the project issues or tasks. (We tend to use the terms *issue* and *task* interchangeably, but in our data model, a task will actually be just one type of issue.) We also want to restrict all the CRUD operations on the issues to be within the context of a specific project. That is, *issues* belong to *projects*. The user must have selected an existing project to work within, prior to being able to perform any CRUD operations on the project's issues.

In order to achieve the previously mentioned outlined goals, we need to:

- Design the database schema and build the objects to support project issues
- Create the Yii model classes that will allow the application to easily interact with the database table(s) we created
- Create the controller class that will house the functionality to allow us to:
  - Create new issues
  - Retrieve a list of existing issues within a project from the database

○ Update/edit existing issues

○ Delete existing issues

• Create views to render user interfaces for these (above) actions

This list is plenty to get us going. Let's get started by making the necessary database changes.

Designing the schema

Back in *Chapter 3*, *The TrackStar Application*, we proposed some initial ideas about the *issue* entity. We proposed that it have a *name*, a *type*, an *owner*, a *requestor*, a *status*, and a *description*. We also mentioned when we created the `tbl_project` table that we would be adding basic audit history information to each table we create, to track the dates, times, and users who update the tables. However, types, owners, requestors, and statuses are themselves their own entities. To keep our model flexible and extensible, we'll model some of these separately. *Owners* and *requestors* are both users of the system and as such will be housed in a separate table called `tbl_user`. We have already introduced the idea of a *user* in the `tbl_project` table, as we added the columns `create_user_id` and `update_user_id` to track the identifier of the user who initially created the project, as well as the user who was responsible for last updating the project details. Even though we have not formally introduced that table yet, these fields are intended to be foreign keys to a `user` table. The `owner_id` and `requestor_id` column in the `tbl_issue` table will also be foreign keys that relate back to this `tbl_user` table.

We could model the type and status attributes in the same manner. However, until our requirements demand this extra complexity in the model, we can keep things simple. The `type` and `status` columns on the `tbl_issue` table will remain integer values that can be mapped to named types and statuses. However, rather than complicating our model by using separate tables, we will model these as basic class constant (`const`) values within the AR model class we create for the issue entity. Don't worry if all of this is a little fuzzy; it will make more sense in the coming sections.

Defining some relationships

Since we are introducing the `tbl_user` table, we need to go back and define the relationship between the users and projects. Back in *Chapter 3, The TrackStar Application*, we specified that users (we called them project members) would be associated with zero or more projects. We also mentioned that projects can also have many (one or more) users. Since projects can have many users and these users can be associated with many projects, we call this a **many-to-many** relationship between projects and users. The easiest way to model a many-to-many relationship in a relational database is to use an association table (also called an assignment table). So we need to add this table to our model as well.

The following figure outlines a basic entity-relationship between the users, projects, and issues. Projects can have zero to many users. A user needs to be associated with at least one project but can be associated with many. Issues belong to one and only one project, while projects can have from zero to many issues. Finally an issue is assigned to (or requested by) one single user.

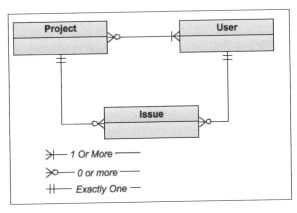

Building objects and their relationships

We have to create three new tables, namely `tbl_issue`, `tbl_user`, and our association table `tbl_project_user_assignment`. You may recall that we introduced Yii database migrations in *Chapter 4, Project CRUD*. As we are now ready to make a change to our database structure, we'll use Yii migrations for this as to better manage the application of these changes.

Since we are adding these to our database all at the same time, we'll do this in one migration. From the command line, change to the `protected/` directory and issue the following command:

```
$ ./yiic migrate create create_issue_user_and_assignment_tables
```

This will result in a new migration file being added to the `protected/migrations/` directory.

Open up this newly created file and implement the safeUp() and safeDown() method as follows:

```
// Use safeUp/safeDown to do migration with transaction
public function safeUp()
{
  //create the issue table
  $this->createTable('tbl_issue', array(
    'id' => 'pk',
     'name' => 'string NOT NULL',
      'description' => 'text',
      'project_id' => 'int(11) DEFAULT NULL',
    'type_id' => 'int(11) DEFAULT NULL',
    'status_id' => 'int(11) DEFAULT NULL',
    'owner_id' => 'int(11) DEFAULT NULL',
    'requester_id' => 'int(11) DEFAULT NULL',
    'create_time' => 'datetime DEFAULT NULL',
    'create_user_id' => 'int(11) DEFAULT NULL',
    'update_time' => 'datetime DEFAULT NULL',
    'update_user_id' => 'int(11) DEFAULT NULL',
     ), 'ENGINE=InnoDB');

  //create the user table
  $this->createTable('tbl_user', array(
    'id' => 'pk',
    'username' => 'string NOT NULL',
      'email' => 'string NOT NULL',
      'password' => 'string NOT NULL',
    'last_login_time' => 'datetime DEFAULT NULL',
    'create_time' => 'datetime DEFAULT NULL',
    'create_user_id' => 'int(11) DEFAULT NULL',
    'update_time' => 'datetime DEFAULT NULL',
    'update_user_id' => 'int(11) DEFAULT NULL',
     ), 'ENGINE=InnoDB');
```

```
    //create the assignment table that allows for many-to-many
//relationship between projects and users
    $this->createTable('tbl_project_user_assignment', array(
        'project_id' => 'int(11) NOT NULL',
        'user_id' => 'int(11) NOT NULL',
        'PRIMARY KEY (`project_id`,`user_id`)',
    ), 'ENGINE=InnoDB');

    //foreign key relationships

    //the tbl_issue.project_id is a reference to tbl_project.id
    $this->addForeignKey("fk_issue_project", "tbl_issue", "project_
id", "tbl_project", "id", "CASCADE", "RESTRICT");

    //the tbl_issue.owner_id is a reference to tbl_user.id
    $this->addForeignKey("fk_issue_owner", "tbl_issue", "owner_id",
"tbl_user", "id", "CASCADE", "RESTRICT");

    //the tbl_issue.requester_id is a reference to tbl_user.id
    $this->addForeignKey("fk_issue_requester", "tbl_issue",
"requester_id", "tbl_user", "id", "CASCADE", "RESTRICT");

    //the tbl_project_user_assignment.project_id is a reference to
tbl_project.id
    $this->addForeignKey("fk_project_user", "tbl_project_user_
assignment", "project_id", "tbl_project", "id", "CASCADE",
"RESTRICT");

    //the tbl_project_user_assignment.user_id is a reference to tbl_
user.id
    $this->addForeignKey("fk_user_project", "tbl_project_user_
assignment", "user_id", "tbl_user", "id", "CASCADE", "RESTRICT");


  }

  public function safeDown()
  {
    $this->truncateTable('tbl_project_user_assignment');
    $this->truncateTable('tbl_issue');
    $this->truncateTable('tbl_user');
    $this->dropTable('tbl_project_user_assignment');
    $this->dropTable('tbl_issue');
    $this->dropTable('tbl_user');
  }
```

Here we have implemented the `safeUp()` and `safeDown()` methods rather than the standard `up()` and `down()` methods. Doing this runs these statements in a database transaction with the intent that they are committed or rolled back as a single unit.

 In fact, since we are using MySQL, these `create table` and `drop table` statements will not be run in a single transaction. Certain MySQL statements cause implicit commits and as such using the `safeUp()` and `safeDown()` methods in this case is not of much use. We will leave this in to help the user understand why Yii migrations offer the `safeUp()` and `safeDown()` methods. See `http://dev.mysql.com/doc/refman/5.5/en/implicit-commit.html` for more details about this.

Now we can run the migration from the command line:

```
$ ./yiic migrate
Yii Migration Tool v1.0 (based on Yii v1.1.12)

Total 1 new migration to be applied:
    m121109_142835_create_issue_user_and_assignment_tables

Apply the above migration? (yes|no) [no]:yes
*** applying m121109_142835_create_issue_user_and_assignment_tables
    > create table tbl_issue ... done (time: 0.064s)
    > create table tbl_user ... done (time: 0.188s)
    > create table tbl_project_user_assignment ... done (time: 0.145s)
    > add foreign key fk_issue_project: tbl_issue (project_id) references tbl_project (id) ... done (time:
0.165s)
    > add foreign key fk_issue_owner: tbl_issue (owner_id) references tbl_user (id) ... done (time: 0.215s)
    > add foreign key fk_issue_requester: tbl_issue (requester_id) references tbl_user (id) ... done (time:
0.149s)
    > add foreign key fk_project_user: tbl_project_user_assignment (project_id) references tbl_project (id)
... done (time: 0.157s)
    > add foreign key fk_user_project: tbl_project_user_assignment (user_id) references tbl_user (id) ... d
one (time: 0.145s)
*** applied m121109_142835_create_issue_user_and_assignment_tables (time: 1.231s)

Migrated up successfully.
```

This migration has created our necessary database objects. Now we can turn our focus to creating our active record model classes.

Creating active record model classes

Now that we have these tables created, we need to create the Yii model AR classes to allow us to easily interact with these tables within the application. We did this when creating the `Project` model class in the previous chapter, by using the Gii code generation tool. We'll remind you of the steps here, but spare you of all the screenshots. Please refer to *Chapter 4, Project CRUD* for the more detailed walkthrough of using the Gii tool to create an active record class.

Creating the Issue model class

Navigate to the Gii tool via `http://localhost/trackstar/index.php?r=gii` and select the **Model Generator** link. Leave the table prefix as **tbl_**. Fill in the **Table Name** field as `tbl_issue`, which will autopopulate the **Model Class** field as **Issue**. Also ensure that the **Build Relations** checkbox is checked. This will ensure that our relationships are automatically created for us in our new model class.

Once the form is filled out, click on the **Preview** button to get a link to a pop up that will show you all of the code that is about to be generated. Then click on the **Generate** button to actually create the new `Issue.php` model class file in the `/protected/models/` directory.

Creating the User model class

This is probably becoming old-hat for you at this point, so we are going to leave the creation of the `User` AR class as an exercise for you. This particular class becomes much more important in the next chapter, when we dive into user authentication and authorization.

You may be asking, "What about the AR class for the `tbl_project_user_assignment` table?". Although one could create an AR class for this table, it is not necessary. The AR model provides an **Object Relational Mapping (ORM)** layer to our application to help us work much more easily with our domain objects. However, *ProjectUserAssignment* is not a domain object of our application. It is simply a construct in a relational database to help us model and manage the many-to-many relationship between the projects and users. Maintaining a separate AR class to handle the management of this table is extra complexity that we can avoid for the time being. We can manage the inserts, updates, and deletes on this table using Yii's DAO directly.

Creating the issue CRUD operations

Now that we have our issue AR class in place, we can turn to building the necessary functionality to manage our project issues. We'll again lean on the Gii code generation tool to help us create the basics of this functionality. We did this in detail for the projects in the previous chapter. I'll remind of you of the basic steps for Issues here, once again:

1. Navigate to the Gii generator menu at `http://localhost/trackstar/index.php?r=gii`, and select the **Crud Generator** link.

2. Fill out the form using **Issue** as the value for the **Model Class** field. This will autopopulate the **Controller ID** to also be **Issue**. The **Base Controller Class** and **Code Template** fields can remain their predefined default values.

3. Click on the **Preview** button to get a list of all the files that the Gii tool is proposing to create. The following screenshot shows this list of files:

Preview Generate	
Code File	**Generate** ☐
controllers/IssueController.php	new ☑
views/issue/_form.php	new ☑
views/issue/_search.php	new ☑
views/issue/_view.php	new ☑
views/issue/admin.php	new ☑
views/issue/create.php	new ☑
views/issue/index.php	new ☑
views/issue/update.php	new ☑
views/issue/view.php	new ☑

4. You can click on each individual link to preview the code to be generated. Once satisfied, click on the **Generate** button to have all of these files created. You should receive the following message of success:

> The controller has been generated successfully. You may try it now.

Using the issue CRUD operations

Let's try this out. Either click on the **try it now** link shown in the previous screenshot or simply navigate to `http://localhost/trackstar/index.php?r=issue`. You should be presented with something similar to what is shown in the following screenshot:

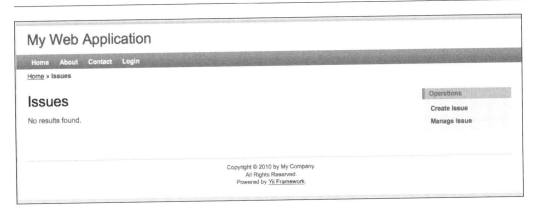

Creating a new issue

Since we have not yet added any new issues, there are none to list. Let's change that and create a new one. Click on the **Create Issue** link. (If this takes you to the login page, then log in using either demo/demo or admin/admin. You'll properly be redirected after a successful login.) You should now see a new Issue-Input form similar to what is shown in the following screenshot:

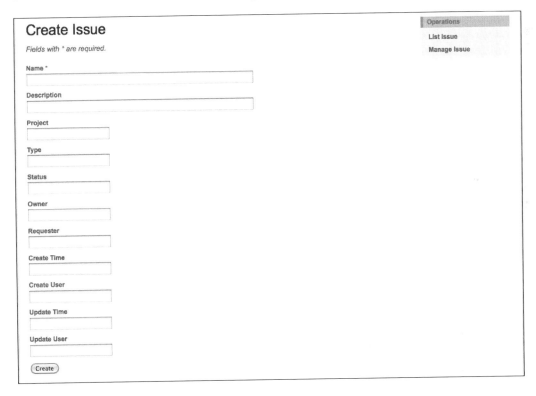

When looking at this input form, we can see that it has an input field for every column in the database table, just as it is defined in the database table. However, as we know from when we designed our schema and built our tables, some of these fields are not direct input fields but rather represent relationships to other entities. For example, rather than having a **Type** freeform text-input field on this form, we should use a drop-down input form field that is populated with choices of the issue types that are allowed. A similar argument could be made for the **Status** field. The **Owner** and **Requester** fields should also be drop-downs, exposing choices of the names of the users who have been assigned to work on the project under which the issue resides. Also, since all issue management should be taking place within the context of a specific project, the **Project** field should not even be a part of this form at all. Lastly, the **Create Time**, **Create User**, **Update Time**, and **Update User** fields are all values that should be calculated and determined once the form is submitted, and should not be available for the user to directly manipulate.

It seems we have identified a number of corrections we would like to make on this initial input form. As we mentioned in the previous chapter, the autocreated, CRUD "scaffolding" code that is generated by the Gii tool is just a starting point. Rarely is it enough on its own to meet all the specific functionality needs of an application.

Adding drop-down fields

We'll start with adding a drop-down for the issue types. Issues have just three types, namely *Bugs*, *Features*, and *Tasks*. What we would like to see when creating a new issue is a drop-down, input-type form field with these three choices. We will achieve this by having the Issue model class itself provide a list of its available types. Since we did not create a separate database table to hold our issue types, we'll add these as class constants directly to our Issue active record model class.

At the top of the Issue model class, add the following three constant definitions:

```
const TYPE_BUG=0;
const TYPE_FEATURE=1;
const TYPE_TASK=2;
```

Now add a new method to this class, Issue::getTypeOptions(), which will return an array based on these defined constants:

```
/**
 * Retrieves a list of issue types
 * @return array an array of available issue types.
 */
public function getTypeOptions()
{
    return array(
```

```
      self::TYPE_BUG=>'Bug',
      self::TYPE_FEATURE=>'Feature',
      self::TYPE_TASK=>'Task',
    );
}
```

We now have a way to retrieve the available list of issue types, but we still don't have a drop-down field in the input form that displays these values that we can choose from. Let's add that now.

Adding the issue type drop-down

Open up the file containing the new issue creation form protected/views/issue/_ form.php and find the lines that correspond to the **Type** field on the form:

```
<div class="row">
  <?php echo $form->labelEx($model,'type_id'); ?>
  <?php echo $form->textField($model,'type_id'); ?>
  <?php echo $form->error($model,'type_id'); ?>
</div>
```

These lines need a little clarification. In order to understand this, we need to refer to some code towards the top of the _form.php file, which is given as follows:

```
<?php $form=$this->beginWidget('CActiveForm', array(
  'id'=>'issue-form',
  'enableAjaxValidation'=>false,
)); ?>
```

This is defining the $form variable using the CActiveForm widget in Yii. **Widgets** are going to be covered in much more detail later. For now, we can understand this code by understanding CActiveForm better. CActiveForm can be thought of as a helper class that provides a set of methods to help us with creating forms that are associated with a data model class. In this case, it is being used to create an input form based on our Issue model class.

To fully understand the variables in our view file, let's also review our controller code that is rendering the view file(s). As has been previously discussed, one way to pass data from the controller to the view is by explicitly declaring an array, the keys of which will be the names of the available variables in the view files. Since this is the create action for a new issue, the controller method rendering the form is `IssueCont roller::actionCreate()`. This method is listed as follows:

```
/**
    * Creates a new model.
    * If creation is successful, the browser will be redirected to the
   'view'
  * page.
   */
  public function actionCreate()
  {
    $model=new Issue;

    // Uncomment the following line if AJAX validation is needed
    // $this->performAjaxValidation($model);

    if(isset($_POST['Issue']))
    {
      $model->attributes=$_POST['Issue'];
      if($model->save())
        $this->redirect(array('view','id'=>$model->id));
    }

    $this->render('create',array(
      'model'=>$model,
    ));
  }
```

Here we see that when the view is being rendered, it is being passed an instance of the `Issue` model class, which will be available in the view as a variable called `$model`.

Now let's go back to the code that is responsible for rendering the **Type** field on the form. The first line is:

```
$form->labelEx($model,'type_id');
```

This line is using the CActiveForm::labelEx() method to render an HTML label for the issue model attribute type_id. It takes in an instance of the model class and the corresponding model attribute for which we want a label generated. The model class Issue:: attributeLabels() method will be used to determine the label. If we take a peek at that method listed below, we see that the attribute type_id is mapped to a label of 'Type', which is exactly what we see rendered as the label to this form field:

```
public function attributeLabels()
{
    return array(
        'id' => 'ID',
        'name' => 'Name',
        'description' => 'Description',
        'project_id' => 'Project',
        'type_id' => 'Type',
        'status_id' => 'Status',
        'owner_id' => 'Owner',
        'requester_id' => 'Requester',
        'create_time' => 'Create Time',
        'create_user_id' => 'Create User',
        'update_time' => 'Update Time',
        'update_user_id' => 'Update User',
    );
}
```

Using the labelEx() method is also what is responsible for our little red asterisks next to our required fields. The labelEx() method will add an additional CSS class name (CHtml::requiredCss, which defaults to 'required') and asterisk (using CHtml::afterRequiredLabel, which defaults to ' <span class="required">*</span>') when the attribute is required.

The next line, <?php echo $form->textField($model,'type_id'); ?>, uses the CActiveForm::textField() method to render a text-input field for our Issue model attribute type_id. Any of the validation rules defined for type_id in the model class Issue::rules() method will be applied as form validation rules to this input form.

Finally the line `<?php echo $form->error($model,'type_id'); ?>` uses the `CActiveForm::error()` method to render any validation errors associated with the `type_id` attribute upon submission.

You can try out this validation with the type field. The `type_id` column is defined as an integer type in our MySQL schema definition, and because of this, Gii generated a validation rule in the `Issue::rules()` method to enforce this:

```
public function rules()
{
    // NOTE: you should only define rules for those attributes that
    // will receive user inputs.
    return array(
      array('name', 'required'),
      array('project_id, type_id, status_id, owner_id, requester_id,
create_user_id, update_user_id', 'numerical', 'integerOnly'=>true),
```

So if we attempt to submit a string value in our **Type** form field, we will receive an inline error right under the field, as depicted in the following screenshot:

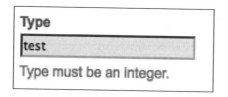

Now that we understand better exactly what we have, we are in a better position to change it. What we need to do is change this field from a free form, text-input field, to a drop-down entry type. It probably comes as little surprise that the `CActiveForm` class has a `dropDownList()` method that will generate a drop-down list for a model attribute. Let's replace the line that calls `$form->textField` (in the file `/protected/views/issue/_form.php`) with the following:

```
<?php echo $form->dropDownList($model,'type_id', $model-
>getTypeOptions()); ?>
```

This still takes the earlier model as the first argument and the model attribute as the second one. The third argument specifies the list of drop-down choices. This should be an array of `value=>display` pairs. We already created our `getTypeOptions()` method in the `Issue.php` model class to return an array of this format, so we can use it directly.

 It should be noted that Yii framework base classes make use of the PHP _get "magic" function. This allows us, in our child classes, to write methods such as `getTypeOptions()` and reference those methods as class properties, using the syntax `->typeOptions`. So we could have also used the equivalent syntax when requesting our issue type options array `$model->typeOptions`.

Save your work and look again at our issue input form. You should see a nice drop-down menu of Issue-type choices in place of the freeform text field, as displayed in the following screenshot:

Adding the status dropdown: do it yourself

We are going to take the same approach for the issue status. As mentioned back in *Chapter 3, The TrackStar application*, when we introduced the application, issues can be in one of the following three statuses:

- Not yet started
- Started
- Finished

We'll create three class constants in our `Issue` model class for the status values. Then we'll create a new method, `Issue::getStatusOptions()`, to return an array of our available issue statuses. And finally, we'll alter the `_form.php` file to render a drop-down of status options rather than a freeform text-input field for the status.

We are going to leave the implementation of the status drop-down to you. You can follow the same approach that we took for the types. After you make this change, the form should look similar to what is shown in the following screenshot:

We should also note that as we change these from freeform text-entry fields to drop-down fields, it is good practice to also add a range validation to our `rules()` method to ensure that the submitted value falls within the range of the values allowed by the drop-down. In the previous chapter, we saw a list of all the validators that the Yii framework provides. The `CRangeValidator` attribute, which uses an alias of *in*, is a good choice to use for defining this validation rule. So we could define such a rule as follows:

```
array('type_id', 'in', 'range'=>self::getAllowedTypeRange()),
```

And then we add a method to return an array of our allowed numerical type values:

```
public static function getAllowedTypeRange()
{
  return array(
    self::TYPE_BUG,
    self::TYPE_FEATURE,
```

```
        self::TYPE_TASK,
    );
}
```

Similarly do this for our `status_id`. We'll also leave this as an exercise for you to implement.

Fixing the owner and requester fields

Another problem we notice with the issue creation form is that the owner and requester fields are also freeform text-input fields. However, we know that these are integer values in the issue table that hold foreign key identifiers to the `id` column of the `tbl_user` table. So we also need to add drop-down fields for these fields. We won't take the exact same approach we did for the type and status attributes, as the issue owners and requesters need to be taken from the `tbl_user` table. Also, since not every user in the system will be associated with the project under which the issue resides, these issues cannot be used as drop-downs populated with the data taken from the entire `tbl_user` table. We need to restrict the list to just those users that are associated with this project.

This brings up another thing we need to address. As mentioned in the *Feature planning* section at the beginning of this chapter, we need to manage our issues within the context of a specific project. That is, a specific project should be chosen before you are able to create a new issue. Currently, our application does not enforce this workflow.

Let's address these changes one by one. First, we will alter the application to enforce a valid project to be identified prior to using any functionality to manage the issues associated with that project. Once a project is chosen, we'll make sure that both our owner and requester drop-down choices are restricted to only the users that are associated with that project.

Enforcing a project context

We want to ensure that a valid project context is present before we allow access to managing the issues. To do this, we are going to implement what is called a filter. A **filter** in Yii is a bit of code that is configured to be executed either before or after a controller action is executed. One common example is if we want to ensure that a user is logged in prior to executing a controller action method. We could write a simple access filter that would check this requirement before the action is executed. Another example is if we want to perform some extra logging or other auditing logic after an action has been executed. We could write a simple audit filter to provide this post-action processing.

In this case, we want to ensure that a valid project has been chosen prior to creating a new issue. So we'll add a project filter to our `IssueController` class to accomplish this.

Defining filters

A filter can be defined either as a controller class method or it can be a separate class. When using the simple-method approach, the method name must begin with the word *filter* and have a specific signature. For example, if we were going to create a filter method called *someMethodName*, our full filter method would look like:

```
public function filterSomeMethodName($filterChain)
{
...
}
```

The other approach is to write a separate class to perform the filter logic. When using the separate-class approach, the class must extend `CFilter` and then override at least one of the `preFilter()` or `postFilter()` methods depending on whether the logic should be executed before the action is invoked, or after.

Adding a filter

So, let's add a filter to our `IssueController` class to handle the checking for a valid project. We'll take the class-method approach.

Open up `protected/controllers/IssueController.php` and add the following method at the bottom of the class:

```
public function filterProjectContext($filterChain)
{
    $filterChain->run();
}
```

Okay, we now have a filter defined. However it does not do much yet. It simply executes `$filterChain->run()`, which continues the filtering process and allows the execution of the action methods that are being filtered by this method. This brings up another point. How do we define which action methods should use this filter?

Specifying the filtered actions

The Yii framework base class for our controller classes is CController. It has a filters() method that needs to be overridden in order to specify the actions on which the filters need to be applied. In fact, this method has already been overridden in our IssueController.php class. This was done for us when we used the Gii tool to autogenerate this class. It already added a simple *accessControl* filter, which is defined in the CController base class, to handle some basic authorization to ensure that the user has sufficient permission to perform certain actions. If you are not already logged in and click on the **Create Issue** link, you will be directed to the login page for authentication before being allowed to create a new issue. The access control filter is responsible for this. We'll be covering it in more detail when we focus on user authentication and authorization in the next chapter.

For now, we just need to add our new filter to this configuration array. To specify that our new filter should be applied to the create action, alter the IssueController::filters() method by adding the highlighted code, as follows:

```
/**
 * @return array action filters
 */
public function filters()
{
  return array(
    'accessControl', // perform access control for CRUD operations
    'projectContext + create', //check to ensure valid project context
  );
}
```

The filters() method should return an array of filter configurations. The previous code returns a configuration that specifies that the projectContext filter, which is defined as a method within the class, should be applied to the actionCreate() method. The configuration syntax allows for the "+" and "-" symbols to be used to specify whether a filter should or should not be applied. For example, if we decided that we wanted this filter to be applied to all the actions except the actionUpdate() and actionView() action methods, we could specify:

```
return array(
        'projectContext - update, view' ,
  );
```

You should not specify both the plus and the minus operators at the same time. Only one should be needed for any given filter configuration. The plus operator says "Only apply the filter to the following actions". The minus operator says "Apply the filter to ALL actions *except* the following". If neither the "+" nor the "-" is in the configuration, the filter will be applied to all the actions.

At the moment, we'll keep this restricted to just the create action. So as defined previously with the + create configuration, our filter method will be called when any user attempts to create a new issue.

Adding filter logic

Okay, so now we have a filter defined and we have configured it to be called upon every attempted actionCreate() method call within the issue controller class. However, it still does not perform the necessary logic. Since we want to ensure the project context before the action is attempted, we need to put the logic in the filter method before the call to $filterChain->run().

We'll add a project property to the controller class itself. We'll then use a querystring parameter in our URLs to indicate the project identifier. Our preaction filter will check to see if the existing project attribute is null; if so, it will use the querystring parameter to attempt to select the project based on the primary key identifier. If successful, the action will execute; if it fails, an exception will be thrown. Here is the relevant code needed to perform all of this:

```
class IssueController extends CController
{
    ....
    /**
    * @var private property containing the associated Project model
instance.
    */
    private $_project = null;

    /**
    * Protected method to load the associated Project model class
        * @param integer projectId the primary identifier of the
associated Project
    * @return object the Project data model based on the primary key
    */
    protected function loadProject($projectId)    {
    //if the project property is null, create it based on input id
    if($this->_project===null)
    {
    $this->_project=Project::model()->findByPk($projectId);
```

```
        if($this->_project===null)
                {
            throw new CHttpException(404,'The requested project does not
    exist.');
                }
        }

        return $this->_project;
    }

    /**
     * In-class defined filter method, configured for use in the above
    filters()
     * method. It is called before the actionCreate() action method is run
    in
     * order to ensure a proper project context
     */
    public function filterProjectContext($filterChain)
    {
    //set the project identifier based on GET input request variables
    if(isset($_GET['pid']))
        $this->loadProject($_GET['pid']);
        else
        throw new CHttpException(403,'Must specify a project before
    performing this action.');

        //complete the running of other filters and execute the requested
    action
        $filterChain->run();

    }
    ...
    }
```

With this in place, if you now attempt to create a new issue by clicking on the **Create Issue** link from the issue listing page at this URL http://localhost/trackstar/index.php?r=issue, you should see an "Error 403" error message, also displaying the error text we specified previously.

This is good. It shows that we have properly implemented the code to prevent a new issue from being created when no project has been identified. The quickest way to get past this error is to simply add a pid querystring parameter to the URL used for creating new issues. Let's do that so we can supply the filter with a valid project identifier and proceed to the form to create a new issue.

Adding the project ID

Back in *Chapter 4, Project CRUD,* we added several new projects to the application as we were testing and implementing the CRUD operations on projects. So it is likely that you still have a valid project in your development database. If not, simply use the application to create a new project again. Once complete, take note of the *project ID* created, as we need to add this ID to the new issue URL.

The link we need to alter is in the view file for the issue listing page /protected/ views/issue/index.php. Towards the top of that file, you will see where the link is defined for creating a new issue in our menu items. This is specified in the following highlighted code:

```
$this->menu=array(
    array('label'=>'Create Issue', 'url'=>array('create')),
    array('label'=>'Manage Issue', 'url'=>array('admin')),
);
```

To add a querystring parameter to this link, we simply append a *name=>value* pair in the defined array for the url parameter. The code we added for the filter is expecting the querystring parameter to be pid (for project id). Also, since we are using the first (project id = 1) project for this example, we will alter the **Create Issue** link as such:

```
array('label'=>'Create Issue', 'url'=>array('create', 'pid'=>1)),
```

Now when you view the issue listing page, you will see that the **Create Issue** hyperlink opens a URL with a querystring parameter appended at the end:

http://localhost/trackstar/index.php?r=issue/create&pid=1

This querystring parameter allows the filter to properly set the project context. So this time when you click on the link, rather than getting the 403 error page, the form to create a new issue will be displayed.

> For more details on using filters in Yii, see http://www. yiiframework.com/doc/guide/1.1/en/basics. controller#filter.

Altering the project details page

Adding the *project id* to the URL for the **Create New Issue** link was a good first step to ensure that our filter was working as expected. However, we have now hardcoded the link to always associate a new issue with the project ID = 1. This of course is not what we want. What we want to do is have the menu option for creating a new issue be a part of the project details page. In this way, once you have chosen a project from the project listing page, the specific project context will be known, and we can dynamically append that project ID to the create new issue link. Let's make that change.

Open up the project details view file /protected/views/project/view.php. At the top of this file, you will notice the menu items contained within the $this->menu array. We need to add another link to create a new issue to the end of this list of defined menu links:

```
$this->menu=array(
    array('label'=>'List Project', 'url'=>array('index')),
    array('label'=>'Create Project', 'url'=>array('create')),
    array('label'=>'Update Project', 'url'=>array('update',
'id'=>$model->id)),
    array('label'=>'Delete Project', 'url'=>'#', 'linkOptions'=>array('s
ubmit'=>array('delete','id'=>$model->id),'confirm'=>'Are you sure you
want to delete this item?')),
    array('label'=>'Manage Project', 'url'=>array('admin')),
    array('label'=>'Create Issue', 'url'=>array('issue/create',
'pid'=>$model->id)),
    );
```

What we have done is moved the menu option to create a new issue for the page that lists the details for a specific project. We used a link similar to the one before, but this time we had to specify the full *controllerID/actionID* pair (issue/create). Also, rather than hardcoding the project ID to be 1, we have used the $model variable within the view file, which is the AR class for the specific project. In this way, regardless of the project we choose, this variable will always reflect the correct project id attribute for that project.

With this in place, we can also remove the other link where we hardcoded the project ID to be 1 in the protected/views/issue/index.php view file.

Now that we have the project context properly set when creating a new issue, we can remove the project field as a user input form field. Open up the view file for the new issue form /protected/views/issue/_form.php. Remove the following lines that are associated with the project input field:

```
<div class="row">
    <?php echo $form->labelEx($model,'project_id'); ?>
    <?php echo $form->textField($model,'project_id'); ?>
    <?php echo $form->error($model,'project_id'); ?>
</div>
```

However, as the project_id attribute will not be submitted with the form, we will need to set the project_id parameter based on the one set from the filter we just implemented. Since we know the associated project ID already, let's explicitly set the Issue::project_id to the value of the id property of the project instance created by our previously implemented filter. So alter the IssueController::actionCreate() method as the following highlighted code suggests:

```
public function actionCreate()
{
    $model=new Issue;
    $model->project_id = $this->_project->id;
```

Now when we submit the form back, the project_id attribute for the issue active record instance will be correctly set. Even though we don't have our owner and requestor dropdowns set yet, we can submit the form and a new issue will be created with the proper project ID set.

Returning back to the owner and requester dropdowns

Finally, we can turn back to what we were setting out to do, which is to change the owner and requester fields to be the drop-down choices of the valid members of that project. In order to properly do this, we need to associate some users with a project. Since user management is the focus of the upcoming chapters, we will do this manually by adding the association directly to the database via direct SQL. Let's add two test users using the following SQL:

```
INSERT INTO tbl_user (email, username, password) VALUES ('test1@
notanaddress.com','User One', MD5('test1')), ('test2@notanaddress.
com','User Two', MD5('test2'));
```

We are using the one-way MD5 hashing algorithm here because of its ease of use and because it is widely available with the 5.x versions of MySQL and PHP. However, it is now known that MD5 is "broken" as a one-way hashing algorithm with regard to security, and it is not suggested that you use this hashing algorithm in a production environment. Please consider using *Bcrypt* for your real production applications. Here are some URLs providing more information on *Bcrypt*:

http://en.wikipedia.org/wiki/Bcrypt

http://php.net/manual/en/function.crypt.php

http://www.openwall.com/phpass/

When you run this on the `trackstar` database, it will create two new users in our system with the IDs 1 and 2. Let's also manually assign these two users to project #1 with the following SQL:

```
INSERT INTO tbl_project_user_assignment (project_id, user_id)
VALUES (1,1), (1,2);
```

After running the previous SQL statements, we have two valid members assigned to project #1.

One of the wonderful features of relational Active Record within Yii is the ability to access the valid members of a project that an issue belongs to, directly from the issue `$model` instance itself. When we used the Gii tool to initially create our issue model class, we ensured that the **Build Relations** checkbox was ticked. This instructed Gii to look at the underlying database and define the relevant relationships. This can be seen in the `relations()` method within `/protected/models/Issue.php`. Since we created this class after adding the appropriate relationships to the database, the method should look something like the following:

```
    /**
     * @return array relational rules.
     */
    public function relations()
    {
        //NOTE: you may need to adjust the relation name and the related
        // class name for the relations automatically generated below.
        return array(
            'requester' => array(self::BELONGS_TO, 'User', 'requester_id'),
            'owner' => array(self::BELONGS_TO, 'User', 'owner_id'),
            'project' => array(self::BELONGS_TO, 'Project', 'project_id'),
        );
    }
```

The //NOTE comment from the previous code snippet suggests that you may have slightly different, or want slightly different, class attribute names and encourages you to adjust them as needed. This array configuration defines properties on the model instance that are themselves other AR instances. With these relations in place, we can access the related AR instances incredibly easily. For example, say we want to access the project to which an issue is associated. We can do so using the following syntax:

```
//create the model instance by primary key:
$issue = Issue::model()->findByPk(1);
//access the associated Project AR instance
$project = $issue->project;
```

Since we created our Project model class prior to having other tables and relationships defined in our database, there are no relations defined yet. However now that we have some relationships defined, we need to add these to the Project::relations() method. Open up the project AR class /protected/models/Project.php and replace the entire relations() method with the following:

```
/**
 * @return array relational rules.
 */
public function relations()
{
return array(
        'issues' => array(self::HAS_MANY, 'Issue', 'project_id'),
        'users' => array(self::MANY_MANY, 'User', 'tbl_project_
user_assignment(project_id, user_id)'),
    );
}
```

With these in place, we can easily access all of the issues and/or users associated with a project with incredibly easy syntax. For example:

```
//instantiate the Project model instance by primary key:
$project = Project::model()->findByPk(1);
//get an array of all associated Issue AR instances
$allProjectIssues = $project->issues;
//get an array of all associated User AR instance
$allUsers = $project->users;
//get the User AR instance representing the owner of
//the first issue associated with this project
$ownerOfFirstIssue = $project->issues[0]->owner;
```

Normally we would have to write complicated SQL join statements to access such related data. Using relational AR in Yii saves us from this complexity and tedium. We can now access these relationships in a very elegant and concise, object-oriented manner that is very easy to read and understand.

Generating the data to populate the dropdowns

We'll follow a similar approach as we did for the status and type drop-down data in order to implement a valid user dropdown. We'll add a getUserOptions() method to our Project model class.

Open up the file /protected/models/Project.php and add the following method to the bottom of the class:

```
/**
 * @return array of valid users for this project, indexed by user IDs
 */
public function getUserOptions()
{
  $usersArray = CHtml::listData($this->users, 'id', 'username');
      return $usersArray;
}
```

Here we are using Yii's CHtml helper class to help us create an array of id=>username pairs from each user associated with the project. Remember that the users property (defined in the relations() method) in the project class mapped to an array of user AR instances. The CHtml::listData() method can take in this list and produce a valid array in a suitable format for CActiveForm::dropDownList().

Now that we have our getUserOptions() method returning the data we need, we should implement the dropdown to display that returned data. We have already used a filter to set the associated project ID from the $_GET request, and we used this value to set the project_id attribute on the new issue instance at the beginning of the IssueController::actionCreate() method. So now, through the lovely power of Yii's relational AR features, we can easily populate our dropdown of users using the associated Project model. Here are the changes we need to make in the issue form:

Open up the view file containing the input form elements /protected/views/issue/_form.php, and find the two text-input field form element definitions for owner_id and requester_id and replace it with the following code:

```
<?php echo $form->textField($model,'owner_id'); ?>
with this:
```

```
<?php echo $form->dropDownList($model,'owner_id', $model->project-
>getUserOptions()); ?>
and also replace this line:
<?php echo $form->textField($model,'requester_id'); ?>
with this:
<?php echo $form->dropDownList($model,'requester_id', $model->project-
>getUserOptions()); ?>
```

Now if we view our issue creation form again, we see two nicely populated drop-down fields for the **Owner** and **Requester**:

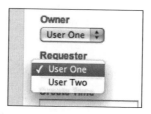

Making one last change

Since we already have the create issue form view file open, let's quickly make one last change. The creation time and user as well as the last updated time and user fields that we have on every table for basic history and auditing purposes should not be exposed to the user. Later we will alter the application logic to automatically populate these fields upon inserts and updates. For now, let's just remove them as inputs on the form.

Just completely remove the following lines from /protected/views/issue/_form. php:

```
<div class="row">
    <?php echo $form->labelEx($model,'create_time'); ?>
    <?php echo $form->textField($model,'create_time'); ?>
    <?php echo $form->error($model,'create_time'); ?>
</div>

<div class="row">
    <?php echo $form->labelEx($model,'create_user_id'); ?>
    <?php echo $form->textField($model,'create_user_id'); ?>
    <?php echo $form->error($model,'create_user_id'); ?>
</div>

  <div class="row">
      <?php echo $form->labelEx($model,'update_time'); ?>
      <?php echo $form->textField($model,'update_time'); ?>
```

```
        <?php echo $form->error($model,'update_time'); ?>
    </div>

    <div class="row">
      <?php echo $form->labelEx($model,'update_user_id'); ?>
      <?php echo $form->textField($model,'update_user_id'); ?>
      <?php echo $form->error($model,'update_user_id'); ?>
    </div>
```

The following screenshot shows what our new issue creation form now looks like with all of these changes:

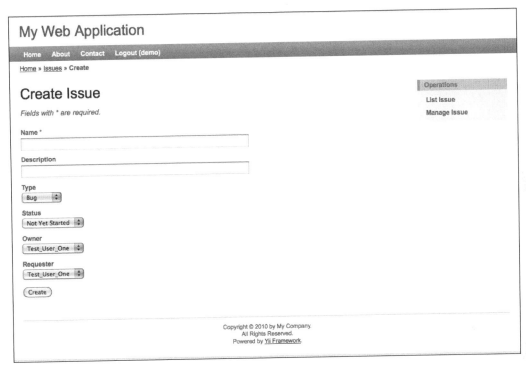

The rest of the CRUD

The goal of this chapter is to implement all the CRUD operations for Issues. We have finalized the creation functionality, but we still need to complete the read, update, and delete of issues. Luckily, most of the foundation has already been laid by using the Gii CRUD generation functionality. However, since we want to manage all the issues within the context of a project, we need to make some adjustments to how we access this functionality.

Listing the issues

Even though there is the `actionIndex()` method in the `IssueController` class that displays a list of all the issues in the database, we don't have a need for this functionality as it is currently coded. Rather than a separate, standalone page that lists all the issues in the database, we want to only list the issues that are associated with a specific project. So we'll alter the application to display the listing of the issues as part of the project details page. Since we are taking advantage of the relational AR model in Yii, it will be a snap to make this change.

Altering the project controller

First let's alter the `actionView()` method in the `ProjectController` class. Since we want to display a list of the issues associated with a specific project, we can do this on the same page as the project details page. The method `actionView()` is the method that displays the project details.

Alter that method to be:

```
/**
 * Displays a particular model.
 * @param integer $id the ID of the model to be displayed
 */
public function actionView($id)
{
        $issueDataProvider=new CActiveDataProvider('Issue',
array(
                'criteria'=>array(
                        'condition'=>'project_id=:projectId',
                        'params'=>array(':projectId'=>$this-
>loadModel($id)->id),
                ),
                'pagination'=>array(
                        'pageSize'=>1,
                ),
        ));

        $this->render('view',array(
                'model'=>$this->loadModel($id),
                'issueDataProvider'=>$issueDataProvider,
        ));

}
```

Here we are using the `CActiveDataProvider` framework class to provide data using `CActiveRecord` objects. It will use the associated AR model class to retrieve data from the database in a manner that can be used very easily with a great, built-in, framework-listing component called `CListView`. We'll use this component to display a list of our issues in the view file. We have used the criteria property to specify the condition that it should only retrieve the issues associated with the project being displayed. We also used the pagination property to limit the issue list to just one issue per page. We set this very low so we can quickly demonstrate the paging features by just adding another issue. We'll demonstrate this soon.

The last thing we did was add this data provider to the array defined in the call to `render()`, to make it available to the view file in a `$issueDataProvider` variable.

Altering the project view file

As we just mentioned, we'll use a framework component called `CListView` to display our list of issues on the project details page. Open up `/protected/views/project/view.php` and add this to the bottom of that file:

```
<br />
<h1>Project Issues</h1>

<?php $this->widget('zii.widgets.CListView', array(
  'dataProvider'=>$issueDataProvider,
  'itemView'=>'/issue/_view',
)); ?>
```

Here we are setting the `dataProvider` property of `CListView` to be our issue data provider that we created above. And then we are configuring it to use the `protected/views/issue/_view.php` file as a template for rendering each item in the data provider. This file was already created for us by the Gii tool when we generated our CRUD for the issues. We are making use of it here to display the issues on the project details page.

> You may recall from way back in *Chapter 1, Meet Yii*, that **Zii** is the official extension library that is packaged with the Yii framework. These extensions are developed and maintained by the core Yii framework team. You can read more about Zii here: `http://www.yiiframework.com/doc/guide/1.1/en/extension.use#zii-extensions`

We need to also make a couple of changes to the /protected/views/issue/_view.
php file that we specified as a layout template for each issue. Alter the entire contents
of that file to be the following:

```
<div class="view">

    <b><?php echo CHtml::encode($data->getAttributeLabel('name')); ?>:</
b>
    <?php echo CHtml::link(CHtml::encode($data->name), array('issue/
view', 'id'=>$data->id)); ?>
    <br />


    <b><?php echo CHtml::encode($data->getAttributeLabel('descripti
on')); ?>:</b>
    <?php echo CHtml::encode($data->description); ?>
    <br />


    <b><?php echo CHtml::encode($data->getAttributeLabel('type_id'));
?>:</b>
    <?php echo CHtml::encode($data->type_id); ?>
<br />


    <b><?php echo CHtml::encode($data->getAttributeLabel('status_id'));
?>:</b>
    <?php echo CHtml::encode($data->status_id); ?>

</div>
```

Now if we save and view our results by looking at the project details page for project
number 1 (http://localhost/trackstar/index.php?r=project/view&id=1),
and assuming you have created at least one example issue under that project (if not,
just use the **Create Issue** link from this page to create one), we should see what is
displayed in the following screenshot:

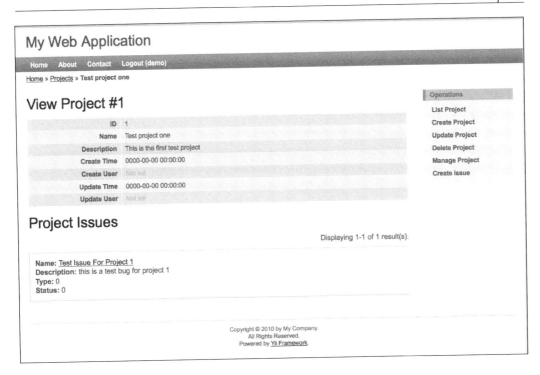

Since we set the pagination property of our data provider very low (remember we set it to just 1), we can add one more issue to demonstrate the built-in paging functionality. Adding one more issue changes the display of the issues to have links that allow us to go from page to page within our project issues' listing, as depicted in the following screenshot:

Final tweaks

We now have a list of our issues associated with a project and are displaying them on the project details page. We also have the ability to view the details of an issue (that is Read them) as well as links to Update and Delete issues. So our basic CRUD operations are in place.

However, there are still a few items that need to be addressed before we can complete this section of our application. One thing we will notice is that the issues display list is showing numeric ID numbers for the **Type, Status, Owner**, and **Requester** fields. We should change this so that the text values for those are displayed instead. Also, since the issues are under a specific project already, it is a bit redundant to have the project ID displayed as part of the issue list data. So we can remove that. Finally, we need to address some of the navigational links that are displayed on the various other issue-related forms to ensure that we are always returning to this project details page as the starting place for all of our issue management.

We'll tackle these one at a time.

Getting the status and type text to display

Previously we added public methods to the Issue AR class, to retrieve the status and type options to populate the dropdowns on the issue creation form. We need to add similar methods on this AR class to return the text for a specific status or type ID.

Add the following two, new public methods to the Issue model class (/protected/models/Issue.php) to retrieve the status and type text for the current issue:

```
/**
 * @return string the status text display for the current issue
 */
public function getStatusText()
{
  $statusOptions=$this->statusOptions;
  return isset($statusOptions[$this->status_id]) ?
$statusOptions[$this->status_id] : "unknown status ({$this->status_
id})";
}

/**
 * @return string the type text display for the current issue
 */
public function getTypeText()
{
  $typeOptions=$this->typeOptions;
```

```
        return isset($typeOptions[$this->type_id]) ? $typeOptions[$this-
    >type_id] : "unknown type ({$this->type_id})";
    }
```

These return the status text value ("Not Yet Started", "Started", or "Finished") and type text value ("Bug", "Feature", or "Task") for the Issue instance.

Adding the text display to the form

Now that we have our two new public methods that will return the valid status and type text for our listing to display, we need to make use of them. Alter the following lines of code in /protected/views/issue/_view.php.

Change this `<?php echo CHtml::encode($data->type_id); ?>` to this:

```
<?php echo CHtml::encode($data->getTypeText()); ?>
```

And this `<?php echo CHtml::encode($data->status_id); ?>` to this:

```
<?php echo CHtml::encode($data->getStatusText()); ?>
```

After these changes, our issues listing page for **Project #1**, http://localhost/ trackstar/index.php?r=issue&pid=1, no longer displays integer values for our issue type and status fields. It now looks like what is displayed in the following screenshot:

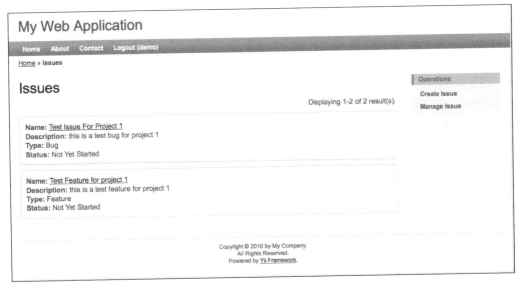

Since we are using the same view file to display our issues listing on our project details page, these changes are reflected there as well.

Changing the issue detail view

We also need to make a few other changes to the details view of the issue. Currently if we view the issue details, it is displayed as in the following screenshot:

View Issue #1

ID	1
Name	Test Issue For Project 1
Description	this is a test bug for project 1
Project	1
Type	0
Status	0
Owner	1
Requester	1
Create Time	0000-00-00 00:00:00
Create User	Not set
Update Time	0000-00-00 00:00:00
Update User	Not set

This is using a view file we have not yet altered. It is still displaying the project ID, which we don't need to display, as well as the **Type** and **Status** as integer values rather than their associated text values. Opening up the view file used to render this display, /protected/views/issue/view.php, we notice that it is using the Zii extension widget CDetailView, which we have not seen before. This is similar to the CListView widget used to display the listing, but is used to display the details of a single data model instance rather than for displaying a list view of many. The following is the relevant code from this file showing the use of this widget:

```php
<?php $this->widget('zii.widgets.CDetailView', array(
    'data'=>$model,
    'attributes'=>array(
        'id',
        'name',
        'description',
        'project_id',
        'type_id',
        'status_id',
        'owner_id',
        'requester_id',
        'create_time',
        'create_user_id',
        'update_time',
```

```
                'update_user_id',
            ),
    )); ?>
```

Here we are setting the data model of the `CDetailView` widget to be the `Issue` model class instance (that is the specific instance we want to display the details of), and then setting a list of attributes of the model instance to be displayed in the rendered detail view. An attribute can be specified as a string in the format of `Name:Type:Label`, of which both `Type` and `Label` are optional, or as an array itself. In this case just the name of the attributes are specified.

If we specify an attribute as an array, we can customize the display further by declaring a value element. We will take this approach in order to specify the model class methods `Issue::getTypeText()` and `Issue::getStatusText()` to be used to get the text values for the **Type** and **Status** fields respectively.

Let's change this use of `CDetailView` to use the following configuration:

```
<?php $this->widget('zii.widgets.CDetailView', array(
    'data'=>$model,
    'attributes'=>array(
        'id',
        'name',
        'description',
        array(
            'name'=>'type_id',
            'value'=>CHtml::encode($model->getTypeText())
        ),
        array(
            'name'=>'status_id',
            'value'=>CHtml::encode($model->getStatusText())
        ),
        'owner_id',
        'requester_id',
        ),
    )); ?>
```

Here we have removed a few attributes from being displayed at all, namely the `project_id`, `create_time`, `update_time`, `create_user_id`, and `update_user_id` attributes. We will handle the population and display of some of these later, but for now we can just remove them from the detail display.

We also changed the declaration of the `type_id` and `status_id` attributes to use an array specification so that we could use the value element. We have specified that the corresponding `Issue::getTypeText()` and `Issue::getStatusText()` methods be used for getting the values of these attributes. With these changes in place, viewing the issue details page shows the following:

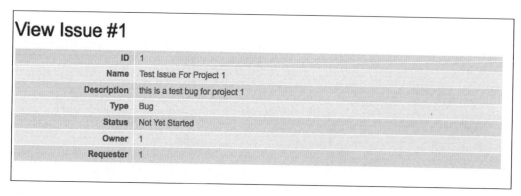

Okay, we are getting much closer to what we want, but there are still a couple of changes we need to make.

Displaying owner and requester names

Things are looking better, but we still see integer identifiers being displayed for the **Owner** and **Requester** rather than the actual usernames. We'll take a similar approach to what we did for the type and status text displays. We'll add two new public methods on the `Issue` model class to return the names of these two properties.

Using relational AR

Since our issues and users are represented as separate database tables and related through a foreign key relationship, we can access the `owner` and `requester` username directly from `$model` in the view file. Utilizing the power of Yii's relational AR model features, displaying the username attribute of the related `User` model class instance is a snap.

As we have mentioned, the model class `Issue::relations()` method is where the relationships are defined. If we take a peek at this method, we see the following:

```
/**
 * @return array relational rules.
 */
public function relations()
{
```

```
    // NOTE: you may need to adjust the relation name and
//the related class name for the relations automatically generated
//below.
    return array(
        'owner' => array(self::BELONGS_TO, 'User', 'owner_id'),
        'project' => array(self::BELONGS_TO, 'Project', 'project_id'),
        'requester' => array(self::BELONGS_TO, 'User', 'requester_id'),
    );
}
```

The highlighted code is what is most relevant for our needs. There are both owner and requester attributes defined as relations to the User model class. These definitions specify that the values of these attributes are User model class instances. The owner_id and requester_id parameters specify the unique primary key of their respective User class instances. So we can access these just as we do our other attributes of the Issue model class.

To display the username of the owner and requester User class instances, we once again change our CDetailView configuration to the following:

```
<?php $this->widget('zii.widgets.CDetailView', array(
    'data'=>$model,
    'attributes'=>array(
        'id',
        'name',
        'description',
        array(
            'name'=>'type_id',
            'value'=>CHtml::encode($model->getTypeText())
        ),
        array(
            'name'=>'status_id',
            'value'=>CHtml::encode($model->getStatusText())
        ),
        array(
        'name'=>'owner_id',
        'value'=>isset($model->owner)?CHtml::encode($model->owner-
>username):"unknown"
        ),
        array(
            'name'=>'requester_id',
            'value'=>isset($model->requester)?CHtml::encode($model-
>requester->username):"unknown"          ),
    ),
)); ?>
```

After making these changes, our issues detail listing is starting to look pretty good. The following screenshot shows the progress we made so far:

View Issue #1

ID	1
Name	Test Issue For Project 1
Description	this is a test bug for project 1
Type	Bug
Status	Not Yet Started
Owner	Test_User_One
Requester	Test_User_One

Making some final navigation tweaks

We are very close to completing the functionality that we set out to implement within this chapter. The only thing left to do is to clean up our navigation just a little. You may have noticed that there are still some options available that allow the user to navigate to an entire listing of issues, or to create a new issue, outside of a project context. For the purposes of our TrackStar application, everything we do with issues should be within the context of a specific project. Earlier we enforced this project context for creating a new issue, which is a good start, but we still need to make a few changes.

One thing that we will notice is that the application still allows the user to navigate to a listing of all issues, across all projects. For example, on an issue detail page, such as `http://localhost/trackstar/index.php?r=issue/view&id=1`, we see that in the right-hand column menu navigation there are the links **List Issue** and **Manage Issue**, corresponding to `http://localhost/trackstar/index.php?r=issue/index` and `http://localhost/trackstar/index.php?r=issue/admin` respectively (remember that to access the admin page, you have to be logged in as `admin/admin`). These still display all the issues across all the projects. So we need to limit this list to a specific project.

Since these links originate from the issue details page and that specific issue has an associated project, we can first alter the links to be passed in a specific project ID, and then use that project ID as the criteria to limit our issue's query in both the `IssueController::actionIndex()` and `IssueController::actionAdmin()` methods.

First let's alter the links. Open up the `/protected/views/issue/view.php` file and locate the array of menu items towards the top of the file. Change the menu configuration to be:

```
$this->menu=array(
    array('label'=>'List Issues', 'url'=>array('index', 'pid'=>$model-
>project->id)),
    array('label'=>'Create Issue', 'url'=>array('create', 'pid'=>$model-
>project->id)),
    array('label'=>'Update Issue', 'url'=>array('update', 'id'=>$model-
>id)),
    array('label'=>'Delete Issue', 'url'=>'#', 'linkOptions'=>array('su
bmit'=>array('delete','id'=>$model->id),'confirm'=>'Are you sure you
want to delete this item?')),
    array('label'=>'Manage Issues', 'url'=>array('admin', 'pid'=>$model-
>project->id)),
);
```

The changes made are highlighted. We have added a new querystring parameter to the **Create Issue** link, as well as to the issue listing page and the issue admin listing page. We already knew that we had to make this change for the create link, since we have previously implemented a filter to enforce that a valid project context be made available prior to creating a new issue. We won't have to make any further changes relative to this link. But for the index and admin links, we will need to alter their corresponding action methods to make use of this new querystring variable.

Since we have already configured a filter to load the associated project using the querysting variable, let's take advantage of this. We'll add to the filter configuration so that our filter method is called prior to both the `IssueController::actionIndex()` and `IssueController::actionAdmin()` methods being executed. Change the `IssueController::filters()` method as such:

```
public function filters()
    {
        return array(
            'accessControl', // perform access control for CRUD operations
            'projectContext + create index admin', //perform a check to
ensure valid project context
        );
    }
```

With this in place, the associated project will be loaded and available for use. Let's use it in our `IssueController::actionIndex()` method. Alter that method to be:

```
public function actionIndex()
{
$dataProvider=new CActiveDataProvider('Issue', array(
    'criteria'=>array(
     'condition'=>'project_id=:projectId',
     'params'=>array(':projectId'=>$this->_project->id),
     ),
   ));
    $this->render('index',array(
     'dataProvider'=>$dataProvider,
    ));
}
```

Here, as we have done before, we are simply adding a condition to the creation of the model data provider to only retrieve the issues associated with the project. This will limit the list of issues to just the ones under the project.

We need to make the same change to the admin listing page. However, this view file /protected/views/issue/admin.php is using the results of the model class Issue::search() method to provide the listing of the issues. So we actually need to make two changes to enforce the project context with this listing.

First we need to alter the IssueController::actionAdmin() method to set the correct project_id attribute on the model instance it is sending to the view. The following highlighted code shows this necessary change:

```
public function actionAdmin()
  {
    $model=new Issue('search');

    if(isset($_GET['Issue']))
      $model->attributes=$_GET['Issue'];

    $model->project_id = $this->_project->id;

    $this->render('admin',array(
      'model'=>$model,
    ));
  }
```

Then we need to add to our criteria in the `Issue::search()` model class method.
The following highlighted code identifies the change that we need to make to
this method:

```
public function search()
    {
        // Warning: Please modify the following code to remove attributes that
        // should not be searched.

        $criteria=new CDbCriteria;

        $criteria->compare('id',$this->id);

        $criteria->compare('name',$this->name,true);

        $criteria->compare('description',$this->description,true);

        $criteria->compare('type_id',$this->type_id);

        $criteria->compare('status_id',$this->status_id);

        $criteria->compare('owner_id',$this->owner_id);

        $criteria->compare('requester_id',$this->requester_id);

        $criteria->compare('create_time',$this->create_time,true);

        $criteria->compare('create_user_id',$this->create_user_id);

        $criteria->compare('update_time',$this->update_time,true);

        $criteria->compare('update_user_id',$this->update_user_id);

        $criteria->condition='project_id=:projectID';

        $criteria->params=array(':projectID'=>$this->project_id);

        return new CActiveDataProvider(get_class($this), array(
            'criteria'=>$criteria,
        ));
    }
```

Here, we have removed the `$criteria->compare()` call using `project_id` with the direct `$criteria->condition()` that the `project_id` value be exactly equal to our project context. With these changes in place, the issues listed on the admin page are now restricted to be only those that are associated with the specific project.

> There are several places throughout the view files under `/protected/views/issues/` that contain links that require a `pid` querystring to be added in order to work properly. We leave it as an exercise to the reader to make the appropriate changes following the same approach as provided in these examples. As we proceed with our application development, we'll assume that all the links to create a new issue or to display a list of issues are properly formatted to contain the appropriate `pid` querystring parameter.

Summary

We were able to cover a lot of different topics in this chapter. Based on the relationship between *issues, projects,* and *users* within our application, the implementation of our issue-management functionality was significantly more complicated than our project entity management that we worked on in the previous chapter. Fortunately, Yii was able to come to our rescue many times to help alleviate the pain of having to write all of the code needed to address this complexity.

We leaned on our good friend Gii for Active Record model creation as well as for the initial implementation of all basic CRUD operations against the issue entity. We again used Yii migrations to help facilitate our needed database schema changes to support our issue functionality. We got to use relational Active Record in Yii, and saw how easy it is to retrieve related database information using this feature. We introduced controller filters as a means to tap into the request life cycle and implement business logic before and/or after controller action methods. And we demonstrated how to use dropdowns in our Yii forms.

We have made a lot of progress on our basic application thus far, and have done so without having to write a lot of code. The Yii framework itself has done most of the heavy lifting. We now have a working application that allows us to manage projects and also manage the issues within those projects. This is the heart of what our application is trying to achieve. We should feel proud of the accomplishments thus far.

However, we still have a long way to go before this application is truly ready for production use. A major missing piece is all of the needed functionality around user management. In the next two chapters, we will be diving into user authentication and authorization. We'll start by showing how Yii user authentication works, and start authenticating our users against the usernames and passwords stored in the database.

6

User Management and Authentication

We have made a lot of progress in a very short amount of time. The basic foundation of our TrackStar application has been laid. We now have the ability to manage projects and issues within projects, which is the primary purpose of this application. Of course, there is still a lot left to do.

Back in *Chapter 3, The TrackStar Application*, when we were introducing this application, we described it as a user-based application that provides the ability to create user accounts and grants access to the application features once a user has been authenticated and authorized. In order for this application to be useful to more than one person we need to add the ability to manage users within projects. This is going to be the focus of the next two chapters.

Feature planning

When we used the `yiic` command-line tool to initially create our TrackStar application, we noticed that basic login functionality was automatically created for us. The login page allows for two username/password credential combinations, `demo/demo` and `admin/admin`. You may recall that we had to log in to the application in order to perform some of our CRUD operations on our project and issue entities in the previous two chapters.

This basic authentication skeleton code provides a great start, but we need to make a few changes in order to support any number of users. We also need to add user CRUD functionality to the application to allow us to manage these multiple users. This chapter is going to focus on extending the authentication model to use the `tbl_user` database table and add the needed functionality to allow for basic user data management.

In order to achieve the above outlined goals, we will need to work on the following:

- Create the controller classes that will house the functionality to allow us to:
    - Create new users
    - Retrieve a list of existing users from the database
    - Update/edit existing users
    - Delete existing users

- Create the view files and presentation tier logic that will:
    - Display the form to allow for new user creation
    - Display a listing of all the existing users
    - Display the form to allow the editing of an existing user
    - Add a delete button so we can delete users

- Make adjustments to the create new user form so that it can be used by external users as a self-registration process

- Alter the authentication process to use the database to validate the login credentials

User CRUD

As we are building a user-based web application, we must have a way to add and manage users. We added a `tbl_user` table to our database in *Chapter 5, Managing Issues*. You may recall that we left it as an exercise to the reader to create the associated AR model class. If you are following along and did not create the necessary user model class, you will need to do so now.

The following is a brief reminder on using the Gii code creation tool to create the model class:

1. Navigate to the Gii tool via `http://localhost/trackstar/index.php?r=gii` and select the **Model Generator** link.

2. Leave the table prefix as `tbl_`. Fill in the **Table Name** field as `tbl_user`, which will autopopulate the **Model Class** name field as **User**.

3. Once the form is filled out, click on the **Preview** button to get a link to a pop up that will show you all of the code about to be generated.

4. Finally, click on the **Generate** button to actually create the new `User.php` model class file in the `/protected/models/` directory.

With the `User` AR class in place, creating the CRUD scaffolding is a snap. We have done this before, using the Gii tool. As a reminder, the following are the necessary steps:

1. Navigate to the tool via `http://localhost/trackstar/index.php?r=gii`.

2. Click on the **Crud Generator** link from the list of available generators.

3. Type in `User` for the **Model Class** name field. The corresponding **Controller ID** will autopopulate with **User**.

4. You will then be presented with options to preview each file prior to generating. Click on the **Generate** button, which will generate all of the associated CRUD files in their proper locations.

With this in place, we can view our user listing page at `http://localhost/trackstar/index.php?r=user/index`. In the previous chapter, we manually created a couple of users in our system so that we could properly handle the relationships between projects, issues, and users. This is why we see a couple of users listed on this page. The following screenshot shows how this page is displayed for us:

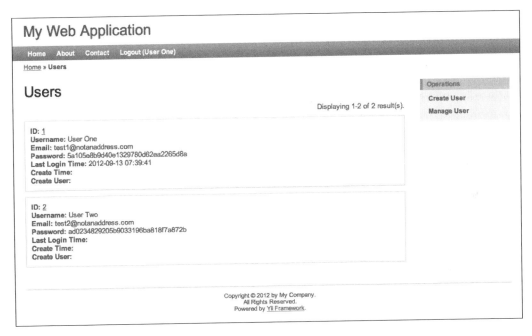

We can also view the new **Create User** form by visiting `http://localhost/trackstar/index.php?r=user/create`. If you are not currently logged in, you will be first routed to the login page before being able to view the form. So you might have to log in using `demo/demo` or `admin/admin` to view this form.

Having created and used our CRUD operation functionality first on our project entity, and then again with issues, we are very familiar at this point with how these features are initially implemented by the Gii code generation tool. The generated code for creating and updating is a great start, but needs some adjusting to meet the specific application requirements. The form we just generated for creating a new user is no exception. It has an input form field for every single column that has been defined in the `tbl_user` table. We don't want to expose all of these fields for user input. The columns for last login time, creation time and user, and update time and user should all be set programmatically after the form is submitted.

Updating our common audit history columns

Back in the previous chapters, when we introduced our **Project** and **Issue** CRUD functionality, we also noticed that our forms had more input fields than they should. Since we have defined all of our database tables to have the same creation and update time and user columns, every one of our autocreated input forms has these fields exposed. We completely ignored these fields when dealing with the project creation form back in *Chapter 4, Project CRUD*. Then, with the new issue creation form in *Chapter 5, Managing Issues*, we took the step to remove the fields from displaying in the form, but we never added in the logic to properly set these values when a new row is added.

Let's take a minute to add in this needed logic. Since all of our entity tables, `tbl_project`, `tbl_issue`, and `tbl_user`, have the same columns defined, we could add our logic to a common base class and then have each of the individual AR classes extend from this new base class. This is a common approach to applying the same functionality to entities of the same type. However, Yii components—that is any instance of `CComponent` or a derived class of `CComponent`, which are typically the majority of your classes in a Yii application—offer you another and arguably more flexible alternative.

Component behavior

Behaviors in Yii are classes implementing the `IBehavior` interface, and whose methods can be used to extend the functionality of components by being attached to the component, rather than the component explicitly extending the class. Behaviors can be attached to multiple components and components can attach multiple behaviors. This re-use of behaviors across components makes them very flexible, and by being able to attach multiple behaviors to the same component, we are able to achieve a kind of *multiple inheritance* for our Yii component classes.

We are going to use this approach to add the needed functionality to our model classes. The reason we are taking this approach, rather than just adding the logic directly to our User model class, is because our other model classes, Issue and Project, also need this same logic. Rather than duplicate the code in every AR model class, placing the functionality in behaviors, and then attaching the behaviors to the model classes, will allow us to properly set these fields for every AR model class in just one place.

In order for a component to use the methods of a behavior, the behavior has to be attached to the component. This is as simple as calling the attachBehavior() method on a component:

```
$component->attachBehavior($name, $behavior);
```

In the previous code, $name is a unique identifier for the behavior within the component. Once attached, the component can call the methods defined in the behavior class:

```
$component->myBehaviorMethod();
```

In the previous code, myBehaviorMethod() is defined in the $behavior class, but can be called as if it was defined in the $component class.

For model classes, we can add our desired behaviors to the behaviors() method, which is the approach we will take for these model classes. Now we just need to create a behavior to attach.

In fact, the Zii extension library, which is packaged with the Yii framework, already has a ready-made behavior that will update our date-time columns, create_time and update_time, which we have on each of our underlying tables. This behavior is called CTimestampBehavior. So, let's put this behavior to use.

Let's start with our User model class. Add the following method to protected/models/User.php:

```
public function behaviors()
{
  return array(
     'CTimestampBehavior' => array(
        'class' => 'zii.behaviors.CTimestampBehavior',
        'createAttribute' => 'create_time',
        'updateAttribute' => 'update_time',
       'setUpdateOnCreate' => true,
     ),
   );
}
```

Here we are attaching the Zii extension library's `CTimestampBehavior` to our `User` model class. We have specified the create time and update time attributes and have also configured the behavior to set the update time when a new record is created. With this in place, we can try it out. Create a new user, and you'll see the `create_time` and `update_time` records being automatically inserted for us. Pretty cool, right?

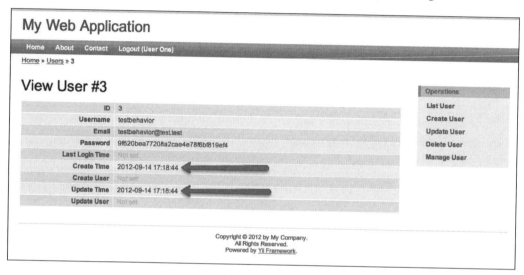

This is great, but we need to repeat this in our other model classes. We could duplicate the `behaviors()` method in each one, and continue to do so as we add more model classes. Alternatively, we could put this in a common base class and have each of our model classes extend this new base class. This way, we would only need to define the `behaviors()` method once.

We need to insert our `create_user_id` and `update_user_id` columns as well when we save and update a record. We could handle this in a number of ways. Since multiple behaviors can be attached to a component, we could create a new behavior, that is similar to `CTimestampBehavior`, which updates the create and update user ID columns. Or, we could simply extend `CTimestampBehavior`, and add the extra functionality to this child class. Or we could tap into the model `beforeSave` event directly and set our necessary fields there. Extending the existing behavior to add this extra functionality would probably make the most sense in a real-world application; however, to demonstrate another approach, let's tap into the active record `beforeSave` event, and do this in a common base class from which all of our AR model classes can extend. This way, you'll have exposure to a couple of different approaches and have more options to choose from when building your own Yii applications.

So, we need to create a new base class for our AR model classes. We'll also make this new class abstract since it should not be instantiated directly. First, go ahead and remove the behaviors() method from the User AR class, as we'll put this in our base class. Then create a new file, protected/models/TrackStarActiveRecord. php, and add the following code:

```php
<?php
abstract class TrackStarActiveRecord extends CActiveRecord
{
    /**
     * Prepares create_user_id and update_user_id attributes before
saving.
     */

    protected function beforeSave()
    {

        if(null !== Yii::app()->user)
            $id=Yii::app()->user->id;
        else
            $id=1;

        if($this->isNewRecord)
            $this->create_user_id=$id;

        $this->update_user_id=$id;

        return parent::beforeSave();
    }

    /**
     * Attaches the timestamp behavior to update our create and update
    times
     */
    public function behaviors()
    {
      return array(
          'CTimestampBehavior' => array(
              'class' => 'zii.behaviors.CTimestampBehavior',
              'createAttribute' => 'create_time',
              'updateAttribute' => 'update_time',
             'setUpdateOnCreate' => true,
          ),
        );
    }

}
```

Here, as discussed, we are overriding the CActiveRecord::beforeSave() method. This is one of the many events that CActiveRecord exposes to allow customization of its process workflow. There are two methods exposed that allow us to tap into the record saving workflow and perform any necessary logic either right before or right after the active record is saved: beforeSave() and afterSave(). In this case, we have decided to explicitly set our create and update user fields just prior to saving the active record, that is just before it is written to the database.

We determine whether or not we are dealing with a new record (that is an insert) or an existing record (that is an update) by using the property $this->isNewRecord, and set our fields appropriately. We then make sure to invoke the parent implementation by returning parent::beforeSave() to ensure it has a chance to do everything it needs to do. We are performing a NULL check on Yii::app()->user to handle instances where we may be using this model class outside of a web application context, for example in a Yii console application (covered in a later chapter). If we don't have a valid user, we are simply defaulting to the first user, id = 1, which we could set up to be a super user.

Also, as discussed, we have moved our behaviors() method to this base class so that all AR model classes that extend it will have this behavior attached.

To try this out, we now need to alter each of the three existing AR classes Project. php, User.php, and Issue.php to extend from our new abstract class rather than directly from CActiveRecord. So, for example, rather than the following:

```
class User extends CActiveRecord
{
...}
```

We need to have:

```
class User extends TrackStarActiveRecord
{
...}
```

We need to make similar changes for our other model classes.

Now if we add another new user, we should see all four of our audit history columns populated with timestamps and user IDs respectively.

With these changes now in place, we should remove these fields from each of the forms for creating new projects, issues, and users (we already removed them from the issues form in the previous chapter). The HTML for these form fields is in the `protected/views/project/_form.php`, `protected/views/issue/_form.php`, and `protected/views/user/_form.php` files. The lines we need to remove from each of these files are as follows:

```
<div class="row">
    <?php echo $form->labelEx($model,'create_time'); ?>
    <?php echo $form->textField($model,'create_time'); ?>
    <?php echo $form->error($model,'create_time'); ?>
</div>

<div class="row">
    <?php echo $form->labelEx($model,'create_user_id'); ?>
    <?php echo $form->textField($model,'create_user_id'); ?>
    <?php echo $form->error($model,'create_user_id'); ?>
</div>

<div class="row">
    <?php echo $form->labelEx($model,'update_time'); ?>
    <?php echo $form->textField($model,'update_time'); ?>
    <?php echo $form->error($model,'update_time'); ?>
</div>

<div class="row">
    <?php echo $form->labelEx($model,'update_user_id'); ?>
    <?php echo $form->textField($model,'update_user_id'); ?>
    <?php echo $form->error($model,'update_user_id'); ?>
</div>
```

And from the user creation form, `protected/views/user/_form.php`, we can also remove the last login time field:

```
<div class="row">
    <?php echo $form->labelEx($model,'last_login_time'); ?>
    <?php echo $form->textField($model,'last_login_time'); ?>
    <?php echo $form->error($model,'last_login_time'); ?>
</div>
```

Since we are removing these from being form inputs, we should also remove the validation rules defined for these fields in the associated rules method. These validation rules are defined to ensure the data submitted by the user is valid and correctly formatted. Removing the rules also prevents them from being able to be a part of the bulk assignment of properties that occurs when we take all of the submitted querystring or post variables and assign their values to our AR model properties. For example, we see lines like the following in our create and update controller actions for AR models:

```
$model->attributes=$_POST['User'];
```

This is doing a mass assignment of all of the model attributes from the posted form fields. As an added security measure, this only works for attributes that have validation rules assigned for them. You can use the `CSafeValidator` as a way to mark model attributes that don't otherwise have any validation rules as being safe for this mass assignment.

Since these fields are not going to be filled in by the user, and we don't need them to be massively assigned, we can remove the rules.

Okay, so let's remove them. Open up `protected/models/User.php` and in the `rules()` method, remove the following two rules:

```
array('create_user_id, update_user_id', 'numerical',
'integerOnly'=>true),
array('last_login_time, create_time, update_time', 'safe'),
```

The project and issue AR classes have similar rules defined, but not identical. When removing those rules, be sure to leave in the rules that do still apply to the user input fields.

The removal of the rule for the `last_login_time` attribute above was intentional. We should remove this from being exposed as a user input field as well. This field needs to be updated automatically upon a successful login. Since we had the view file open and were removing the other fields, we decided to remove this one now as well. However, we will wait to add the necessary application logic until after we make a few other changes and cover a few other topics.

Actually, while we still have our hands in this validation rules method for the `User` class, we should make another change. We want to ensure that the e-mail as well as the username for every user is unique. We should validate this requirement when the form is submitted. Also, we should validate that the data submitted for the e-mail conforms to a standard e-mail format. You may recall from back in *Chapter 4*, *Project CRUD* that we introduced Yii's built-in validators, and two of these are perfect for our needs. We'll use the `CEmailValidator` and `CUniqueValidator` classes to achieve our validation needs. We can quickly add these rules by adding the following two lines of code to this `rules()` method:

```
array('email, username', 'unique'),
array('email', 'email'),
```

The entire `User::rules()` method should now look like the following:

```
public function rules()
    {
        // NOTE: you should only define rules for those attributes that
        // will receive user inputs.
        return array(
            array('email', 'required'),
array('email, username, password', 'length', 'max'=>255,
array('email, username', 'unique'),
array('email', 'email'),
            // The following rule is used by search().
            // Please remove those attributes that should not be searched.
            array('id, email, username, password, last_login_time,
create_time, create_user_id, update_time, update_user_id', 'safe',
'on'=>'search'),
        );
    }
```

The *unique* declaration in the above rule is an alias that refers to Yii's built-in validator, `CUniqueValidator`. This validates the uniqueness of the model class attribute against the underlying database table. With the addition of this validation rule, we will receive an error when attempting to enter either an e-mail and/or username that already exists in the database. Also, with the addition of the e-mail validation, we will receive an error when the value in the e-mail form field is not of a correct e-mail format.

When we first created our `tbl_user` table in the previous chapter, we added two test users so we would have some data to play with. The first of these two users has an e-mail address of `test1@notanaddress.com`. Try to add another user using this same e-mail. The following screenshot shows the error message received and the highlighting of the field in error after such an attempt:

Submitting a value that is not in a valid e-mail format will also produce an error message.

Adding a password confirmation field

In addition to the changes we just made, we should add a new field to force the user to confirm the password they entered. This is a standard practice on user registration forms and helps the user not to make a mistake when entering this important piece of information. Fortunately, Yii comes with another built-in validator, `CCompareValidator`, which does exactly what you think it might do. It compares the values of two attributes, and returns an error if they are not equal.

In order to take advantage of this built-in validation, we need to add a new attribute to our model class. Add the following attribute to the top of the `User` model AR class:

```
public $password_repeat;
```

We named this attribute by appending `_repeat` to the name of the attribute we want to compare against. The compare validator will allow you to specify any two attributes to compare, or compare an attribute to a constant value. If no comparison attribute or value is specified when declaring the compare rule, it will default to looking for an attribute beginning with the same name as the one being compared, with the addition of `_repeat` appended to the end. This is why we named the attribute in this manner. Now we can add a simple validation rule to the `User::rules()` method as follows:

```
array('password', 'compare'),
```

If not using the `_repeat` convention, you would need to specify the attribute with which you want the comparison performed. For example, if we wanted to compare the `$password` attribute to an attribute named `$confirmPassword`, we could use:

```
array('password', 'compare', 'compareAttribute'=>'confirmPassword'),
```

Since we have explicitly added the `$password_repeat` attribute to the user AR class, and there is no validation rule defined for it, we need to also tell the model class to allow this field to be set in a bulk manner when the `setAttributes()` method is called. As previously mentioned, we do this by explicitly adding our new attribute to the *safe* attributes list for our `User` model class. To do this, add the following to the `User::rules()` array:

```
array('password_repeat', 'safe'),
```

Let's make one more change to our validation rules. All of the fields we currently have on the user form should be required. Currently, our required rule is only being applied to the `email` field. While we are making changes to this `User::rules()` method, let's add username and password to this list as well:

```
array('email, username, password, password_repeat', 'required'),
```

 For more information on validation rules, see: `http://www.yiiframework.com/doc/guide/1.1/en/form.model#declaring-validation-rules`

Okay, now all of our rules are set. However, we still need to add the password confirmation field to the form. Let's do that now.

To add this field, open up `protected/views/user/_form.php`, and add the following code block below the password field:

```
<div class="row">
    <?php echo $form->labelEx($model,'password_repeat'); ?>
    <?php echo $form->passwordField($model,'password_repeat',array('si
ze'=>60,'maxlength'=>255)); ?>
    <?php echo $form->error($model,'password_repeat'); ?>
</div>
```

With all of these form changes in place, the **Create User** form should look as depicted in the following screenshot:

And now, if we attempt to submit the form with different values in the **Password** and **Password Repeat** fields, we will be met with an error as shown in the following screenshot:

Hash the password

One last change we should make before we leave the new user creation process is to create a hashed version of the user's password before we store it in our database. It is a very common practice to apply a one-way hashing algorithm on sensitive user information before adding it to persistent storage.

We will add this logic to the `User.php` AR class by taking advantage of another method of `CActiveRecord` that allows us to customize the default active record workflow. This time we'll override the `afterValidate()` method and apply a basic one-way hash to the password after we validate all the input fields, but before we save the record.

 Similar to our use of the `CActiveRecord::beforeSave()` method when setting our create and update timestamps, here we are overriding the `CActiveRecord::beforeValidate()` method. This is one of the many events that `CActiveRecord` exposes to allow customization of its process workflow. As a quick reminder, if you do not explicitly send `false` as a parameter when calling the `save()` method on an AR class, the validation process will be triggered. This process performs the validations as specified in the `rules()` method within the AR class. There are two methods exposed that allow us to tap into the validation workflow and perform any necessary logic either right before or right after the validation is performed, that is, `beforeValidate()` and `afterValidate()`. In this case, we have decided to hash the password just after performing the validation.

Open up the `User` AR class and add the following to the bottom of the class:

```
/**
 * apply a hash on the password before we store it in the database
 */
protected function afterValidate()
{
   parent::afterValidate();
if(!$this->hasErrors())
   $this->password = $this->hashPassword($this->password);
}

/**
 * Generates the password hash.
 * @param string password
   * @return string hash
 */
 public function hashPassword($password)
{
   return md5($password);
}
```

We mentioned this in the previous chapter, but it is worth mentioning again. We are using the one-way MD5 hashing algorithm here because of its ease of use and that it is widely available on 5.x Versions of MySQL and PHP. However, it is now known that MD5 is "broken" as a one-way hashing algorithm with regard to security and it is not suggested that you use this hashing algorithm in a production environment. Please consider using Bcrypt for your real, production applications. The following are some URLs providing more information on Bcrypt:

- http://en.wikipedia.org/wiki/Bcrypt
- http://php.net/manual/en/function.crypt.php
- http://www.openwall.com/phpass/

With this in place, it will hash the password just after all of the other attribute validations have successfully passed.

This approach works fine for brand new records, but for updates, if the user is not updating his/her password information, it runs the risk of hashing an already hashed value. We could handle this in a number of ways, but to keep things simple for now, we will need to ensure we ask the user to supply a valid password every time they desire to update their user data.

We now have the ability to add new users to our application. Since we initially created this form using the Gii tool's **Crud Generator** link, we also have read, update, and delete functionality for users. Try it out by adding some new users, viewing a list of them, update some of the information, and then delete a few of the entries to ensure everything is working as expected. (Remember that you will need to be logged in as admin, as opposed to demo, in order to perform the deletes.)

Authenticating users using the database

As we know, a basic login form and user authentication process was created for us simply by using the yiic command to create our new application. This authentication scheme is very simple. It interrogates the input form's username/password values, and if they are either demo/demo or admin/admin, it passes, otherwise it fails. This is obviously not intended to be a permanent solution, but rather a foundation on which to build. We are going to build upon this by altering the authentication process to use our tbl_user database table that we already have as part of our model. But before we start changing the default implementation, let's take a closer look at how Yii implements an authentication model.

Introducing the Yii authentication model

Central to the Yii authentication framework is an application component called **user**, which, in the most general case, is an object implementing the IWebUser interface. The specific class used by our default implementation is the framework class, CWebUser. This user component encapsulates all the identity information for the current user of the application. This component was configured for us as part of the autogenerated application code when we initially created our application using the yiic tool. The configuration can be seen in the protected/config/main.php file, under the components array element:

```
'user'=>array(
  // enable cookie-based authentication
  'allowAutoLogin'=>true,
),
```

Since it is configured as an application component, with the name 'user', we can access it at any place throughout our application using Yii::app()->user.

We also notice that the class property, allowAutoLogin, is being set here as well. This property is false by default, but setting it to true enables user information to be stored in persistent browser cookies. This data is then used to automatically authenticate the user upon subsequent visits. This is what will allow us to have a **Remember Me** checkbox on the login form so that, if the user chooses, they can be automatically logged into the application upon subsequent visits to the site.

The Yii authentication framework defines a separate entity to house the actual authentication logic. This is called an **identity class**, and in general can be any class that implements the IUserIdentity interface. One of the primary roles of this class is to encapsulate the authentication logic to easily allow for different implementations. Depending on the application requirements, we may need to validate a username and password against values stored in a database, or allow users to log in with their OpenID credentials, or integrate with an existing LDAP approach. Separating the logic that is specific to the authentication approach from the rest of the application login process allows us to easily switch between such implementations. The identity class provides this separation.

When we initially created our application, a user identity class file, namely `protected/components/UserIdentity.php`, was generated for us. It extends the Yii framework class, `CUserIdentity`, which is a base class for authentication implementations that uses a username and password. Let's take a closer look at the code that was generated for this class:

```php
<?php
/**
 * UserIdentity represents the data needed to identity a user.
 * It contains the authentication method that checks if the provided
 * data can identify the user.
 */
class UserIdentity extends CUserIdentity
{
  /**
   * Authenticates a user.
   * The example implementation makes sure if the username and
password
   * are both 'demo'.
   * In practical applications, this should be changed to authenticate
   * against some persistent user identity storage (e.g. database).
   * @return boolean whether authentication succeeds.
   */
  public function authenticate()
  {
    $users=array(
      // username => password
      'demo'=>'demo',
      'admin'=>'admin',
    );
    if(!isset($users[$this->username]))
      $this->errorCode=self::ERROR_USERNAME_INVALID;
    else if($users[$this->username]!==$this->password)
      $this->errorCode=self::ERROR_PASSWORD_INVALID;
    else
      $this->errorCode=self::ERROR_NONE;
    return !$this->errorCode;
  }
}
```

The bulk of the work in defining an identity class is the implementation of the `authenticate()` method. This is where we place the code that is specific to the authentication approach. This implementation simply uses the hardcoded username/password values of `demo/demo` and `admin/admin`. It checks these values against the username and password class properties (properties defined in the parent class, `CUserIdentity`) and if they don't match, it will set and return an appropriate error code.

In order to better understand how these pieces fit into the entire end-to-end authentication process, let's walk through the logic starting with the login form. If we navigate to the login page, `http://localhost/trackstar/index.php?r=site/login`, we see a simple form allowing the input of a username, a password, and an optional checkbox for the **Remember Me Next Time** functionality that we discussed before. Submitting this form invokes the logic contained in the `SiteController::actionLogin()` method. The following sequence diagram depicts the class interaction that occurs during a successful login from the time the form is submitted.

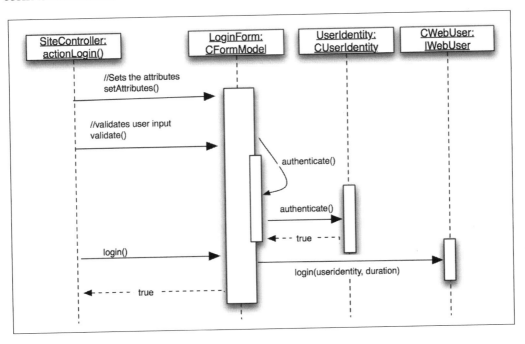

The process starts with setting the class attributes on the form model class, LoginForm, to the form values submitted. The LoginForm->validate() method is then called, which validates these attribute values based on the rules defined in the rules() method. This method is defined as follows:

```
public function rules()
{
    return array(
        // username and password are required
        array('username, password', 'required'),
        // rememberMe needs to be a boolean
        array('rememberMe', 'boolean'),
        // password needs to be authenticated
        array('password', 'authenticate'),
    );
}
```

The last of these rules stipulates that the password attribute be validated using the custom method authenticate(), which is also defined in the LoginForm class as follows:

```
/**
 * Authenticates the password.
 * This is the 'authenticate' validator as declared in rules().
 */
public function authenticate($attribute,$params)
{
    $this->_identity=new UserIdentity($this->username,$this-
>password);
    if(!$this->_identity->authenticate())
        $this->addError('password','Incorrect username or password.');
}
```

Continuing to follow the sequence diagram, the password validation within LoginForm calls the authenticate() method within the same class. This method creates a new instance of the authentication identity class being used, in this case it is /protected/components/UserIdentity.php, and then calls its authenticate() method. This method, UserIdentity::authenticate() is as follows:

```
/**
 * Authenticates a user.
 * The example implementation makes sure if the username and
password
 * are both 'demo'.
 * In practical applications, this should be changed to authenticate
 * against some persistent user identity storage (e.g. database).
```

```
 * @return boolean whether authentication succeeds.
 */
public function authenticate()
{
  $users=array(
    // username => password
    'demo'=>'demo',
    'admin'=>'admin',
  );
  if(!isset($users[$this->username]))
    $this->errorCode=self::ERROR_USERNAME_INVALID;
  else if($users[$this->username]!==$this->password)
    $this->errorCode=self::ERROR_PASSWORD_INVALID;
  else
    $this->errorCode=self::ERROR_NONE;
  return !$this->errorCode;
}
```

This is implemented to use the username and password to perform its authentication. In this implementation, as long as the username/password combination is either demo/demo or admin/admin, this method will return true. Since we are walking through a successful log in, the authentication succeeds and then the SiteController calls the LoginForm::login() method, which looks as follows:

```
/**
 * Logs in the user using the given username and password in the
model.
 * @return boolean whether login is successful
 */
public function login()
{
  if($this->_identity===null)
  {
    $this->_identity=new UserIdentity($this->username,$this-
>password);
    $this->_identity->authenticate();
  }
  if($this->_identity->errorCode===UserIdentity::ERROR_NONE)
  {
    $duration=$this->rememberMe ? 3600*24*30 : 0; // 30 days
    Yii::app()->user->login($this->_identity,$duration);
    return true;
  }
  else
    return false;
}
```

And we can see that this in turn calls `Yii::app()->user->login` (that is `CWebUser::login()`), passing in the `CUserIdentity` class instance as well as a duration to which to set the cookie for autologin.

By default, the web application is configured to use the Yii framework class, `CWebuser` as the user application component. Its `login()` method takes in an identity class and an optional duration parameter used to set the time to live on the browser cookie. In the previous code, we see that this is set to 30 days if the **Remember Me** checkbox was checked when the form was submitted. If you do not pass in a duration, it is set to zero. A value of zero will result in no cookie being created at all.

The `CWebUser::login()` method takes the information contained in the identity class and saves it in persistent storage for the duration of the user session. By default, this storage is the PHP session storage.

After all of this is completed, the `login()` method on `LoginForm` that was initially called by our controller class returns `true`, which indicates a successful log in. The controller class then redirects to the URL value in `Yii::app()->user->returnUrl`. You can set this on certain pages throughout the application if you want to ensure that the user be redirected back to their previous page, that is wherever they were in the application before they decided (or were forced) to log in. This value defaults to the application entry URL.

Changing the authenticate implementation

Now that we understand the entire authentication process, we can easily see where we need to make the change to use our `tbl_user` table to validate the username and password credentials submitted via the login form. We can simply alter the `authenticate()` method in the user identity class to verify the existence of a matching row with the supplied username and password values. Since, at the moment, there is nothing else in our `UserIdentity.php` class except the authenticate method, let's completely replace the contents of this file with the following code:

```php
<?php

/**
 * UserIdentity represents the data needed to identity a user.
 * It contains the authentication method that checks if the provided
 * data can identity the user.
 */

class UserIdentity extends CUserIdentity
{
```

```
   private $_id;

   public function authenticate()
   {
      $user=User::model()->find('LOWER(username)=?',array(strtolower($th
is->username)));
      if($user===null)
         $this->errorCode=self::ERROR_USERNAME_INVALID;
      else if(!$user->validatePassword($this->password))
         $this->errorCode=self::ERROR_PASSWORD_INVALID;
      else
      {
         $this->_id=$user->id;
         $this->username=$user->username;
$this->setState('lastLogin', date("m/d/y g:i A", strtotime($user-
>last_login_time)));
         $user->saveAttributes(array(
            'last_login_time'=>date("Y-m-d H:i:s", time()),
         ));
         $this->errorCode=self::ERROR_NONE;
      }
      return $this->errorCode==self::ERROR_NONE;
   }

   public function getId()
   {
      return $this->_id;
   }
}
```

And since we are going to have our User model class do the actual password validation, we also need to add the following method to our User model class:

```
/**
 * Checks if the given password is correct.
 * @param string the password to be validated
 * @return boolean whether the password is valid
 */
public function validatePassword($password)
{
   return $this->hashPassword($password)===$this->password;
}
```

There are a few things going on with this new code that should be pointed out. First, it is now attempting to retrieve a row from the `tbl_user` table, by way of creating a new `User` model AR class instance, where the username is the same as the `UserIdentity` class's attribute value (remember that this is set to be the value from the login form). Since we enforced the uniqueness of the username when creating a new user, this should find at most one matching row. If it does not find a matching row, an error message is set to indicate the username is incorrect. If a matching row is found, it compares the passwords by calling our new `User::validatePassword()` method. If the password fails the validation, it sets an error message to indicate an incorrect password.

If the authentication is successful, a couple of other things happen before the method returns. First, we have set a new attribute on the `UserIdentity` class for the user ID. The default implementation in the parent class is to return the username for the ID. Since we are using a database, and have a numeric primary key as our unique user identifier, we want to make sure this is what is set and returned throughout the application when the user ID is requested. For example, when the code `Yii::app()->user->id` is executed, we want to make sure that the unique ID from the database is returned, not the username.

Extending user attributes

The second thing happening here is the setting of an attribute on the user identity to be the last login time returned from the database, and then also updating the `last_login_time` field in the database to be the current time. The specific code from the previous snippet doing this is as follows:

```
$this->setState('lastLogin', date("m/d/y g:i A", strtotime($user-
>last_login_time)));
$user->saveAttributes(array(
  'last_login_time'=>date("Y-m-d H:i:s", time()),
));
```

The user application component, `CWebUser`, derives its user attributes from the explicit ID and name attributes defined in the identity class, and then from `name=>value` pairs set in an array called the `identity states`. These are the extra user values that can be persisted throughout a user's session. As an example of this, we are setting the attribute named `lastLogin` to be the value of the `last_login_time` field in the database. This way, at any place throughout the application, this attribute can be accessed via:

```
Yii::app()->user->lastLogin;
```

The reason we take a different approach when storing the last login time versus the ID is that *ID* just happens to be an explicitly defined property on the CUserIdentity class. So, other than *name* and *ID*, all other user attributes that need to be persisted throughout the session can be set in a similar manner.

 When cookie-based authentication is enabled (by setting CWebUser::allowAutoLogin to be true), the persistent information will be stored in the cookie. Therefore, you should *not* store sensitive information (for example, your password) in the same manner as we have stored the user's last login time.

With these changes in place, you will now need to provide a correct username and password combination for a user defined in the tbl_user table in the database. Using demo/demo or admin/admin will, of course, no longer work. Give it a try. You should be able to login as any one of the users you created earlier in this chapter. If you followed along and have the same user data as we do, the credentials Username: User One, Password: test1 should work.

 Now that we have altered the login process to authenticate against the database, we won't be able to access the delete functionality for any of our project, issue, or user entities. The reason for this is that there are authorization checks in place to ensure that the user is an admin prior to allowing access. Currently, none of our database users have been configured to be authorized administrators. Don't worry, authorization is the focus of the next chapter, so we will be able to access that functionality again very soon.

Displaying the last login time on the home page

Now that we are updating the last login time in the database, and saving it to persistent session storage when logging in, let's go ahead and display this time on our welcome screen that a user will see after a successful log in. This will also help make us feel better that all of this is working as expected.

Open up the default view file that is responsible for displaying our home page `protected/views/site/index.php`. Add the following highlighted lines of code just below the welcome statement:

```
<h1>Welcome to <i><?php echo CHtml::encode(Yii::app()->name); ?></i></
h1>
<?php if(!Yii::app()->user->isGuest):?>
<p>
    You last logged in on <?php echo Yii::app()->user->lastLogin; ?>.
</p>
<?php endif;?>
```

And since we are in there, let's go ahead and remove all of the other autogenerated help text, which is everything else below the lines we just added. Once you save and log in again, you should see something similar to the following screenshot, which displays the welcome message followed by a formatted time indicating your last successful log in:

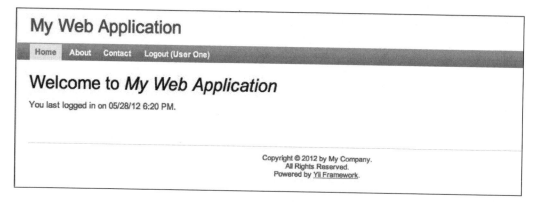

Summary

This chapter was the first of two where we focus on user management, authentication, and authorization. We created the ability to manage CRUD operations for application users, making many adjustments to the new user creation process along the way. We added a new base class for all of our active record classes so that we can easily manage our audit history table columns that are present on all of our tables. We also updated our code to properly manage the user's last login time that we are storing in the database. In doing so, we learned about tapping into the CActiveRecord validation workflow to allow for prevalidation/postvalidation and presaving/postsaving processing.

We then focused on understanding the Yii authentication model in order to enhance it to meet our application requirements so that the user credentials are validated against the values stored in the database.

Now that we have covered authentication, we can turn our focus to the second part of Yii's auth-and-auth framework, *authorization*. This is the focus of the next chapter.

7
User Access Control

User-based web applications, like our TrackStar application, typically need to control access to certain functionality based on who is making the request. When we speak of *user access control*, we are referring, at a high level, to some questions the application needs to ask when requests are being made. These questions are:

- Who is making the request?
- Does that user have the appropriate permission to access the requested functionality?

The answers to these questions help the application respond appropriately.

The work completed in *Chapter 6, User Management and Authorization* provides our application with the ability to answer the first of these questions. The application now allows users to establish their own authentication credentials and validates the username and password when a user logs in. After a successful login, the application knows exactly who is making subsequent requests.

In this chapter, we will focus on helping the application answer the second question. Once the user has provided appropriate identification, the application needs a way to determine if they also have permission to perform the requested action. We'll extend our basic authorization model by taking advantage of Yii's user access control features. Yii provides both a **simple access control filter** as well as a more sophisticated **Role Based Access Control (RBAC)** implementation as a means to help us address our user authorization requirements. We'll take a closer look at both of these as we work to implement the user access requirements for the TrackStar application.

Feature planning

When we first introduced our TrackStar application back in *Chapter 3, The TrackStar Application,* we mentioned the application has two high-level user states, namely anonymous and authenticated. This simply makes a distinction between a user that has successfully logged in (authenticated), and one who has not (anonymous). We also introduced the idea of authenticated users having different roles within a project. Within a specific project, a user can be in one of the following three roles:

- A **project owner** has *all* administrative access to the project
- A **project member** has *some* administrative access, but has more limited access compared to the project owner
- A **project reader** has *read-only* access. Such users cannot change the content of a project

The focus of this chapter is to implement an approach to manage the access control granted to application users. We need a way to create and manage our roles and permissions, assign them to users, and enforce the access control rules we want for each user role.

In order to achieve the goals outlined earlier, we will focus on the following throughout this chapter:

- Implement a strategy to force the user to log in before gaining access to any project or issue-related functionality
- Create user roles and associate those roles with a specific permission structure
- Implement the ability to assign users to roles (and their associated permissions)
- Ensure our role and permission structure exists on a per-project basis (that is, allow users to have different permissions within different projects)
- Implement the ability to associate users to projects and at the same time to roles within that project
- Implement the necessary authorization access checking throughout the application to appropriately grant or deny access to the application user based on their permissions

Luckily, Yii comes with a lot of built-in functionality to help us implement these requirements. So, let's get started.

Access control filter

We first introduced *filters* back in *Chapter 5, Managing Issues* when we enforced a valid project context before allowing issue functionality to be used. If you recall, we added a class method filter `filterProjectContext()` to the `IssueController` class as a way to ensure we had a valid project context before we performed any actions on an Issue entity. Yii provides a similar approach for handling simple access control on an action-by-action basis within controllers.

The Yii framework provides a filter called `accessControl`. This filter can be directly used in controller classes to provide an authorization scheme to verify whether or not a user can access a specific controller action. In fact, the astute reader will remember that when we were implementing the `projectContext` filter back in *Chapter 5, Managing Issues*, we noticed that this access control filter was already included in the filters list for both our `IssueController` and `ProjectController` classes, as follows:

```
/**
 * @return array action filters
 */
public function filters()
{
return array(
'accessControl', // perform access control for CRUD operations
);
}
```

This was included in the autogenerated code produced by using the Gii CRUD code generator tool. The autogenerated code also overrides the `accessRules()` method, which is necessary in order to use the access control filter. It is in this method where you define the actual authorization rules.

The default implementation for our CRUD actions is set up to allow anyone to view a list of existing issues and projects. However, it restricts the access of creating and updating to authenticated users, and further restricts the delete action to a special *admin* user. You might remember that when we first implemented CRUD operations on projects, we had to log in before we were able to create new ones. The same was true when dealing with issues and again with users. The mechanism controlling this authorization and access is exactly this access control filter. Let's take a closer look at this implementation within the `ProjectController.php` class file.

There are two methods relevant to access control in the `ProjectController` class: `filters()` and `accessRules()`. The `filters()` method configures the filter:

```php
/**
 * @return array action filters
 */
public function filters()
{
return array(
'accessControl', // perform access control for CRUD operations
);
}
```

And the `accessRules()` method, which is used to define the authorization rules used by the access filter, is shown as follows:

```php
/**
 * Specifies the access control rules.
 * This method is used by the 'accessControl' filter.
 * @return array access control rules
 */
public function accessRules()
{
return array(
array('allow',  // allow all users to perform 'index' and 'view'
actions
'actions'=>array('index','view'),
'users'=>array('*'),
),
array('allow', // allow authenticated user to perform 'create' and
'update' actions
'actions'=>array('create','update'),
'users'=>array('@'),
),
array('allow', // allow admin user to perform 'admin' and 'delete'
actions
'actions'=>array('admin','delete'),
'users'=>array('admin'),
),
array('deny',  // deny all users
'users'=>array('*'),
),
);
}
```

The `filters()` method is already familiar to us. It is where we specify all the filters to be used in the controller class. In this case, we have only one, `accessControl`, which refers to a filter provided by the Yii framework. This filter uses the other method, `accessRules()`, which defines the rules that drive the access restrictions.

In the `accessRules()` method, there are four rules specified. Each rule is represented as an array. The first element of the array is either *allow* or *deny*. These indicate the granting or denying of access respectively. The rest of the array consists of `name=>value` pairs specifying the remaining parameters of the rule.

Let's look at the first rule defined earlier:

```
array('allow',   // allow all users to perform 'index' and 'view'
actions
'actions'=>array('index','view'),
'users'=>array('*'),
),
```

This rule allows the `actionIndex()` and `actionView()` controller actions to be executed by any user. The asterisk (*), used in the value for the `'users'` element, is a special character used to specify any user (anonymous, authenticated, or otherwise).

Now let's look at the second rule defined:

```
array('allow', // allow authenticated user to perform 'create' and
'update' actions
'actions'=>array('create','update'),
'users'=>array('@'),
),
```

This allows for any authenticated user to access the `actionCreate()` and `actionUpdate()` controller actions. The `@` special character is a way to specify any authenticated user.

The third rule is defined in the following code snippet:

```
array('allow', // allow admin user to perform 'admin' and 'delete'
actions
'actions'=>array('admin','delete'),
'users'=>array('admin'),
),
```

This rule specifies that a specific user, named `admin`, is allowed access to the `actionAdmin()` and `actionDelete()` controller actions.

Finally, let's have a closer look at the fourth rule:

```
array('deny',   // deny all users
'users'=>array('*'),
),
```

This rule denies all users access to all controller actions. We'll elaborate on this one a little more in a minute.

Access rules can be defined using a number of context parameters. The rules mentioned earlier are specifying actions and users to create the rule context, but there are several other parameters you can use. A few of these are given as follows:

- **Controllers**: Specifies an array of controller IDs to which the rule should apply.

- **Roles**: Specifies a list of authorization items (roles, operations, and permissions) to which the rule applies. This makes use of the RBAC feature we will be discussing in the next section.

- **IPs**: Specifies a list of client IP addresses to which this rule applies.

- **Verbs**: Specifies which HTTP request types (GET, POST, and so on) apply to this rule.

- **Expression**: Specifies a PHP expression whose value indicates whether or not the rule should be applied.

- **Actions**: Specifies the action method, by use of the corresponding action ID, to which the rule should match.

- **Users**: Specifies the users to which the rule should apply. The current application user's name attribute is used for matching. The following three special characters can also be used here:

  1. *: any user

  2. ?: anonymous users

  3. @: authenticated users

If no users are specified, the rule will apply to all users.

The access rules are evaluated one by one in the order they are specified. The first rule that matches the current pattern determines the authorization result. If this rule is an allow rule, the action can be executed; if it is a `deny` rule, the action cannot be executed; if none of the rules match the context, the action can still be executed. It is for this reason that the fourth rule mentioned earlier is defined. If we did not define a rule that denied all actions to all users at the end of our rules list, then we would not achieve our desired access restrictions. As an example, take the second rule. It specifies that authenticated users are allowed access to the `actioncreate()` and `actionUpdate()` actions. However, it does not stipulate that anonymous users be denied access. It says nothing about anonymous users. The fourth rule mentioned earlier ensures that all other requests that do not match one of the first three specific rules be denied access.

With this already in place, altering our application to deny access to all project, issue, and user related functionality for anonymous users is a snap. All we have to do is change the special character "*" of the users array value to the "@" special character. This will only allow authenticated users to access the `actionIndex()` and `actionView()` controller actions. All other actions are already restricted to authenticated users.

Now, we could make this change, three times, in each of our project, issue, and user controller class files. However, we have a base controller class from which each of these extend, namely the `Controller` class in the file `protected/components/Controller.php`. So, we can add our CRUD access rules in this one file, and then remove it from each of the child classes. We can also take advantage of the `controllers` context parameter when defining our rules so that it will only apply to these three controllers.

First, let's add the necessary method to our base controller class. Open up `protected/components/Controller.php` and add the following method:

```php
/**
 * Specifies the access control rules.
 * This method is used by the 'accessControl' filter.
 * @return array access control rules
 */
public function accessRules()
{
return array(
array('allow',  // allow all users to perform 'index' and 'view'
actions
'controllers'=>array('issue','project','user'),
'actions'=>array('index','view'),
'users'=>array('@'),
),
array('allow', // allow authenticated user to perform 'create' and
'update' actions
```

```
    'controllers'=>array('issue','project','user'),
    'actions'=>array('create','update'),
    'users'=>array('@'),
    ),
    array('allow', // allow admin user to perform 'admin' and 'delete'
    actions
    'controllers'=>array('issue','project','user'),
    'actions'=>array('admin','delete'),
    'users'=>array('admin'),
    ),
    array('deny',   // deny all users
    'controllers'=>array('issue','project','user'),
    'users'=>array('*'),
    ),
    );
    }
```

The highlighted code in the previous code snippet shows the changes we made. We have added the `controllers` parameter to each of our rules and changed the users for the index and view actions to only allow authenticated users.

Now we can remove this method from each of the specified controllers. Open up all three of the `ProjectController.php`, `IssueController.php`, and `UserController.php` files and remove their respective `accessRules()` methods.

After making these changes, the application will require a login prior to accessing any of our *project*, *issue*, or *user* functionality. We still allow anonymous user access to the `SiteController` class action methods, which we kept because this is where our login actions are located. We obviously have to be able to access the login page if we are not already logged in.

Role based access control

Now that we have used the simple access control filter to limit access to authenticated users, we need to turn focus to meeting some more specific access control needs of our application. As we mentioned, users will play certain roles within a project. The project will have users of type *owner*, who can be thought of as project administrators. They will be granted all access to manipulate the project. The project will also have users of type *member*, who will be granted some access to project functionality, but a proper subset of what owners are able to perform. Finally, the project can have users of type *reader*, who are only able to view project-related content and not alter it in any way. To achieve this type of access control based on the role of a user, we turn to the Role Based Access Control feature of Yii, also referred to more simply as RBAC.

RBAC is an established approach in computer systems security to managing the access permissions of authenticated users. In short, the RBAC approach defines roles within an application. Permissions to perform certain operations are also defined and then associated with roles. Users are then assigned to a role and through the role association, acquire the permissions defined for that role. There is plenty of documentation available for the curious reader about the general RBAC concept and approach. Wikipedia, for example, `http://en.wikipedia.org/wiki/Role-based_access_control`. We'll focus on the specifics of Yii's implementation of the RBAC approach.

Yii's implementation of RBAC is simple, elegant, and powerful. At the foundation of RBAC in Yii is the idea of the **authorization item**. The authorization item is simply a permission to do things in the application. These permissions can be categorized as *roles*, *tasks*, or *operations*, and, as such, form a permission hierarchy. Roles can consist of tasks (or other roles), tasks can consist of operations (or other tasks), and operations are the most granular permission level.

For example, in our TrackStar application, we need a role of type *owner*. So, we would create an authorization item of type *role* and call it "owner". This role could then consist of tasks such as a "user management" and "issue management". These tasks could then further consist of the atomic operations that make up these tasks. Continuing the example, the "user management" task could consist of the operations "create new user", "edit user", and "delete user". This hierarchy allows for inheritance of these permissions so that, given this example, if a user is assigned to the owner role, they inherit the permission to perform create, edit, and delete operations on the user.

Typically in RBAC, you assign a user to one or more roles and the user inherits the permissions that have been assigned to those roles. This holds true for RBAC in Yii as well. However, in Yii, we can associate users to any authorization item, not just the ones of type *role*. This allows us the flexibility to associate a specific permission to a user at any level of granularity. If we only want to grant the "delete user" operation to a specific user, and not give them all the access that an owner role would have, we can simply associate the user to this atomic operation. This makes RBAC in Yii very flexible.

Configuring the authorization manager

Before we can establish an authorization hierarchy, assign users to roles, and perform access permission checking, we need to configure the authorization manager application component, authManager. This component is responsible for storing the permission data and managing the relationships between permissions. It also provides the methods to check whether or not a user has access to perform a particular operation. Yii provides two types of authorization managers CPhpAuthManager and CDbAuthManager. CPhpAuthManager uses a PHP script file to store the authorization data. CDbAuthManager, as you might have guessed, stores the authorization data in a database. The authManager is configured as an application component. Configuring the authorization manager consists simply of specifying which of these two types to use and then setting its initial class property values.

We'll use the database implementation for our application. To make this configuration, open up the main configuration file, protected/config/main.php, and add the following to the application components array:

```
// application components
'components'=>array(
...
'authManager'=>array(
'class'=>'CDbAuthManager',
'connectionID'=>'db',
),
```

This establishes a new application component named authManager, specifies the class type to be CDbAuthManager, and sets the connectionID class property to be our database connection component. Now we can access this anywhere in our application using Yii::app()->authManager.

Creating the RBAC database tables

As mentioned, the CDbAuthManager class uses database tables to store the permission data. It expects a specific schema. That schema is identified in the framework file YiiRoot/framework/web/auth/schema.sql. It is a simple, yet elegant, schema consisting of three tables, AuthItem, AuthItemChild, and AuthAssignment.

The `AuthItem` table holds the information defining the authorization item that is the role, task, or operation. The `AuthItemChild` table houses the parent/child relationships that form our hierarchy of authorization items. Finally, the `AuthAssignment` table is an association table that holds the association between a user and an authorization item.

So, we need to add this table structure to our database. Just as we have done previously, we'll use database migrations to make these changes. From the command line, navigate to the `/protected` directory of the TrackStar application, and create the migration:

```
$ cd /Webroot/trackstar/protected
$ ./yiic migrate create create_rbac_tables
```

This will create a new migration file under the `protected/migrations/` directory named according to the migration file naming conventions (for example, `m120619_015239_create_rbac_tables.php`). Implement the `up()` and `down()` migration methods as follows:

```
public function up()
{
//create the auth item table
$this->createTable('tbl_auth_item', array(
'name' =>'varchar(64) NOT NULL',
'type' =>'integer NOT NULL',
'description' =>'text',
'bizrule' =>'text',
'data' =>'text',
'PRIMARY KEY (`name`)',
), 'ENGINE=InnoDB');

//create the auth item child table
$this->createTable('tbl_auth_item_child', array(
'parent' =>'varchar(64) NOT NULL',
'child' =>'varchar(64) NOT NULL',
'PRIMARY KEY (`parent`,`child`)',
), 'ENGINE=InnoDB');

//the tbl_auth_item_child.parent is a reference to tbl_auth_item.name
$this->addForeignKey("fk_auth_item_child_parent", "tbl_auth_item_
child", "parent", "tbl_auth_item", "name", "CASCADE", "CASCADE");

//the tbl_auth_item_child.child is a reference to tbl_auth_item.name
```

```
$this->addForeignKey("fk_auth_item_child_child", "tbl_auth_item_
child", "child", "tbl_auth_item", "name", "CASCADE", "CASCADE");

//create the auth assignment table
$this->createTable('tbl_auth_assignment', array(
'itemname' =>'varchar(64) NOT NULL',
'userid' =>'int(11) NOT NULL',
'bizrule' =>'text',
'data' =>'text',
'PRIMARY KEY (`itemname`,`userid`)',
), 'ENGINE=InnoDB');

//the tbl_auth_assignment.itemname is a reference
//to tbl_auth_item.name
$this->addForeignKey(
"fk_auth_assignment_itemname",
"tbl_auth_assignment",
"itemname",
"tbl_auth_item",
"name",
"CASCADE",
"CASCADE"
);

//the tbl_auth_assignment.userid is a reference
//to tbl_user.id
$this->addForeignKey(
"fk_auth_assignment_userid",
"tbl_auth_assignment",
"userid",
"tbl_user",
"id",
"CASCADE",
"CASCADE"
);
}

public function down()
{
$this->truncateTable('tbl_auth_assignment');
```

```
$this->truncateTable('tbl_auth_item_child');
$this->truncateTable('tbl_auth_item');
$this->dropTable('tbl_auth_assignment');
$this->dropTable('tbl_auth_item_child');
$this->dropTable('tbl_auth_item');
}
```

After you save these changes, run the migration to create the needed structure:

$ ./yiic migrate

Once the necessary structure is created, you will see a message `Migrated up successfully` on the screen.

Since we stayed with our database table naming conventions, we need to alter our `authManager` component configuration to specify our specific table names. Open up `/protected/config/main.php`, and add the table name specification to the `authManager` component:

```
// application components
'components'=>array(

...
'authManager'=>array(
'class'=>'CDbAuthManager',
'connectionID'=>'db',
'itemTable' =>'tbl_auth_item',
'itemChildTable' =>'tbl_auth_item_child',
'assignmentTable' =>'tbl_auth_assignment',
),
```

Now the authorization manager component will know exactly which tables we want it to use to manage our authorization structure.

> If you need a reminder on how to use Yii database migrations, refer back to *Chapter 4, Project CRUD* where this concept was first introduced.

Creating the RBAC authorization hierarchy

After adding these tables to our `trackstar` database, we need to populate them with our roles and permissions. We will do this using the API provided by the `authmanager` component. To keep things simple, we are going to only define roles and basic operations. We will not set up any formal RBAC tasks for now. The following diagram displays the basic hierarchy we wish to define:

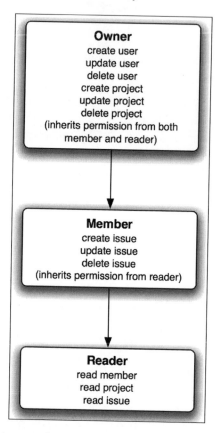

The diagram shows the top-down inheritance. So, owners have all the permissions listed in the Owner box, plus they inherit all the permissions from both the member and reader roles. Likewise, member inherits permissions from reader. What we now need to do is establish this permission hierarchy in the application. As previously mentioned, one way to do this is to write code to utilize the `authManager` API.

As an example of using the API, the following code creates a new role and a new operation, and then adds the relationship between the role and the permission:

```
$auth=Yii::app()->authManager;
$role=$auth->createRole('owner');
$auth->createOperation('createProject','create a new project');
$role->addChild('createProject');
```

Walking through this code, we first get an instance of the `authManager`. We then use its `createRole()`, `createOperation()`, and `addChild()` API methods to create a new `owner` role, and a new operation named `createProject`. We then add the permission to the owner role. This only demonstrates the creation of a small part of our needed hierarchy; all of the remaining relationships we outlined in the previous diagram need to be created in a similar manner.

We could create a new database migration, and place our code there in order to populate our permission hierarchy. However, we are going to take a different approach in order to demonstrate using console commands in your Yii applications. We are going to write a simple shell command to be executed at the command line. This will extend the command options of the `yiic` command-line tool we used to create our initial application.

Writing a console application command

We introduced the `yiic` command-line tool back in *Chapter 2*, *Getting Started*, when we created a new "Hello, World!" application, and again in *Chapter 4*, *Project CRUD* when we used it to initially create the structure of our TrackStar web application. We have continued to use it when creating and running our database migrations.

The `yiic` tool is a console application in Yii that executes tasks in the form of commands. We have used the `webapp` command to create new applications, and the `migrate` command to create new migration files and execute our database migrations. Console applications in Yii are easily extended by writing custom commands, and this is exactly what we are going to do. We are going to extend the `yiic` command tool set by writing a new command-line tool to allow us to build our RBAC authorization.

Writing a new command for a console application is quite simple. A command is simply a class that extends from `CConsoleCommand`. It works similarly to a controller class in that it will parse the input command-line options and dispatch the request to the specified action within the command class, the default being `actionIndex()`. The name of the class should be exactly the same as the desired command name, followed by "Command". In our case, our command will simply be "Rbac", so we'll name our class `RbacCommand`. Lastly, in order to make this command available to the `yiic` console application, we need to save our class into the `/protected/commands/` directory, which is the default location for console commands.

So, create a new file /protected/commands/RbacCommand.php. The contents for this file are too long to be included, but can be easily obtained from the downloadable code for this chapter, or from gist.github.com/jeffwinesett. The individual snippet for this is available at https://gist.github.com/3779677.

The comments in the downloadable code should help tell the story of what is happening here. We override the base class implementation of getHelp() to add an additional description line. We'll show how to display the help in a minute. All of the real action happens in the two actions we added, actionIndex() and actionDelete(). The former creates our RBAC hierarchy, and the latter removes it. They both ensure the application has a vaild authManager application component defined. Then both actions allow the user to have a last chance to cancel the request before proceeding. If the user of this command indicates they want to continue, the request will proceed. Both of our actions will proceed to clear all previously entered data in the RBAC tables and the actionIndex() method will create a new authorization hierarchy. The hierarchy that is created here is exactly the one we discussed previously.

We can see that, even based on our fairly simple hierarchy, there is still a significant amount of code needed. Typically, one would need to develop a more intuitive **Graphical User Interface (GUI)** wrapped around these authorization manager APIs to provide an easy interface to manage roles, tasks, and operations. The approach we have taken here is a great solution for establishing a quick RBAC permission structure, but not ideal for the long-term maintenance of a permission structure that might change significantly.

 In a real-world application, you will most likely need a different, more interactive tool to help maintain the RBAC relationships. The Yii extension library (http://www.yiiframework.com/extensions/) does provide some packaged solutions for this.

With this file in place, if we now ask the `yiic` tool for help, we'll see our new command as one of the available options:

```
$cd /Webroot/trackstar/protected/
$./yiic help
Yii command runner (based on Yii v1.1.12)
Usage: ./yiic <command-name> [parameters...]

The following commands are available:
 - message
 - migrate
 - rbac
 - shell
 - webapp

To see individual command help, use the following:
    ./yiic help <command-name>
```

Our `rbac` does show up in the list. However, before we can try to execute it, we need to configure the `authManager` for our console application. As you may recall, when running console applications, a different configuration file is loaded, namely `/protected/config/console.php`. We need to add the same `authManager` component to this file as we did previously to the `main.php` configuration file. Open up `console.php` and add the following to the components list:

```
'authManager'=>array(
'class'=>'CDbAuthManager',
'connectionID'=>'db',
'itemTable' =>'tbl_auth_item',
'itemChildTable' =>'tbl_auth_item_child',
'assignmentTable' =>'tbl_auth_assignment',
),
```

With this in place, we can now try out our new command:

```
$cd /Webroot/trackstar/protected/
$./yiic help rbac
Usage: ./yiic rbac <action>
Actions:
    index
    delete
DESCRIPTION
    This command generates an initial RBAC authorization hierarchy.
```

This is exactly the help text that we added to our `getHelp()` method in our command class. You can certainly be more verbose and add more detail as desired. Let's actually run the command. Since `actionIndex()` is the default, we don't have to specify the action:

```
$./yiic rbac
This command will create three roles: Owner, Member, and Reader
 and the following permissions:
create, read, update and delete user
create, read, update and delete project
create, read, update and delete issue
Would you like to continue? [yes|no] yes
Authorization hierarchy successfully generated.
```

Our command has completed and we have added the appropriate data to our new database tables to generate our authorization hierarchy.

Since we also added an `actionDelete()` method to remove our hierarchy, you can try that one out as well:

```
$ ./yiic rbac delete
```

Once you are done trying these out, make sure you run the command again to add the hierarchy, as we need it to be in place as we continue.

Assigning users to roles

Everything we have done thus far establishes an authorization hierarchy, but it does not yet assign permissions to users. We accomplish this by assigning users to one of the three roles we created, *owner*, *member*, or *reader*. For example, if we wanted to associate the user whose unique user ID is 1 with the `member` role, we would execute the following:

```
$auth=Yii::app()->authManager;
$auth->assign('member',1);
```

Once these relationships are established, checking a user's access permission is a simple matter. We simply ask the application user component whether or not the current user has the permission. For example, if we wanted to check whether or not the current user is allowed to create a new issue, we could do so with the following syntax:

```
if( Yii::app()->user->checkAccess('createIssue'))
{
    //perform needed logic
}
```

In this example, we assigned user ID 1 to the role of `member` and since in our authorization hierarchy the member role inherits the `createIssue` permission, this `if()` statement would evaluate to `true`, assuming we were logged in to the application as user 1.

We will be adding this authorization assignment logic as part of the business logic executed when adding a new member to a project. We'll be adding a new form that allows us to add users to projects, and the ability to choose a role as part of the process. But first we need to address one other aspect of how user roles need to be implemented within this application, namely, they need to apply on a per-project basis.

Adding RBAC roles to users on a per-project basis

We now have a basic RBAC authorization model in place, but these relationships apply to the application as a whole. Our needs for the TrackStar application are slightly more complex. We need to assign roles to users within the context of projects, not just globally across the application. We need to allow users to be in different roles, depending on the project. For example, a user may be in the `reader` role of one project, a `member` of a second project, and an `owner` of some third project. Users can be associated with many projects, and the role they are assigned needs to be specific to the project.

The RBAC framework in Yii does not have anything built-in that we can take advantage of to meet this requirement. The RBAC model is only intended to establish relationships between roles and permissions. It does not know (nor should it) anything about our TrackStar projects. In order to achieve this extra dimension to our authorization hierarchy, we need to alter our database structure to contain an association between a user, project, and role. If you recall from back in *Chapter 5*, *Managing Issues* we have already created a table, `tbl_project_user_assignment`, to hold the association between a user and a project. We can alter this table to also contain the role assigned to the user within the project. We'll add a new migration to alter our table:

```
$ cd /Webroot/trackstar/protected/
$ ./yiic migrate create add_role_to_tbl_project_user_assignment
```

Now open up the newly created migration file and implement the following up()
and down() methods:

```
public function up()
{
$this->addColumn('tbl_project_user_assignment', 'role',
'varchar(64)');
//the tbl_project_user_assignment.role is a reference
     //to tbl_auth_item.name
$this->addForeignKey('fk_project_user_role', 'tbl_project_user_
assignment', 'role', 'tbl_auth_item', 'name', 'CASCADE', 'CASCADE');
}

public function down()
{
$this->dropForeignKey('fk_project_user_role', 'tbl_project_user_
assignment');
$this->dropColumn('tbl_project_user_assignment', 'role');
}
```

Finally run the migration:

```
$./yiic migrate

Yii Migration Tool v1.0 (based on Yii v1.1.12)

Total 1 new migration to be applied:
    m120620_020255_add_role_to_tbl_project_user_assignment

Apply the above migration? (yes|no) [no]:yes
*** applying m120620_020255_add_role_to_tbl_project_user_assignment
    > add column role varchar(64) to table tbl_project_user_assignment .
.. done (time: 0.100s)
    > add foreign key fk_project_user_role: tbl_project_user_assignment
(role) references tbl_auth_item (name) ... done (time: 0.222s)
*** applied m120620_020255_add_role_to_tbl_project_user_assignment (time
: 0.324s)

Migrated up successfully.
```

You will see the message Migrated up successfully at the end of the screen.

Now our table is set up to allow us to make the role association along with the
association between a user and a project.

Adding RBAC business rules

While the database table shown earlier will hold the basic information to answer the question as to whether a user is assigned to a role within the context of a particular project, we still need our RBAC `auth` hierarchy to answer questions concerning whether or not a user has permission to perform a certain functionality. Although the RBAC model in Yii does not know about our TrackStar projects, it does have a very powerful feature of which we can take advantage. When you create authorization items or assign an item to a user, you can associate a snippet of PHP code that will be executed during the `Yii::app()->user->checkAccess()` call. When defined, this bit of code must return `true` before the user would be granted that permission.

One example of the usefulness of this feature is in the context of applications that allow users to maintain personal profile information. Often in this case, the application would like to ensure that a user has the permission to update only their own profile information and no one else's. In this case we could create an authorization item called "updateProfile", and then associate a business rule that checks if the current user's ID is the same as the user ID associated with the profile information.

In our case, we are going to associate a business rule with the role assignment. When we assign a user to a specific role, we will also associate a business rule that will check the relationship within the context of the project. The `checkAccess()` method also allows us to pass in an array of additional parameters for the business rule to use to perform its logic. We'll use this to pass in the current project context so that the business rule can call a method on the `Project` AR class in order to determine whether or not the user is assigned to that role within that project.

The business rule we'll create will be slightly different for each role assignment. For example, the one we'll use when assigning a user to the owner role will look like the following:

```
$bizRule='return isset($params["project"]) && $params["project"]-
>isUserInRole("owner");';
```

The ones for the roles `member` and `reader` will be similar.

We will also have to pass in the project context when we call the `checkAccess()` method. So now when checking if a user has access to, for example, the `createIssue` operation, the code would look like the following:

```
//add the project AR instance to the input params
$params=array('project'=>$project);
//pass in the params to the checkAccess call
if(Yii::app()->user->checkAccess('createIssue',$params))
{
    //proceed with issue creation logic
}
```

In the previous code, the $project variable is the Project AR class instance associated with the current project context (remember that almost all functionality in our application occurs within the context of a project). This class instance is what is used in the business rule. The business rule calls a method, Project::isUserInRole(), in order to determine if the user is in the role for the specific project.

Implementing the new project AR methods

Now that we have altered our database structure to house the relationship between user, role, and project, we need to implement the required logic to manage and verify the data in this table. We will be adding public methods to the project AR class to handle adding and removing data from this table as well as verifying the existence of rows.

We need to add the public method to the Project AR class that will take in a role name and a user ID and create the association between role, user, and project. Open up the protected/models/Project.php file and add the following method:

```
public function assignUser($userId, $role)
{
$command = Yii::app()->db->createCommand();
$command->insert('tbl_project_user_assignment', array(
'role'=>$role,
'user_id'=>$userId,
'project_id'=>$this->id,
));
}
```

Here we are using the Yii framework query builder approach to directly insert into the database table, rather than using the active record approach. Since tbl_project_user_assignement is just an association table, and does not represent a main domain object of our model, it is sometimes easier to manage the data in these types of tables in a more direct manner than using the active record approach.

 For more information on using Query Builder in Yii, visit: http://www.yiiframework.com/doc/guide/1.1/en/ database.query-builder

We'll also need to be able to remove a user from a project, and in doing so, remove the association between a user and the project. So, let's also add a method to do that.

Add the following method to the `Project` AR class:

```
public function removeUser($userId)
{
$command = Yii::app()->db->createCommand();
$command->delete(
'tbl_project_user_assignment',
'user_id=:userId AND project_id=:projectId',
array(':userId'=>$userId,':projectId'=>$this->id));
}
```

This simply deletes the row from the table that houses the association between the role, the user, and the project.

We have now implemented the methods for adding and removing our associations. We need to add functionality to determine whether or not a given user is associated with a role within the project. We will also add this as a public method to our `Project` AR class.

Add the following method to the bottom of the `Project` AR model class:

```
public function allowCurrentUser($role)
{
$sql = "SELECT * FROM tbl_project_user_assignment WHERE project_
id=:projectId AND user_id=:userId AND role=:role";
$command = Yii::app()->db->createCommand($sql);
$command->bindValue(":projectId", $this->id, PDO::PARAM_INT);
$command->bindValue(":userId", Yii::app()->user->getId(), PDO::PARAM_
INT);
$command->bindValue(":role", $role, PDO::PARAM_STR);
return $command->execute()==1;
}
```

This method is showing how to execute the SQL directly, rather than using the query builder. The query builder is very useful, but for simple queries, it is sometimes easier to just execute the SQL directly, utilizing Yii's Data Access Objects (DAO).

For more information on Yii's Data Access Objects and directly executing SQL in Yii, see:

http://www.yiiframework.com/doc/guide/1.1/en/database.dao

Adding users to projects

Now we need to put all of this together. In *Chapter 6, User Management and Authorization* we added the ability to create new users of the application. However, we do not yet have a way to assign users to specific projects, and further, assign them to roles within these projects. Now that we have our RBAC approach in place, we need to build this new functionality.

The implementation of this functionality involves several coding changes. However, we have provided similar examples of the type of changes needed, and have covered all of the related concepts when implementing functionality in previous chapters. Consequently, we will move pretty quickly through this, and pause only briefly to highlight just a few things we have not yet seen. At this point, the reader should be able to make all of these changes without much help, and is encouraged to do so as a hands-on exercise. To further encourage this exercise, we'll first list everything we are going to do to fulfill this new feature requirement. You can then close the book and try some of these out yourself before looking further down at our implementation.

To achieve this goal we will perform the following:

1. Add a public static method called `getUserRoleOptions()` to the `Project` model class that returns a valid list of role options using the `auth` manager's `getRoles()` method. We will use this to populate a roles selection drop-down field in the form, so that we can select the user role when adding a new user to a project.

2. Add a new public method called `isUserInProject($user)` to the `Project` model class to determine if a user is already associated with a project. We will use this in our validation rules upon form submission so that we don't attempt to add a duplicate user to a project.

3. Add a new form model class called `ProjectUserForm`, extending from `CFormModel` for a new input form model. Add to this form model class three attributes, namely `$username`, `$role`, and `$project`. Also add validation rules to ensure that both the username and the role are required input fields, and that the username should further be validated via a custom `verify()` class method.

This verify method should attempt to create a new UserAR class instance by finding a user matching the input username. If the attempt was successful, it should continue to associate the user to a project using the `assignUser($userId, $role)` method that we already added earlier. We will also need to associate the user to the role in our RBAC hierarchy implemented earlier in this chapter. If no user was found matching the username, it needs to set and return an error. (If needed, review the `LoginForm::authenticate()` method as an example of a custom validation rule method.)

4. Add a new view file under views/project called `adduser.php` to display our new form for adding users to projects. This form only needs two input fields, *username* and *role*. The role should be a drop-down choice listing.

5. Add a new controller action method called `actionAdduser()` to the `ProjectController` class and alter its `accessRules()` method to ensure it is accessible by authenticated members. This new action method is responsible for rendering the new view to display the form and handle the post back when the form is submitted.

Again, we encourage the reader to attempt these changes on their own first. We list our code changes in the following sections.

Altering the project model class

To the `Project` class, we add two new public methods, one of them static so it can be called without the need for a specific class instance:

```
/**
 * Returns an array of available roles in which a user can be placed
when being added to a project
 */
public static function getUserRoleOptions()
{
return CHtml::listData(Yii::app()->authManager->getRoles(), 'name',
'name');
}


/*
 * Determines whether or not a user is already part of a project
 */
public function isUserInProject($user)
{
```

```
$sql = "SELECT user_id FROM tbl_project_user_assignment WHERE project_
id=:projectId AND user_id=:userId";
$command = Yii::app()->db->createCommand($sql);
$command->bindValue(":projectId", $this->id, PDO::PARAM_INT);
$command->bindValue(":userId", $user->id, PDO::PARAM_INT);
return $command->execute()==1;
}
```

Adding the new form model class

Just as it was used in the approach for the login form, we are going to create a new
form model class as a central place to house our form input parameters and to
centralize the validation. This is a fairly simple class that extends from the Yii class
CFormModel and has attributes that map to our form input fields, as well as one to
hold the valid project context. We need the project context to be able to add users
to projects. The entire class is too long to list here, but can be easily obtained from
the downloadable code that accompanies this chapter. The standalone snippet is
available at https://gist.github.com/3779690.

In the following code snippet, we have listed just the parts we have not seen before:

```
class ProjectUserForm extends CFormModel
{
...
        public function assign()
{
if($this->_user instanceof User)
{
//assign the user, in the specified role, to the project
$this->project->assignUser($this->_user->id, $this->role);
//add the association, along with the RBAC biz rule, to our RBAC
hierarchy
        $auth = Yii::app()->authManager;
$bizRule='return isset($params["project"]) && $params["project"]-
>allowCurrentUser("'.$this->role.'");';
$auth->assign($this->role,$this->_user->id, $bizRule);
                return true;
}
            else
{
$this->addError('username','Error when attempting to assign this user
to the project.');
return false;
}
        }
```

For simplicity, in the createUsernameList() method, we are selecting *all* users from the database to use for the username list. If there are a large number of users, this may result in suboptimal performance. To optimize performance, you may need to filter and limit this in cases where there are a large number of users.

The part of the downloadable code that we listed above is the assign() method where we are adding a bizRule to the association between the user and role in RBAC:

```
$auth = Yii::app()->authManager;
$bizRule='return isset($params["project"]) && $params["project"]-
>isUserInRole("'.$this->role.'");';
$auth->assign($this->role,$user->id, $bizRule);
```

We create an instance of the Authmanager class that we used to establish the assignment of the user to the role. However, before we make that assignment, we create the business rule. The business rule uses the $params array by first checking the existence of a project element in the array, and then calls the isUserInRole() method on the project AR class, which is the value of that array element. We explicitly pass in the role name to this method. We then call the AuthManager::assign() method to make the association between the user and the role.

We have also added a simple public method, createUsernameList(), to return an array of all the usernames in the database. We will use this array to populate the data of one of Yii's UI widgets, CJuiAutoComplete, which we will use for the username input form element. As its name suggests, as we type in the input form field, it will provide choice suggestions based on the elements in this array.

Adding the new action method to the project controller

We need a controller action to handle the initial request to display the form for adding a new user to a project. We placed this in the ProjectController class and named it actionAdduser(). The code for this is as follows:

```
    /**
     * Provides a form so that project administrators can
     * associate other users to the project
     */
    public function actionAdduser($id)
    {
      $project = $this->loadModel($id);
      if(!Yii::app()->user->checkAccess('createUser',
      array('project'=>$project)))
```

```
{
    throw new CHttpException(403,'You are not authorized to perform
    this action.');
}


$form=new ProjectUserForm;
// collect user input data
if(isset($_POST['ProjectUserForm']))
{
    $form->attributes=$_POST['ProjectUserForm'];
    $form->project = $project;
    // validate user input
    if($form->validate())
    {
        if($form->assign())
        {
            Yii::app()->user->setFlash('success',$form->username . "
            has been added to the project." );
            //reset the form for another user to be associated if desired
            $form->unsetAttributes();
            $form->clearErrors();
        }
    }
}
$form->project = $project;
$this->render('adduser',array('model'=>$form));
}
```

This is all pretty familiar to us at this point. It handles both the initial GET request to display the form as well as the POST request after the form is submitted. It follows very much the same approach as our `SiteController::actionLogin()` method. The highlighted code in the previous code snippet is, however, something we have not seen before. If the submitted form request is successful, it sets what is called a **flash message**. A flash message is a temporary message stored briefly in the session. It is only available in the current and the next requests. Here we are using the `setFlash()` method of our `CWebUser` application user component to store a temporary message that the request was successful. When we talk about the view in the next section, we will see how to access this message and display it to the user.

One other change we have to make is to the base controller class method
`Controller::accessRules()`. As you recall, we added our access rules to this base
class so that they apply to each of our user, issue, and project controller classes. We
need to add in this new action name to the basic access rules list so that a logged in
user is allowed to access this action:

```
public function accessRules()
{
return array(
array('allow',  // allow all users to perform 'index' and 'view'
actions
'controllers'=>array('issue','project','user'),
'actions'=>array('index','view','addUser'),
'users'=>array('@'),
),
```

Adding the new view file to display the form

Our new action method is calling `->render('adduser')` to render a view file, so we
need to get that created. The following is the full listing of our implementation for
`protected/views/project/adduser.php`:

```
<?php
$this->pageTitle=Yii::app()->name . ' - Add User To Project';
$this->breadcrumbs=array(
$model->project->name=>array('view','id'=>$model->project->id),
'Add User',
);
$this->menu=array(
array('label'=>'Back To Project', 'url'=>array('view','id'=>$model-
>project->id)),
);
?>

<h1>Add User To <?php echo $model->project->name; ?></h1>

<?php if(Yii::app()->user->hasFlash('success')):?>
<div class="successMessage">
<?php echo Yii::app()->user->getFlash('success'); ?>
</div>
<?phpendif; ?>

<div class="form">
<?php $form=$this->beginWidget('CActiveForm'); ?>
```

```
<p class="note">Fields with <span class="required">*</span> are
required.</p>

<div class="row">
<?php echo $form->labelEx($model,'username'); ?>
<?php
$this->widget('zii.widgets.jui.CJuiAutoComplete', array(
'name'=>'username',
'source'=>$model->createUsernameList(),
'model'=>$model,
'attribute'=>'username',
'options'=>array(
'minLength'=>'2',
),
'htmlOptions'=>array(
'style'=>'height:20px;'
),
));
?>
<?php echo $form->error($model,'username'); ?>
</div>

<div class="row">
<?php echo $form->labelEx($model,'role'); ?>
<?php
echo $form->dropDownList($model,'role',
Project::getUserRoleOptions()); ?>
<?php echo $form->error($model,'role'); ?>
</div>


<div class="row buttons">
<?php echo CHtml::submitButton('Add User'); ?>
</div>

<?php $this->endWidget(); ?>
</div>
```

We have seen most of this before. We are defining active labels and active form elements that tie directly to our `ProjectUserForm` form model class. We populate our dropdown using the static method we implemented earlier on the project model class. We populate our Zii library autocomplete widget (`CJuiAutoComplete`) data with the method `createUsernameList()` we added to the project user form model class. We also added a simple link to the menu options to take us back to the project details page.

The highlighted code in the previous code snippet is new to us. This is an example of using the flash message that we introduced and used in the `actionAdduser()` method. We access the message we set using `setFlash()` by asking the same user component if it has a flash message, using `hasFlash('succcess')`. We feed the `hasFlash()` method the exact name we gave it when we set the message. This is a nice way to present the user with some simple feedback about their previous request.

One other small change we made was to add a simple link from the project details page so we could access this from the application. The following highlighted line was added to the project `view.php` view file's menu array:

```
$this->menu=array(
...
array('label'=>'Add User To Project', 'url'=>array('project/adduser',
'id'=>$model->id)),
);
```

This gives us access to the new form when viewing the details of a project.

Putting it all together

With all of these changes in place, we can navigate to our new form by viewing one of the project details pages. For example, when viewing project ID #1 via `http://localhost/trackstar/index.php?r=project/view&id=1`, in the right-hand side column menu of operations is a hyperlink **[Add User To Project]** and clicking on that link should display the following page:

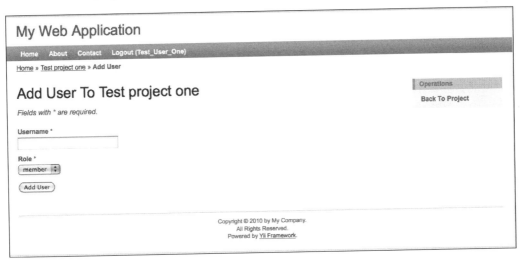

You can use the forms we have built previously to create new projects and users to ensure you have a few of them added to the application. Then you can play around with adding users to projects. As you type in the **Username** field, you will see suggestions for autocompletion. If you attempt to add a user that is not in the user database table, you should see an error telling you so. If you attempt to enter a user that has already been added to the project, you will receive an error telling you so. And upon successful additions, you will see a short flash message indicating success.

Now that we have the ability to assign users to projects and add them to our RBAC authorization hierarchy, we should alter our logic for when we are adding a new project. When a new project is added, it should assign the user who is adding the project as the owner of the project. This way, the creator of the project will have full administrative access to the project. I will leave this as homework for the reader. You can view a solution to this exercise by downloading the available source code for the TrackStar application that accompanies this book.

Checking authorization level

The last thing we need to do to complete what we set out to do in this chapter is to add the authorization checks for the different functionality we have implemented. Earlier in this chapter we outlined, and then implemented, the RBAC authorization hierarchy for the different roles we have. Everything is in place to allow or deny access to functionality based on the permissions that have been granted to users within projects, with one exception. We have not yet implemented the authorization checks necessary when attempting to request functionality. The application is still using the simple access filter that is defined on each of our project, issue, and user controllers. We'll do this for one of our permissions and then leave the remaining implementation as an exercise for the reader.

We see from looking back at our authorization hierarchy that only project owners should be able to add new users to a project. So, let's add this authorization check. We'll hide the link for adding a user on the project details page unless the current user is in the *owner* role for that project (before implementing, you should make sure you have added at least one owner and one member or reader to a project so you can test them when complete). Open up the `protected/views/project/view.php` view file where we placed the link in the menu items for adding a new user. Remove that array element from the menu array items, and then push it on the end of the array only if the `checkAccess()` method returns `true`. The following code shows how the menu items should be defined:

```
$this->menu=array(
array('label'=>'List Project', 'url'=>array('index')),
array('label'=>'Create Project', 'url'=>array('create')),
```

```
array('label'=>'Update Project', 'url'=>array('update', 'id'=>$model-
>id)),
array('label'=>'Delete Project', 'url'=>'#', 'linkOptions'=>array('su
bmit'=>array('delete','id'=>$model->id),'confirm'=>'Are you sure you
want to delete this item?')),
array('label'=>'Manage Project', 'url'=>array('admin')),
array('label'=>'Create Issue', 'url'=>array('issue/create',
'pid'=>$model->id)),

);
if(Yii::app()->user->checkAccess('createUser',array('project'=>$mod
el)))
{
$this->menu[] = array('label'=>'Add User To Project',
'url'=>array('adduser', 'id'=>$model->id));
}
```

This implements the same approach we discussed earlier in the chapter. We call `checkAccess()` on the current user and send in the name of the permission we want to check. Also, since our roles are within the context of projects, we send in the project model instance as an array input. This will allow the business rule to execute, which has been defined in the authorization assignment. Now if we log in as a project owner for a particular project and navigate to that project details page, we'll see the menu option for adding a new user to the project. Conversely, if we log in as a user in the `member` or `reader` role of that same project, and again navigate to the details page, this link will not display.

This, of course, will not prevent a savvy user from gaining access to this functionality by navigating using the URL directly. For example, even while logged in to the application as a user in the `reader` role for, say, project #1, if I navigate directly to `http://localhost/trackstar/index.php?r=project/adduser&id=1` I can still access the form.

To prevent this, we need to add our access check directly to the action method itself. So, in the `ProjectController::actionAdduser()` method in the project controller class, we can add the check:

```
public function actionAdduser($id)
{
$project = $this->loadModel($id);
if(!Yii::app()->user->checkAccess('createUser',
array('project'=>$project)))
{
throw new CHttpException(403,'You are not authorized to perform this
action.');
}

$form=new ProjectUserForm;
```

Now when we attempt to access this URL directly, we will be denied access unless we are in the project *owner* role for the project.

We won't go through implementing the access checks for all of the other functionality. Each would be implemented in a similar manner. We leave this as an exercise for the reader. This implementation is not necessary in order to continue to follow along with the remaining code examples throughout the book.

Summary

We have covered a lot in this chapter. First we were introduced to the basic access control filter that Yii provides as one method to allow and deny access to specific controller action methods. We used this approach to ensure that users be logged in to that application before gaining access to any of the main functionality. We then took a detailed walk through Yii's RBAC model, which allows for a much more sophisticated approach to access control. We built an entire user authorization hierarchy based on application roles. In the process, we were introduced to writing console applications in Yii, and to some of the benefits of this wonderful feature. We then built in new functionality to allow the addition of users to projects and being able to assign them to appropriate roles within those projects. Finally, we discovered how to implement the needed access checks throughout the application to utilize the RBAC hierarchy to appropriately grant/deny access to feature functionality.

In the next chapter, we are going to add even more functionality for users, one of which is the ability to leave comments on our project issues.

8
Adding User Comments

With the implementation of user management throughout the two previous chapters, our Trackstar application is really starting to take shape. The bulk of our primary application feature functionality is now behind us. We can now start to focus on some of the nice-to-have features. The first of these that we will tackle is the ability for users to leave comments on the project issues.

The ability for users to engage in dialog about project issues is an important part of what any issue tracking tool should provide. One way to achieve this is to allow users to leave comments directly on the issues. The comments will form a conversation about the issue and provide immediate as well as historical context to help track the full lifespan of any issue. We will also use comments to demonstrate the use of Yii widgets and how to establish a portlet model for delivering content to the user (for more on portlets, see `http://en.wikipedia.org/wiki/Portlet`).

Feature planning

The goal of this chapter is to implement feature functionality in the Trackstar application that allows users to leave and read comments on issues. When the user is viewing the detail of any project issue, they should be able to read all comments previously added as well as create a new comment on the issue. We also want to add a small fragment of content or portlet to the project listing page to display a list of recent comments left on all of the issues. This will be a nice way to provide a window into recent user activity and allow easy access to the latest issues that have active conversations.

The following is a list of high-level tasks we will need to complete in order to achieve these goals:

1. Design and create a new database table to support comments.
2. Create the Yii AR class associated with our new comments table.
3. Add a form directly to the issue details page to allow users to submit comments.
4. Display a list of all comments associated with an issue directly on its details page.
5. Take advantage of Yii widgets to display a list of the most recent comments on the projects listing page.

Creating the model

We first need to create a new table to house our comments. As you might expect, we will use a database migration to make this addition to our database structure:

```
$ cd /Webroot/trackstar/protected

$ ./yiic migrate create create_user_comments_table
```

The up() and down() methods are as follows:

```
public function up()
{
  //create the issue table
  $this->createTable('tbl_comment', array(
    'id' => 'pk',
        'content' => 'text NOT NULL',
        'issue_id' => 'int(11) NOT NULL',
    'create_time' => 'datetime DEFAULT NULL',
    'create_user_id' => 'int(11) DEFAULT NULL',
    'update_time' => 'datetime DEFAULT NULL',
    'update_user_id' => 'int(11) DEFAULT NULL',
  ), 'ENGINE=InnoDB');

  //the tbl_comment.issue_id is a reference to tbl_issue.id
    $this->addForeignKey("fk_comment_issue", "tbl_comment", "issue_id", "tbl_issue", "id", "CASCADE", "RESTRICT");

  //the tbl_issue.create_user_id is a reference to tbl_user.id
    $this->addForeignKey("fk_comment_owner", "tbl_comment", "create_user_id", "tbl_user", "id", "RESTRICT, "RESTRICT");
```

```
        //the tbl_issue.updated_user_id is a reference to tbl_user.id
        $this->addForeignKey("fk_comment_update_user", "tbl_comment",
  "update_user_id", "tbl_user", "id", "RESTRICT", "RESTRICT");


    }

    public function down()
    {
        $this->dropForeignKey('fk_comment_issue', 'tbl_comment');
        $this->dropForeignKey('fk_comment_owner', 'tbl_comment');
        $this->dropForeignKey('fk_comment_update_user', 'tbl_comment');
        $this->dropTable('tbl_comment');
    }
```

In order to implement this database change, we need to run the migration:

```
  $ ./yiic migrate
```

Now that our database table is in place, creating the associated AR class is a snap. We have seen this many times throughout the previous chapters. We know exactly how to do this. We simply use the Gii code creation tool's **Model Generator** command and create an AR class called Comment, based on our newly created table tbl_comment. If needed, refer back to *Chapter 4, Project CRUD* and *Chapter 5, Managing Issues*, for all the details on using this tool to create model classes.

After using the Gii tool to create the model class for comments, you'll notice that the code generated for us already has some relations defined. These are based on the foreign key relationships we defined on the tbl_comments table. The following is what was created for us:

```
  /**
    * @return array relational rules.
    */
   public function relations()
   {
      // NOTE: you may need to adjust the relation name and the related
      // class name for the relations automatically generated below.
      return array(
         'updateUser' => array(self::BELONGS_TO, 'User', 'update_user_
  id'),
         'issue' => array(self::BELONGS_TO, 'Issue', 'issue_id'),
         'createUser' => array(self::BELONGS_TO, 'User', 'create_user_
  id'),
       );
    }
```

We can see that we have a relationship that specifies a comment belongs to an issue. But we also need to define the one-to-many relationship between an issue and its comments. One issue can have many comments. This change needs to be made in the Issue model class.

 Had we created our comment model at the same time we created our Issue model, this relation would have been created for us.

In addition to this, we will also add a relationship as a statistical query to easily retrieve the number of comments associated with a given issue. Here are the changes we make to the Issue::relations() method:

```
public function relations()
{
    return array(
        'requester' => array(self::BELONGS_TO, 'User', 'requester_id'),
        'owner' => array(self::BELONGS_TO, 'User', 'owner_id'),
        'project' => array(self::BELONGS_TO, 'Project', 'project_id'),
        'comments' => array(self::HAS_MANY, 'Comment', 'issue_id'),
        'commentCount' => array(self::STAT, 'Comment', 'issue_id'),
    );
}
```

This establishes the one-to-many relationship between an issue and comments. It also defines a statistical query to allow us to easily retrieve the total comment count for any given issue instance.

 Statistical query

The commentCount relation defined previously is a new type of relation we have not seen before. In addition to relational queries, Yii also offers what is called a statistical or aggregational relationship. These are very useful in cases where there is a one-to-many (HAS_MANY) or many-to-many (MANY_MANY) relationship between objects. In such cases, we can define statistical relationships to allow us to easily get the total number of related objects. We have taken advantage of this in the previous relationship declarations to allow us to easily retrieve the total number of comments for any given issue instance. For more information on using statistical queries in Yii, refer to http://www.yiiframework.com/doc/guide/1.1/en/database.arr#statistical-query.

We also need to change our newly created `Comment` AR class to extend our custom `TrackStarActiveRecord` base class, so that it benefits from the logic we placed in the `beforeSave()` method. Simply alter the beginning of the class definition, as follows:

```
<?php
     /**
     * This is the model class for table "tbl_comment".
     */
    class Comment extends TrackStarActiveRecord
    {
```

We'll make one last small change to the definitions in the `Comment::relations()` method. The relational attributes were named for us when the class was created. Let's change the one named `createUser`, to `author`, as this related user represents the author of the comment. This is just a semantic change, but it will help to make our code easier to read and understand. Change the definition from `'createUser' => array(self::BELONGS_TO, 'User', 'create_user_id')`, to `'author' => array(self::BELONGS_TO, 'User', 'create_user_id')`.

Creating the comment CRUD

Now that we have our AR model class in place, creating the CRUD scaffolding to manage the related entity is easy. Simply use the Gii code generation tool's **Crud Generator** command with the AR class name, `Comment`, as the argument. We have seen this many times in previous chapters, so we won't go through it in detail again here. If needed, refer back to *Chapter 4, Project CRUD* and *Chapter 5, Managing Issues*, for all the details on using the Gii tool to create CRUD scaffolding code. Although we will not immediately implement full CRUD operations for our comments, it is nice to have the scaffolding for the other operations in place.

After using Gii's Crud Generator, and as long as we are logged in, we should now be able to view the autogenerated comment submission form via the following URL:

```
http://localhost/trackstar/index.php?r=comment/create
```

Altering the scaffolding to meet our requirements

As we have seen many times before, we often have to make adjustments to the autogenerated scaffolding code in order to meet the specific requirements of the application. For one, our autogenerated form for creating a new comment has an input field for every single column defined in the `tbl_comment` database table. We don't actually want all of these fields to be part of the form. In fact, we want to greatly simplify this form to only have a single input field for the comment content. What's more, we don't want the user to access the form via the previously mentioned URL, but rather only by visiting an issue details page. The user will add comments on the same page where they are viewing the details of the issue. We want to build towards something like what is depicted in the following screenshot:

View Issue #1

Id	1
Name	Test Bug
Description	bug one
Project	Not set
Type	0
Status	0
Owner	Not set
Requester	Not set
Create Time	Not set
Create User	Not set
Update Time	Not set
Update User	Not set

2 comments

Test User One:
on December 31, 1969 at 07:00 pm
Hello There

Test User One:
on December 31, 1969 at 07:00 pm
another comment

Leave a Comment

*Fields with * are required.*

Content *

[   ]

(Create)

In order to achieve this, we are going to alter our `Issue` controller class to handle the post of the comment form as well as alter the issue details view to display the existing comments and new comment creation form. Also, since comments should only be created within the context of an issue, we'll add a new method to the issue model class to create new comments.

Adding a comment

As mentioned, we are going to have the issue instance create its own comments. For this, we want to add a method to the `Issue` AR class. Here is that method:

```
/**
 * Adds a comment to this issue
 */
public function addComment($comment)
{
    $comment->issue_id=$this->id;
    return $comment->save();
}
```

This method ensures the proper setting of the comment issue ID before saving the new comment. That is, when an instance of `Issue` creates a new comment, it is understood that the comment belongs to that issue.

With this method in place, we can now turn our focus to the issue controller class. Since we want the comment creation form to display from and post its data back to the `IssueController::actionView()` method, we will need to alter that method. We will also add a new protected method to handle the form post request. First, alter the `actionView()` method to be the following:

```
public function actionView($id)
{
    $issue=$this->loadModel($id);
    $comment=$this->createComment($issue);
    $this->render('view',array(
      'model'=>$issue,
        'comment'=>$comment,
    ));
}
```

Then, add the following protected method to create a new comment and handle the form post request for creating a new comment for this issue:

```
/**
 * Creates a new comment on an issue
 */
protected function createComment($issue)
{
    $comment=new Comment;
    if(isset($_POST['Comment']))
    {
        $comment->attributes=$_POST['Comment'];
        if($issue->addComment($comment))
        {
            Yii::app()->user->setFlash('commentSubmitted',"Your comment has
been added." );
            $this->refresh();
        }
    }
    return $comment;
}
```

Our new protected method, `createComment()`, is responsible for handling the POST request submitted when a user is leaving a new comment on an issue. If the comment is successfully created, we set a flash message to display to the user and also do a page refresh so that our new comment will display. Of course, we still need to alter our view file to make all of this display to the user. The changes made to `IssueController::actionView()` are responsible for calling this new method and also for feeding the new comment instance to the view for display.

Displaying the form

Now, we need to alter our view. First we are going to create a new view file to render the display of our comments and the comment input form. We intend to display this view file within another view file. As such, we don't want to display all of the general page components, such as the header navigation and footer information, again. View files that are intended to be displayed within other view files, or without any extra decoration, are called **partial** views. You can then use the controller method `renderPartial()`, as opposed to the `render()` method. Using `renderPartial()` will only render the content contained within that view file and will not decorate the display with any other content. We will be discussing this in much more detail in *Chapter 10, Making it Look Good*, when we discuss using layouts and decorating your view files.

Yii uses a naming convention of a leading underscore (_) when creating partial view files. Since we'll render this as a partial view, we'll stick with the naming conventions and begin the filename with a leading underscore. Create a new file called _ comments.php under the protected/views/issue/ directory and add the following code to that file:

```php
<?php foreach($comments as $comment): ?>
<div class="comment">
        <div class="author">
      <?php echo CHtml::encode($comment->author->username); ?>:
  </div>

  <div class="time">
      on <?php echo date('F j, Y \a\t h:i a',strtotime($comment->create_
time)); ?>
    </div>

    <div class="content">
      <?php echo nl2br(CHtml::encode($comment->content)); ?>
    </div>
        <hr>
</div><!-- comment -->
<?php endforeach; ?>
```

This file accepts an array of comment instances as an input parameter and displays them one by one. We now need to alter the view file for the issue detail to use this new file. We do this by opening up protected/views/issue/view.php and adding the following to the end of the file:

```php
<div id="comments">
  <?php if($model->commentCount>=1): ?>
    <h3>
        <?php echo $model->commentCount>1 ? $model->commentCount . '
comments' : 'One comment'; ?>
    </h3>

    <?php $this->renderPartial('_comments',array(
      'comments'=>$model->comments,
    )); ?>
  <?php endif; ?>

  <h3>Leave a Comment</h3>

  <?php if(Yii::app()->user->hasFlash('commentSubmitted')): ?>
    <div class="flash-success">
```

```
    <?php echo Yii::app()->user->getFlash('commentSubmitted'); ?>
  </div>
<?php else: ?>
  <?php $this->renderPartial('/comment/_form',array(
    'model'=>$comment,
  )); ?>
<?php endif; ?>

</div>
```

Here we are taking advantage of the statistical query property, commentCount, which we added earlier to our Issue AR model class. This allows us to quickly determine if there are any comments available for the specific issue. If there are comments, it proceeds to render them using our _comments.php display view file. It then displays the input form that was created for us when we used the Gii Crud Generator functionality. It will also display the simple flash message set upon a successfully saved comment.

One last change we need to make is to the comment input form itself. As we have seen many times in the past, the form created for us has an input field for every column defined in the underlying tbl_comment table. This is not what we want to display to the user. We want to make this a simple input form where the user only needs to submit the comment content. So, open up the view file that houses the input form, that is protected/views/comment/_form.php, and edit it to be as follows:

```
<div class="form">
<?php $form=$this->beginWidget('CActiveForm', array(
  'id'=>'comment-form',
  'enableAjaxValidation'=>false,
)); ?>
    <p class="note">Fields with <span class="required">*</span> are
required.</p>
      <?php echo $form->errorSummary($model); ?>
      <div class="row">
  <?php echo $form->labelEx($model,'content'); ?>
  <?php echo $form->textArea($model,'content',array('rows'=>6,
'cols'=>50)); ?>
  <?php echo $form->error($model,'content'); ?>
  </div>

  <div class="row buttons">
    <?php echo CHtml::submitButton($model->isNewRecord ? 'Create' :
'Save'); ?>
  </div>

<?php $this->endWidget(); ?>

</div>
```

With all of this in place, we can visit an issue listing page to see the comment form. For example, if we visit `http://localhost/trackstar/index.php?r=issue/view&id=111`, we see the following comment input form at the bottom of the page:

If we attempt to submit the comment without specifying any content, we see the error as depicted in the following screenshot:

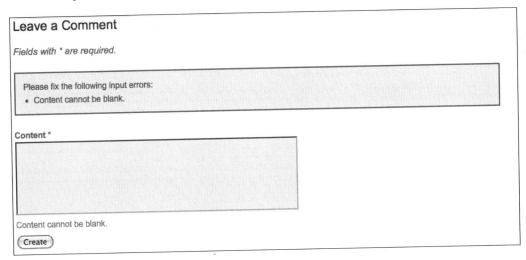

And then, if we are logged in as User One and we submit the comment My first test comment, we are presented with the following display:

One comment

User One:
on July 1, 2012 at 11:13 am
My first test comment

Leave a Comment

Your comment has been added.

Creating a recent comments widget

Now that we have the ability to leave comments on issues, we are going to turn our focus to the second goal of this chapter. We want to display a list of all of the recent comments that have been left on various issues across all of the projects. This will provide a nice snapshot of user communication activity within the application. We also want to build this small block of content in a manner that will allow it to be easily reused in various different locations throughout the site. This is very much in the style of myriad web portal applications across the internet. These small snippets of content are often referred to as **portlets**, and is why we referred to building portlet architecture at the beginning of this chapter. Again, you can refer to http://en.wikipedia.org/wiki/Portlet for more information on this topic.

Introducing CWidget

Lucky for us, Yii is ready-made to help us achieve this architecture. Yii provides a component class called CWidget, which is perfect for achieving this type of architecture. A Yii **widget** is an instance of the CWidget class (or a child class thereof), and is a presentational component typically embedded in a view file to display self-contained, reusable user interface features. We are going to use a Yii widget to build a recent comments component and display it on the main project details page so we can see comment activity across all issues related to the project. To demonstrate the ease of re-use, we'll take it one step further and also display a list of recent comments across all projects on the projects listings page.

Named scopes

To begin creating our widget, we are going to first alter our Comment AR model class to return the most recently added comments. To do this, we are going to take advantage of another feature within Yii's AR model classes—named scopes.

Named scopes allow us to specify a named query, which provides an elegant way to define SQL where conditions when retrieving lists of AR objects. Named scopes are typically defined in the CActiveRecord::scopes() method as name=>criteria pairs. For example, if we want to define a named scope called recent that would return the five most recent comments; we could create the Comment::scopes() method as such:

```
class Comment extends TrackStarActiveRecord
{
  ...
  public function scopes()
  {
    return array(
      'recent'=>array(
        'order'=>'create_time DESC',
        'limit'=>5,
      ),
    );
  }
  ...
}
```

Now, we can easily retrieve a list of recent comments, using the following syntax:

```
$comments=Comment::model()->recent()->findAll();
```

You can also chain named scopes together. If we had defined another named scope, for example, approved (if our application were to have an approval process before comments would be displayed), we could get a list of the most recent approved comments, thus:

```
$comments=Comment::model()->recent()->approved()->findAll();
```

You can see that by chaining these together, we have a flexible and powerful way to retrieve our objects in specific contexts.

Named scopes must appear to the left of a find call (find, findAll, findByPk, and so on) and also can only be used in a class-level context. The named scope method call must be used along with ClassName::model(). See http://www.yiiframework.com/doc/guide/1.1/en/database.ar#named-scopes for more information on named scopes.

Named scopes can also be parameterized. In the earlier recent named scope for comments, we hardcoded the limit in the criteria to be 5. However, we may want to be able to specify the limit number when we call the method. This is how we will set up our named scope for comments. To add parameters, we specify the named scope a bit differently. Rather than use the scopes() method to declare our scope, we define a new public method whose name is the same as the scope name. Add the following method to the Comment AR class:

```
public function recent($limit=5)
{
   $this->getDbCriteria()->mergeWith(
     array(
      'order'=>'t.create_time DESC',
       'limit'=>$limit,
     )
   );
   return $this;
}
```

One thing to note about this query condition is the use of t in the order value. This is to help in the event that this is used along with another related table that has the same column name. Obviously, when two tables that are being joined have columns with the same name, we have to make a distinction between the two in our query. For example, if we use this in the same query where we are retrieving Issue AR information, both tbl_issue and tbl_comment tables have the create_time column defined. We are trying to order by this column in the tbl_comment table and not the one defined in the issue table. In relational AR query in Yii, the alias name for the primary table is fixed as t, while the alias name for a relational table, by default, is the same as the corresponding relation name. So, in this case, we specify t.create_time to indicate that we want to use the primary table's column.

More on relational AR queries in Yii

With this method in place, we could combine the named scope with an eager loading approach to also retrieve related Issue AR instances. For example, let's say we want to get the last ten comments left on issues related to a project whose ID is 1. We could use the following to do so:

```
$comments = Comment::model()->with(array('issue'=>array('condition'=>'
project_id=1')))->recent(10)->findAll();
```

This query is new to us. We have not been using many of these options in our previous queries. Previously, we were using different approaches to execute relational queries:

- Load the AR instance
- Access the relational properties defined in the `relations()` method

For example, if we wanted to query for all of the issues associated with, say, project ID #1, we would have been using something similar to the following two lines of code:

```
// First retrieve the project whose ID is 1
$project=Project::model()->findByPk(1);

// Then retrieve the project's issues (a relational query is actually
being performed behind the scenes here)
$issues=$project->issues;
```

This familiar approach uses what is referred to as **lazy loading**. When we first create the project instance, the query does not return all of the associated issues. It only retrieves the associated issues upon a subsequent, explicit request for them, that is when `$project->issues` is executed. This is referred to as "lazy" because it waits to load the issues until they are requested at a later time.

This approach is very convenient and can also be very efficient, especially in those cases where the associated issues are not required. However, in other circumstances, this approach can be somewhat inefficient. For example, if we wanted to retrieve the issue information across *N* projects, then using this lazy approach would involve executing *N* join queries. Depending on how large *N* is, this could be very inefficient. In these situations, we have another option. We can use what is called **eager loading**.

The eager loading approach retrieves the related AR instances at the same time as the main AR instances are requested. This is accomplished by using the `with()` method in concert with either the `find()` or `findAll()` methods for AR query. Sticking with our project example, we could use eager loading to retrieve all issues for all projects by executing the following single line of code:

```
//retrieve all project AR instances along with their associated issue
AR instances
$projects = Project::model()->with('issues')->findAll();
```

Now, in this case, every project AR instance in the `$projects` array already has its associated `issues` property populated with an array of `Issue` AR instances. This result has been achieved by using just a single join query.

So, let's look back at our example of retrieving the last ten comments for a specific project:

```
$comments = Comment::model()->with(array('issue'=>array('condition'=>'
project_id=1')))->recent(10)->findAll();
```

We are using the eager loading approach to retrieve the issues along with the comments, but this one is slightly more complex. This query specifies a single join between the `tbl_comment` and `tbl_issue` tables. This relational AR query would basically execute something similar to the following SQL statement:

```
SELECT tbl_comment.*, tbl_issue.* FROM tbl_comment LEFT OUTER JOIN
tbl_issue ON (tbl_comment.issue_id=tbl_issue.id) WHERE (tbl_issue.
project_id=1) ORDER BY tbl_comment.create_time DESC LIMIT 10;
```

Armed with the knowledge about the benefits of lazy loading versus eager loading in Yii, we should make an adjustment to how the issue model is loaded within the `IssueController::actionView()` method. Since we have altered the issues' detail view to display our comments, including the author of the comment, we know it will be more efficient to use the eager loading approach to load our comments along with their respective authors when we make the call to `IssueController::loadModel()`. To do this, we can add an additional parameter as a simple input flag to indicate whether or not we want to load the comments as well.

Alter the `IssueController::loadModel()` method as follows:

```
    public function loadModel($id, $withComments=false)
    {
      if($withComments)
        $model = Issue::model()->with(array('comments'=>array('with'=>'a
uthor')))->findByPk($id);
      else
        $model=Issue::model()->findByPk($id);
      if($model===null)
        throw new CHttpException(404,'The requested page does not
exist.');
      return $model;
    }
```

There are three places where the `loadModel()` method is called in the `IssueController` method: `actionView`, `actionUpdate`, and `actionDelete`. We only need the associated comments when we are viewing the issue details. So, we have made the default to not retrieve the associated comments. We just need to alter the `actionView()` method to add `true` to the `loadModel()` call.

```
public function actionView($id)
{
    $issue=$this->loadModel($id, true);
    ....
}
```

With this in place, we will load the issue along with all of its associated comments, and for each comment, we'll load the associated author information, all with just one database call.

Creating the widget

We are now ready to create our new widget to make use of all the previously mentioned changes to display our recent comments.

As we previously mentioned, a widget in Yii is a class that extends from the framework class, `CWidget`, or one of its child classes. We'll add our new widget to the `protected/components/` directory, as the contents of this directory are already specified in the main configuration file to be autoloaded within the application. This way, we won't have to explicitly import the class every time we wish to use it. We'll call our widget `RecentComments` and add a `.php` file of the same name to this directory. Add the following class definition to this newly created `RecentComments.php` file:

```
<?php
/**
    * RecentCommentsWidget is a Yii widget used to display a list of
recent comments
    */
class RecentCommentsWidget extends CWidget
{
    private $_comments;
    public $displayLimit = 5;
    public $projectId = null;

    public function init()
        {
            if(null !== $this->projectId)
```

```
        $this->_comments = Comment::model()->with(array('issue'=>a
rray('condition'=>'project_id='.$this->projectId)))->recent($this-
>displayLimit)->findAll();
        else
            $this->_comments = Comment::model()->recent($this-
>displayLimit)->findAll();
        }

    public function getData()
    {
        return $this->_comments;
    }

    public function run()
    {
        // this method is called by CController::endWidget()
        $this->render('recentCommentsWidget');
    }
}
```

The primary work involved when creating a new widget is to override the `init()` and `run()` methods of the base class. The `init()` method initializes the widget and is called after its properties have been initialized. The `run()` method executes the widget. In this case, we simply initialize the widget by requesting recent comments based on the `$displayLimit` and `$projectId` properties, using the query we discussed previously. The execution of the widget itself simply renders its associated view file, which we have yet to create. View files for widgets, by convention, are placed in a `views/` directory within the same directory where the widget resides and are named the same as the widget, except starting with a lowercase letter. Sticking with this convention, create a new file whose fully qualified path is `protected/components/views/recentCommentsWidget.php`. Once created, add the following to that file:

```
<ul>
    <?php foreach($this->getData() as $comment): ?>
        <div class="author">
            <?php echo $comment->author->username; ?> added a comment.
        </div>
        <div class="issue">
            <?php echo CHtml::link(CHtml::encode($comment->issue->name),
array('issue/view', 'id'=>$comment->issue->id)); ?>
        </div>

    <?php endforeach; ?>
</ul>
```

This calls the `RecentCommentsWidget::getData()` method, which returns an array of comments. It then iterates over each of them, displaying who added the comment and the associated issue on which the comment was left.

In order to see the results, we need to embed this widget into an existing controller view file. As previously mentioned, we want to use this widget on the projects listing page to display all recent comments across all projects, and also on a specific project details page to display the recent comments for just that specific project.

Let's start with the projects listing page. The view file responsible for displaying that content is `protected/views/project/index.php`. Open up that file and add the following at the bottom:

```php
<?php $this->widget('RecentCommentsWidget'); ?>
```

If we view the projects listing page `http://localhost/trackstar/index.php?r=project` now, we see something similar to the following screenshot:

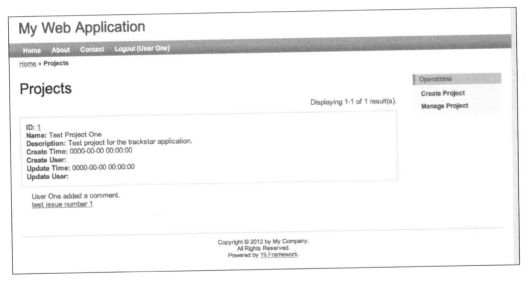

We have now embedded our new recent comments data within the page, simply by calling the widget. This is nice, but we can take our little widget one step further to have it display in a consistent manner with all other potential *portlets* in the application. We can do this by taking advantage of another class provided to us by Yii, `CPortlet`.

Introducing CPortlet

CPortlet is part of Zii, the official extension class library that comes packaged with Yii. It provides a nice base class for all portlet-style widgets. It will allow us to render a nice title as well as a consistent HTML markup, so that all portlets across the application can be easily styled in a similar manner. Once we have a widget that renders content, such as our RecentCommentsWidget, we can simply use the rendered content of our widget as the content for CPortlet, which itself is a widget, as it also extends from CWidget. We can do this by placing our call to the RecentComments widget between a beginWidget() and an endWiget() call for CPortlet, as follows:

```php
<?php $this->beginWidget('zii.widgets.CPortlet', array(
    'title'=>'Recent Comments',
));

$this->widget('RecentCommentsWidget');

$this->endWidget(); ?>
```

Since CPortlet provides a title property, we set it to be something meaningful for our portlet. We then use the rendered content of the RecentComments widget to provide the content for the portlet widget. The end result of this is depicted in the following screenshot:

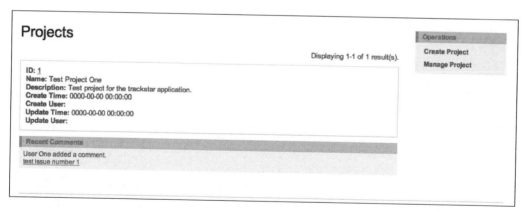

This is not a huge change from what we had previously, but we have now placed our content into a consistent container that is already being used throughout the site. Note the similarity between the right-hand column menu content block and our newly created, recent comments content block. I am sure it will come as no surprise to you that this right-hand column menu block is also displayed within a `CPortlet` container. Taking a peek in `protected/views/layouts/column2.php`, which is a file that the `yiic webapp` command autogenerated for us when we initially created the application, reveals the following code:

```php
<?php
  $this->beginWidget('zii.widgets.CPortlet', array(
    'title'=>'Operations',
  ));
  $this->widget('zii.widgets.CMenu', array(
    'items'=>$this->menu,
    'htmlOptions'=>array('class'=>'operations'),
  ));
  $this->endWidget();
?>
```

So, it seems that the application has been taking advantage of portlets all along!

Adding our widget to another page

Let's also add our portlet to the project details page and restrict the comments to just those associated with the specific project.

Add the following at the end of the `protected/views/project/view.php` file:

```php
<?php $this->beginWidget('zii.widgets.CPortlet', array(
  'title'=>'Recent Comments On This Project',
));

$this->widget('RecentCommentsWidget', array('projectId'=>$model->id));

$this->endWidget(); ?>
```

This is basically the same thing we added to the projects listing page, except we are initializing the widget's `$projectId` property by adding an array of name=>value pairs to the call.

If we visit a specific project details page now, we should see something similar to the following screenshot:

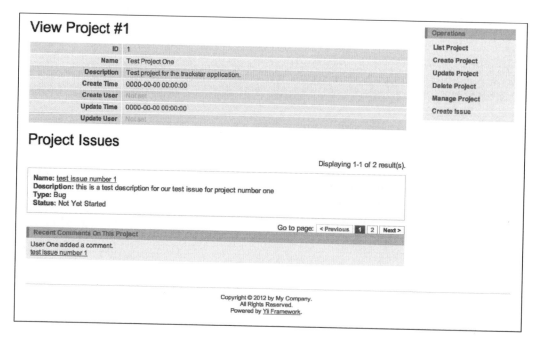

This preceding screenshot shows the details page for **Project #1**, which has one associated issue with just one comment on that issue, as depicted in the screenshot. You may need to add a few issues and comments on those issues in order to generate a similar display. We now have a way to display recent comments with a few different configurable parameters anywhere throughout the site, in a consistent and easily maintainable manner.

Summary

With this chapter, we have started to flush out our Trackstar application with the functionality that has come to be expected of most user-based web applications today. The ability for users to communicate with each other within the application is an essential part of a successful issue management system.

As we created this essential feature, we were able to look deeper into how to write relational AR queries. We were also introduced to content components called widgets and portlets. This introduced us to an approach to developing small content blocks and being able to use them anywhere throughout the application. This approach greatly increases re-use, consistency, and ease of maintenance.

In the next chapter, we'll build upon the recent comments widget created here and expose the content generated by our widget as an RSS feed to allow users to track application or project activity without having to visit the application.

Adding an RSS Web Feed

9

In the previous chapter, we added the ability for the user to leave comments on issues and to display a list of these comments, utilizing portlet architecture to allow us to easily and consistently display that listing anywhere throughout the application. In this chapter, we are going to build upon this feature and expose this list of comments as an RSS data feed. Furthermore, we are going to use the existing feed functionality available in another open source framework, Zend Framework, to demonstrate just how easy it is for a Yii application to integrate with other frameworks and libraries.

Feature planning

The goal of this chapter is to create an RSS feed using the content created from our user-generated comments. We should allow users to subscribe to a comment feed that spans all projects as well as subscribe to individual project feeds. Luckily, the widget functionality we built previously already has the capability to return a list of recent comments across all projects as well as restrict the data to one specific project. So, we have already coded the appropriate methods to access the necessary data. The bulk of this chapter will focus on putting that data in the correct format to be published as an RSS feed and on adding links to our application to allow users to subscribe to these feeds.

The following is a list of high-level tasks we will be completing in order to achieve these goals:

- Downloading and installing Zend Framework into the Yii application
- Creating a new action in a controller class to respond to the feed request and return the appropriate data in an RSS format
- Altering our URL structure for ease of use
- Adding our newly created feed to both the project listings page as well as to each individual project details page

A little background–content syndication, RSS, and Zend Framework

Web content syndication has been around for many years but has only gained enormous popularity over the past few years. Web content syndication refers to publishing information in a standardized format so that it can easily be used by other websites and easily consumed by reader applications. Many news sites have long been electronically syndicating their content, but the massive explosion of web logs (also known as blogs) across the internet has turned content syndication, known as feeds, into an expected feature of almost every website. Our TrackStar application will be no exception.

Really Simple Syndication (RSS) is an XML format specification that provides a standard for web content syndication. There are other formats that could be used, but due to the overwhelming popularity of RSS among most websites, we will focus on delivering our feed in this format.

Zend is known as "The PHP Company". One of the products they offer to assist in application development is Zend Framework. The framework provides components that can be incorporated into other framework applications. Yii is flexible enough to allow us to use pieces of other frameworks. We will be using just one component of the Zend Framework library, called Zend_Feed, so that we don't have to write all of the underlying "plumbing" code to generate our RSS-formatted web feeds. For more on Zend_Feed, visit http://www.zendframework.com/manual/en/zend.feed.html.

Installing Zend Framework

Since we are using Zend Framework to help support our RSS needs, we first need to download and install the framework. To download the framework files, visit http://www.zend.com/community/downloads. Since we will only be utilizing a single component of this framework, the minimal version of the framework will suffice. We are using Version 1.1.12.

When you expand the downloaded framework file, you should see the following high-level directory and file structure:

- INSTALL.txt
- LICENSE.txt
- README.txt
- bin/
- library/

In order to use this framework within our Yii application, we need to move some of the files within our application's directory structure. Let's create a new directory called `vendors/`, under the `/protected` directory within our application. Then, move the Zend Framework directory `/library/Zend` underneath this newly created directory. After everything is in place, ensure that `protected/vendors/Zend/Feed.php` exists in the TrackStar application.

Using Zend_Feed

Zend_Feed is a small component of Zend Framework that encapsulates all of the complexities of creating web feeds behind a simple, easy-to-use interface. It will help us get a working, tested, RSS-compliant data feed in place in very little time. All we will need to do is format our comment data in a manner expected by Zend_Feed, and it will do the rest.

We need a place to house the code to handle the requests for our feed. We could create a new controller for this, but to keep things simple, we'll just add a new action method to our main `CommentController.php` file to handle the requests. Rather than add to the method a little at a time, we'll list the entire method here, and then talk through what it is doing.

```
Open up CommentController.php and add the following public method:
/**
 * Uses Zend Feed to return an RSS formatted comments data feed
 */
public function actionFeed()
{
  if(isset($_GET['pid']))
  {
    $comments = Comment::model()->with(array(
              'issue'=>array(
                'condition'=>'project_id=:projectId',
                'params'=>array(':projectId'=>intval($_GET['pid'])),
              )))->recent(20)->findAll();
  }
  else
    $comments = Comment::model()->recent(20)->findAll();

    //convert from an array of comment AR class instances to an
  name=>value array for Zend
    $entries=array();

    foreach($comments as $comment)
```

```
        {
                $entries[]=array(
                        'title'=>$comment->issue->name,
                        'link'=>CHtml::encode($this->createAbsoluteUrl('issue/
view',array('id'=>$comment->issue->id))),
                        'description'=> $comment->author->username . '
says:<br>' . $comment->content,
                        'lastUpdate'=>strtotime($comment->create_time),
                        'author'=>CHtml::encode($comment->author->username),
                );
        }

        //now use the Zend Feed class to generate the Feed
        // generate and render RSS feed
        $feed=Zend_Feed::importArray(array(
                'title'   => 'Trackstar Project Comments Feed',
                'link'    => $this->createAbsoluteUrl(''),
                'charset' => 'UTF-8',
                'entries' => $entries,
        ), 'rss');

        $feed->send();

    }
```

This is all fairly simple. First, we check the input request querystring for the existence of a pid parameter, which we take to indicate a specific project ID. Remember that we want to optionally allow the data feed to restrict the content to comments associated with a single project. Next, we use the same method that we used in the previous chapter to populate our widget to retrieve a list of up to 20 recent comments, either across all projects, or if the project ID is specified, specific to that project.

You may remember that this method returns an array of Comment AR class instances. We iterate over this returned array and convert the data into the format accepted by the Zend_Feed component. Zend_Feed accepts a simple array containing elements that are themselves arrays containing the data for each comment entry. Each individual entry is a simple associative array of name=>value pairs. To comply with the specific RSS format, each of our individual entries must minimally contain a title, a link, and a description. We have also added two optional fields, one called lastUpdate, which Zend_Feed translates to the RSS field, pubDate, and one to specify the author.

There are a few extra helper methods we take advantage of in order to get the data in the correct format. For one, we use the controller's `createAbsoluteUrl()` method, rather than just the `createUrl()` method, in order to generate a fully qualified URL. Using `createAbsoluteUrl()` will generate a link similar to the following:

`http://localhost/trackstar/index.php?r=issue/view&id=5` as opposed to just `/index.php?r=issue/view&id=5`

Also, to avoid errors such as `unterminated entity reference` generated from PHP's `DOMDocument::createElement()` method, which is used by `Zend_Feed` to generate the RSS XML, we need to convert all applicable characters to HTML entities by using our handy helper function, `CHtml::encode`. So, we encode the link so that a URL that looks like `http://localhost/trackstar/index.php?r=issue/view&id=5` will be converted to `http://localhost/trackstar/index.php?r=issue/view&amp;id=5`.

We need to also do this for our other data that will be in the RSS format. Both the description and title fields are generated as a CDATA block, so using encode is not necessary on these.

Once all of our entries have been properly populated and formatted, we use Zend_Feed's `importArray()` method, which accepts an array to construct the RSS feed. Finally, once the feed class is built from the input array of entries and returned, we call the `send()` method on that class. This returns the properly formatted RSS XML and appropriate headers to the client.

We need to make a couple of configuration changes to the `CommentController.php` file and class before this will work. We need to include a few of the Zend framework files in our comment controller. Add the following statements to the top of `CommentController.php`:

```
Yii::import('application.vendors.*');
require_once('Zend/Feed.php');
require_once('Zend/Feed/Rss.php');
```

Finally, alter the `CommentController::accessRules()` method to allow any user to access our newly added `actionFeed()` method:

```
public function accessRules()
  {
    return array(
      array('allow',  // allow all users to perform 'index' and 'view'
actions
          'actions'=>array('index','view','feed'),
          'users'=>array('*'),
      ),
```

This is really all there is to it. If we now navigate to `http://localhost/trackstar/index.php?r=comment/feed`, we can view the results of our efforts. Since browsers handle the display of RSS feeds differently, your experience might differ from the following screenshot. The following screenshot is what you should see if viewing in the Firefox browser:

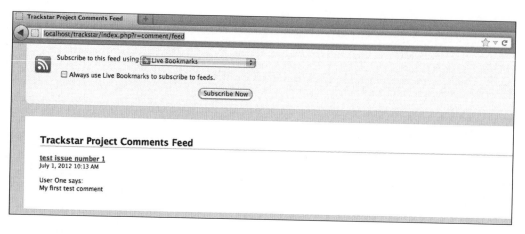

However, viewing in the Chrome browser, we see the raw XML being displayed, as seen in the following screenshot:

```xml
<?xml version="1.0" encoding="UTF-8"?>
<rss xmlns:content="http://purl.org/rss/1.0/modules/content/" version="2.0">
  <channel>
    <title><![CDATA[Trackstar Project Comments Feed]]></title>
    <link>/trackstar/index.php?r=comment/feed</link>
    <description><![CDATA[]]></description>
    <pubDate>Sun, 08 Jul 2012 18:03:28 -0400</pubDate>
    <generator>Zend_Feed</generator>
    <docs>http://blogs.law.harvard.edu/tech/rss</docs>
    <item>
      <title><![CDATA[test issue number 1]]></title>
      <author>User One</author>
      <link>http://localhost/trackstar/index.php?r=issue/view&amp;id=1</link>
      <description><![CDATA[User One says:<br>My first test comment]]></description>
      <pubDate>Sun, 01 Jul 2012 11:13:53 -0400</pubDate>
    </item>
  </channel>
</rss>
```

This may depend on your version. You may also be prompted to select the available RSS reader extensions to install, such as the Google Reader or RSS Feed Reader extensions for Chrome.

Creating user-friendly URLs

So far, throughout our development, we have been using the default format of our Yii application URL structure. This format, discussed back in *Chapter 2, Getting Started*, in the section called *Reviewing our request routing*, uses a querystring approach. We have the main parameter "r", which stands for *route*, followed by a controllerID/actionID pair, and then optional querystring parameters, as needed by the specific action methods being called. The URL we created for our new feed is no exception. It is a long, cumbersome, and arguably ugly URL. There has got to be a better way! Well, in fact there is.

We could make the previously mentioned URL look cleaner and more self-explanatory by using the so-called *path* format, which eliminates the query string and puts the GET parameters into the path info part of the URL:

Taking our comment feed URL as an example, instead of `http://localhost/ trackstar/index.php?r=comment/feed`, we would have `http://localhost/ trackstar/index.php/comment/feed/`.

What's more, we don't need to specify the entry script for each request. And we can also take advantage of Yii's request routing configuration options to remove the need to specify the controllerID/actionID pair as well. Our request could then look like this:

`http://localhost/trackstar/commentfeed`

Also, it is common, especially with feed URLs, to have the `.xml` extension specified at the end. So, it would be nice if we could alter our URL to look like the following:

`http://localhost/trackstar/commentfeed.xml`

This greatly simplifies the URL for users and is also an excellent format for URLs to be properly indexed into major search engines (often referred to as "search engine friendly URLs"). Let's see how we can use Yii's URL management features to alter our URL to match this desired format.

Using the URL manager

The built-in URL manager in Yii is an application component that can be configured in the `protected/config/main.php` file. Let's open up that file and add a new URL manager component declaration to the components array:

```
'urlManager'=>array(
    'urlFormat'=>'path',
),
```

As long as we stick with the default and name the component `urlManager`, we do not need to specify the class of the component because it is predeclared to be `CUrlManager.php` in the `CWebApplication.php` framework class.

With this one simple addition, our URL structure has changed to the path format throughout the site. For example, previously, if we wanted to view a specific issue whose ID is 1, we made the request using the following URL:

```
http://localhost/trackstar/index.php?r=issue/view&id=1
```

Now, with these changes in place, our URL looks like this:

```
http://localhost/trackstar/index.php/issue/view/id/1
```

You'll notice that the changes we have made have affected all the URLs generated throughout the application. To see this, visit our feed again by going to `http://localhost/trackstar/index.php/comment/feed/`. We notice that all of our issue links have been reformatted to this new structure for us. This is all thanks to our consistent use of the controller methods and other helper methods to generate our URLs. We can alter the URL format in just one single configuration file, and the changes will automatically propagate throughout the application.

Our URLs are looking better, but we still have the entry script, `index.php`, specified and we are not yet able to append the `.xml` suffix at the end of our feed URL. So, let's hide the `index.php` file as part of the URL and also set up the request routing to understand that a request for `commentfeed.xml` actually means a request for `CommentController::actionFeed()`. Let's actually tackle the latter first.

Configuring routing rules

Yii URL manager allows us to specify rules that define how URLs are parsed and created. A rule consists of defining a route and a pattern. The pattern is used to match the path information part of the URL to determine which rule is used to parse or create URLs. The pattern may contain named parameters using the syntax `ParamName:RegExp`. When parsing a URL, a matching rule will extract these named parameters from the path info and put them into the `$_GET` variable. When a URL is being created by the application, a matching rule will extract the named parameters from `$_GET` and put them into the path info part of the created URL. If a pattern ends with `/*`, it means additional GET parameters may be appended to the path info part of the URL.

To specify URL rules, set the `CUrlManager` file's `rules` property as an array of rules in the format `pattern=>route`.

As an example, let's look at the two following rules:

```
'urlManager'=>array(
   'urlFormat'=>'path',
   'rules'=>array(
   'issues'=>'issue/index',
   'issue/<id:\d+>/*'=>'issue/view',
   ),
)
```

There are two rules specified in this code. The first rule says that if the user requests the URL `http://localhost/trackstar/index.php/issues`, it should be treated as `http://localhost/trackstar/index.php/issue/index`, and the same applies when constructing such a URL. So, for example, if we are creating the URL in our application using a controller's `createUrl('issue/index')` method, it would generate `/trackstar/index.php/issues` rather than `/trackstar/index.php/issue/index`.

The second rule contains a named parameter, `id`, which is specified using the `<ParamName:RegExp>` syntax. It says that, for example, if the user requests the URL `http://localhost/trackstar/index.php/issue/1`, it should be treated as `http://localhost/trackstar/index.php/issue/view/id/1`. The same also applies when constructing such a URL.

The route can also be specified as an array itself to allow the setting of other attributes such as the URL suffix and whether or not the route should be considered case-sensitive. We'll take advantage of these as we specify the rule for our comment feed.

Let's add the following rule to our `urlManager` application component configuration:

```
'urlManager'=>array(
        'urlFormat'=>'path',
        'rules'=>array(   'commentfeed'=>array('comment/feed',
 'urlSuffix'=>'.xml', 'caseSensitive'=>false),
        ),
    ),
```

Here, we have used the `urlSuffix` attribute to specify our desired URL `.xml` suffix.

Now we can access our feed by using the following URL:

`http://localhost/trackstar/index.php/commentFeed.xml`

Removing the entry script from the URL

Now we just need to remove the index.php part from the URL. This is done in two steps, as follows:

1. Alter the web server configuration to reroute all requests that don't correspond to existing files or directories to index.php.

2. Set the urlManager component's showScriptName property to false.

The first step takes care of how the application routes the requests, while the latter takes care of how URLs will be created throughout the application.

Since we are using Apache HTTP Server, we can perform the first step by creating a .htaccess file in the application root directory and adding the following directives to that file:

```
# Turning on the rewrite engine is necessary for the following rules
and features.
# FollowSymLinks must be enabled for this to work.
<IfModule mod_rewrite.c>
  Options +FollowSymlinks
  RewriteEngine On
</IfModule>


# Unless an explicit file or directory exists, redirect all request to
Yii entry script
<IfModule mod_rewrite.c>
  RewriteCond %{REQUEST_FILENAME} !-f
  RewriteCond %{REQUEST_FILENAME} !-d
  RewriteRule . index.php
</IfModule>
```

 This approach is only for Apache HTTP Server. You will need to consult the web server rewrite rules if using a different web server. Also note that this information could be placed in the main Apache configuration file as an alternative to using the .htaccess file approach.

With this .htaccess file in place, we can now visit our feed by navigating to http://localhost/trackstar/commentfeed.xml (or http://localhost/trackstar/commentFeed.xml, since we set the case sensitivity to false).

However, even with this in place, if we use one of the controller methods or one of our CHtml helper methods in our application to create our URL, say by executing `$this->createAbsoluteUrl('comment/feed');` in a controller class, it will generate the following URL, with `index.php` still in the URL:

```
http://localhost/trackstar/index.php/commentfeed.xml
```

In order to instruct it to not use the entry script name when generating URLs, we need to set that property on the `urlManager` component. We do this again in the `main.php` configuration file, as follows:

```
'urlManager'=>array(
    'urlFormat'=>'path',
    'rules'=>array(
        'commentfeed'=>array('comment/feed', 'urlSuffix'=>'.xml',
'caseSensitive'=>false),
    ),
    'showScriptName'=>false,
),
```

In order to handle the addition of the project ID in the URL, we need to restrict the comment feed data to comments associated to specific projects, and for that we need to add one other rule, as follows:

```
'urlManager'=>array(
        'urlFormat'=>'path',
        'rules'=>array(
            '<pid:\d+>/commentfeed'=>array('comment/feed',
'urlSuffix'=>'.xml', 'caseSensitive'=>false),
            'commentfeed'=>array('comment/feed', 'urlSuffix'=>'.xml',
'caseSensitive'=>false),
        ),
        'showScriptName'=>false,
),
```

This rule also uses the `<Parameter:RegEx>` syntax to specify a pattern to allow for a project ID to be specified before the `commentfeed.xml` part of the URL. With this rule in place, we can restrict our RSS feed to comments specific to a project. For example, if we just want the comments associated with Project #2, the URL format would be:

```
http://localhost/trackstar/2/commentfeed.xml
```

Adding the feed links

Now that we have created our feed and altered the URL structure to make it more user and search engine friendly, we need to add the ability for users to subscribe to the feed. One way to do this is to add the following code before rendering the pages in which we want to add the RSS feed link. Let's do this for both the project listing page as well as a specific project details page. We'll start with the project listings page. This page is rendered by the `ProjectController::actionIndex()` method. Alter that method as follows:

```php
public function actionIndex()
{
    $dataProvider=new CActiveDataProvider('Project');

    Yii::app()->clientScript->registerLinkTag(
        'alternate',
        'application/rss+xml',
        $this->createUrl('comment/feed'));

    $this->render('index',array(
        'dataProvider'=>$dataProvider,
    ));
}
```

The highlighted code shown here adds the following to the `<head>` tag of the rendered HTML:

```html
<link rel="alternate" type="application/rss+xml" href="/commentfeed.
xml" />
```

In many browsers, this will automatically generate a little RSS feed icon in the address bar. The following screenshot depicts what this icon looks like in the Safari address bar:

We make a similar change to add this link to a specific project details page. The rendering of these pages is handled by the `ProjectController::actionView()` method. Alter that method to the following:

```
public function actionView($id)
  {
    $issueDataProvider=new CActiveDataProvider('Issue', array(
      'criteria'=>array(
        'condition'=>'project_id=:projectId',
        'params'=>array(':projectId'=>$this->loadModel($id)->id),
      ),
      'pagination'=>array(
        'pageSize'=>1,
      ),
    ));

    Yii::app()->clientScript->registerLinkTag(
        'alternate',
        'application/rss+xml',
        $this->createUrl('comment/feed',array('pid'=>$this-
>loadModel($id)->id)));


    $this->render('view',array(
      'model'=>$this->loadModel($id),
      'issueDataProvider'=>$issueDataProvider,
    ));

  }
```

This is almost the same as what we added to the index method, except that we are specifying the project ID so that our comment entries are restricted to just those associated with that project. A similar icon will now display in the address bar on our project details page. Clicking on these icons allow the user to subscribe to these comment feeds.

> The `registerLinkTag()` method allows you to also specify the media attribute as the fourth argument, and then you can further specify other supported attributes as an array of name=>value pairs, as a fifth argument. See http://www.yiiframework.com/doc/api/1.1/CClientScript/#registerLinkTag-detail for more information on using this method.

Summary

This chapter demonstrated just how easy it is to integrate Yii with other external frameworks. We specifically used the popular Zend Framework to demonstrate this and were able to quickly add an RSS compliant web feed to our application. Though we specifically used Zend_Feed, we really demonstrated how to integrate any of the Zend Framework components into the application. This further extends the already very extensive feature offering of Yii, making Yii applications incredibly feature rich.

We also learned about the URL management features within Yii and altered our URL format throughout the application to be more user and search engine friendly. This is the first step in improving upon the look and feel of our application, something we have very much neglected to this point. In the next chapter, we are going to take a closer look at the presentation tier of Yii applications. Styles, themes, and generally making things look good is the focus of the next chapter.

10
Making It Look Good

In the previous chapter, we started to add a little beauty to our application by making our URLs more attractive to both the user and to search engine bots that crawl the site. In this chapter, we are going to turn our focus more to the look and feel of our application by covering the topics of layouts and themes in Yii. We will be focusing on the approach one takes and the tools available to help design the frontend of a Yii application rather than the design itself. So this chapter will focus more on how to make your applications look good, rather than spending a lot of time specifically designing our TrackStar application to actually be good-looking.

Feature planning

This chapter aims to focus on the frontend. We want to create a new look for our site that is reusable and able to be implemented dynamically. We also want to accomplish this without overwriting or otherwise removing our current design. Finally, we are going to dig into the internationalization features of Yii to better understand how to accommodate users from different geographic regions.

The following is a list of high-level tasks that we will need to complete in order to achieve these goals:

- To create a new theme for our application by creating a new layout, CSS, and other asset files needed to provide the application with a new frontend design
- To use the internationalization and localization features of Yii to help translate a portion of our application to a new language

Designing with layouts

One thing that you may have noticed is that we have added a lot of functionality to our application without adding any explicit navigation to access this functionality. Our home page has not yet changed from the default application we built. We still have the same navigation items as we did when we first created our new application. We need to change our basic navigation to better reflect the underlying functionality present in the application.

Thus far, we have not fully covered how our application is using all of the view files responsible for displaying the content. We know that our view files are responsible for our data display and for housing the HTML sent back in response to each page request. When we create new controller actions, we often create new views to handle the display of the returned content from these action methods. Most of these views are very specific to the action methods they support and are not used across multiple pages. However there are some things, such as the main menu navigation, that are used across multiple pages throughout the site. These types of UI components are better suited to reside in what are called layout files.

A **layout** in Yii is a special view file used to decorate other view files. Layouts typically contain markup or other user interface components that are common across multiple view files. When using a layout to render a view file, Yii embeds the view file into the layout.

Specifying a layout

There are two main places where a layout can be specified. One is the property called $layout of the CWebApplication itself. This defaults to protected/views/layouts/main.php. As is the case with all application settings, this can be overridden in the main configuration file protected/config/main.php. For example, if we created a new layout file protected/views/layouts/newlayout.php and wanted to use this new file as our application-wide layout file, we could alter our main config.php file to set the layout property as such:

```
return array(
   ...
   'layout'=>'newlayout',
```

The filename is specified without the .php extension and is relative to the $layoutPath property of CWebApplication, which defaults to Webroot/protected/views/layouts (which itself could be overridden in a similar manner if this location does not suit your application's needs).

The other place to specify the layout is by setting the $layout property of the controller class. This allows for more granular control of the layout on a controller-by-controller basis. This is the way it was specified when we generated the initial application. Using the yiic tool to create our initial application automatically created a controller base class Webroot/protected/components/Controller.php, from which all of our other controller classes extend. Opening up this file reveals that the $layout property has been set to column1. Setting the layout file at the more granular controller level will override the setting in the CWebApplication class.

Applying and using a layout

The use of a layout file is implicit in the call to the CController::render() method. That is, when you make the call to the render() method to render a view file, Yii will embed the contents of the view file into the layout file specified in either the controller class or the one specified at the application level. You can avoid applying any layout decoration of the rendered view file by calling the CController::renderPartial() method instead.

As previously mentioned, a layout file is typically used to decorate other view files. One example use of a layout is to provide a consistent header and footer layout to each and every page. When the render() method is called, what happens behind the scenes is that a call is first sent to renderPartial() on the specified view file. The output of this is stored in a variable called $content, which is then made available to the layout file. So a very simple layout file might look like the following:

```html
<!DOCTYPE html>
<html>
<head>
<title>Title of the document</title>
</head>
<body>
  <div id="header">
    Some Header Content Here
  </div>

  <div id="content">
    <?php echo $content; ?>
  </div>

  <div id="footer">
      Some Footer Content Here
  </div>
</body>
</html>
```

In fact let's try this out. Create a new file called `newlayout.php` and place it in the default directory for layout files, called `/protected/views/layouts/`. Add the preceding HTML content to this file and save it. Now we'll put this to use by altering our site controller to use this new layout. Open up `SiteController.php` and override the layout property set in the base class by explicitly adding it to this class, as such:

```
class SiteController extends Controller
{

    public $layout='newlayout';
```

This will set the layout file to `newlayout.php`, but only for this controller. Now every time we make the call to the `render()` method within `SiteController`, the `newlayout.php` layout file will be used.

One page that `SiteController` is responsible for rendering is the login page. Let's take a look at that page to verify these changes. If we navigate to `http://localhost/trackstar/site/login` (assuming we are not already logged in), we now see something similar to the following screenshot:

Some Header Content Here

Login

Please fill out the following form with your login credentials:

Fields with * are required.

Username *
Password *

Hint: You may login with demo/demo or admin/admin.

☐ Remember me next time
(Login)
Some Footer Content Here

If we simply comment out the `$layout` attribute we just added and refresh the login page again, we'll be back to using the original `main.php` layout and our page will now be back to what it looked like earlier.

Deconstructing the main.php layout file

So far, all of our application pages have been using the `main.php` layout file to provide the primary layout markup. Before we start making changes to our page layout and design, it would serve us well to take a closer look at this main layout file. You can view it in its entirety from the downloadable code for this chapter, or view the standalone file at `https://gist.github.com/3781042`.

The first five lines will probably look somewhat familiar to you:

```
<!DOCTYPE html PUBLIC "-//W3C//DTD XHTML 1.0 Transitional//EN"
"http://www.w3.org/TR/xhtml1/DTD/xhtml1-transitional.dtd">
<html xmlns="http://www.w3.org/1999/xhtml" xml:lang="en" lang="en">
<head>
  <meta http-equiv="Content-Type" content="text/html; charset=utf-8"
/>
  <meta name="language" content="en" />
```

These lines define a standard, HTML document-type declaration, followed by a starting `<html>` element and then the start of our `<head>` element. Within the `<head>` tag, we first have a `<meta>` tag to declare the standard XHTML-compliant uft-8 character encoding, followed by another `<meta>` tag that specifies English as the primary language in which the website is written.

Introducing the Blueprint CSS framework

The next several lines beginning with the comment `<!—blueprint CSS framework -->` may be less familiar to you. Another great thing about Yii is that it utilizes other best-in-breed frameworks when appropriate, and the Blueprint CSS framework is one such example.

The Blueprint CSS framework was included in the application as a by-product of using the `yiic` tool when we initially created our application. It is included to help standardize the CSS development. Blueprint is a CSS Grid framework. It helps standardize your CSS, provides cross-browser compatibility, and provides consistency in HTML element placement, helping reduce CSS errors. It comes with many screen- and print-friendly layout definitions and helps jumpstart your design by providing all of the CSS that you need, to get something that looks good and is in place. For more on the Blueprint framework, visit `http://www.blueprintcss.org/`.

So the following lines of code are required and specific to the Blueprint CSS framework:

```
<!-- blueprint CSS framework -->
<link rel="stylesheet" type="text/css" href="<?php echo Yii::app()-
>request->baseUrl; ?>/css/screen.css" media="screen, projection" />
<link rel="stylesheet" type="text/css" href="<?php echo Yii::app()-
>request->baseUrl; ?>/css/print.css" media="print" />
<!--[if lt IE 8]>
<link rel="stylesheet" type="text/css" href="<?php echo Yii::app()-
>request->baseUrl; ?>/css/ie.css" media="screen, projection" />
<![endif]-->
```

The call to `Yii::app()->request->baseUrl;` is used here to get the relative URL to the application.

Understanding the Blueprint installation

Yii by no means requires the use of Blueprint. However since the default application generated does include the framework, understanding its installation and use will be beneficial.

The typical installation of Blueprint involves first downloading the framework files and then placing three of its `.css` files into the Yii application's main `css` directory. If we take a peek under the main `Webroot/css` directory within our TrackStar application, we already see the inclusion of these three files:

- `ie.css`
- `print.css`
- `screen.css`

So luckily for us, the basic installation has already been completed. In order to take advantage of the framework, the previous `<link>` tags need to be placed under the `<head>` tag for each web page. This is why these declarations are made in the layout file.

The next two `<link>` tags are as follows:

```
<link rel="stylesheet" type="text/css" href="<?php echo Yii::app()-
>request->baseUrl; ?>/css/main.css" />
<link rel="stylesheet" type="text/css" href="<?php echo Yii::app()-
>request->baseUrl; ?>/css/form.css" />
```

These <link> tags define some custom css definitions used to provide layout declarations in addition to the ones specified in the Blueprint files. You should always place any custom definitions below the ones provided by Blueprint so that your custom declarations take precedence.

Setting the page title

Setting a specific and meaningful page title on a per page basis is important for indexing your website pages in search engines, and helpful to users who want to bookmark specific pages of your site. The next line in our main layout file specifies the page title in the browser:

```
<title><?php echo CHtml::encode($this->pageTitle); ?></title>
```

Remember that $this in a view file refers to the controller class instance that initially rendered the view. The $pageTitle attribute is defined down in Yii's CController base class and will default to the action name followed by the controller name. This is easily customized in the specific controller class or even within each specific view file.

Defining a page header

It is often the case that websites are designed to have consistent header content repeated across many pages. The next few lines in our main layout file define the area for a page header:

```
<body>
<div class="container" id="page">

  <div id="header">
    <div id="logo"><?php echo CHtml::encode(Yii::app()->name); ?></div>
  </div><!-- header -->
```

The first <div> tag with a class of container is required by the Blueprint framework in order to display the content as a grid.

> Again, using the Blueprint CSS Grid framework or any other CSS framework is not at all a requirement of Yii. It is just there to help you jumpstart your design layout if desired.

The next three lines lay out the first of the main content we see on these pages. They display the name of the application in large letters. So far this has been displaying the text **My Web Application**. I am sure that it has been driving some of you crazy. Although we may change this later to use a logo image, let's go ahead and change this to the real name of our application, **TrackStar**.

We could hardcode this name right here in the HTML. However, if we alter our application configuration to reflect our new name, the changes will be propagated everywhere throughout the site, wherever `Yii::app()->name` is being used. I am sure that you could make this simple change in your sleep at this point. Simply open up the main `config.php` file `/protected/config/main.php` where our application configuration settings are defined, and change the value of the `name` property from `'name'=>'My Web Application'`, to the new value `'name'=>'TrackStar',`.

Save the file, refresh your browser, and the header on the home page should now look something similar to the following screenshot:

One thing we immediately notice in the previous screenshot is that the change has been made in two places. It just so happens that the view file responsible for our home page content, `/protected/views/site/index.php`, also uses the application name property. Since we made the change in the application configuration file, our change is reflected in both places.

Since the name property is something you may decide to change at some point, it is good practice to also define the application `id` property. This property is used by the framework to create unique signed keys as a prefix to access session variables, cached data, and other tokens. If there is no `id` property specified, the `name` property will be used. So changing it could render this data invalid. Let's also define an `id` property for our application. This is added to `protected/config/main.php`, just as we did for the `name` property. We can use the same value for this as we are using for our name:

```
'id'=>'TrackStar',
```

Displaying menu navigation items

The main site's navigation controls are often repeated across multiple pages in a web application, and housing this in a layout makes it very easy to re-use. The next block of markup and code in our main layout file defines the top-level menu items:

```
<div id="mainmenu">
  <?php $this->widget('zii.widgets.CMenu',array(
    'items'=>array(
      array('label'=>'Home', 'url'=>array('/site/index')),
      array('label'=>'About', 'url'=>array('/site/page',
'view'=>'about')),
      array('label'=>'Contact', 'url'=>array('/site/contact')),
      array('label'=>'Login', 'url'=>array('/site/login'),
'visible'=>Yii::app()->user->isGuest),
      array('label'=>'Logout ('.Yii::app()->user->name.')',
'url'=>array('/site/logout'), 'visible'=>!Yii::app()->user->isGuest)
    ),
  )); ?>
</div><!-- mainmenu -->
```

Here we see that one of the Zii components called CMenu is being used. We introduced Zii back in *Chapter 8, Adding User Comments*. To jog your memory, the Zii extension library is a set of extensions developed by the Yii developer team. This library comes packaged with the core Yii framework. Any of these extensions can easily be used within a Yii application, simply by referring to the desired extension class file using a path alias in the form of zii.path.to.ClassName. The root alias zii is predefined by the application and the rest of the path is relative to this framework directory. Since this Zii menu extension resides on your filesystem at YiiRoot/zii/widgets/CMenu.php, we can simply use zii.widgets.CMenu when referring to this in our application code.

CMenu takes in an array of associative arrays that provide the menu items. Each item array consists of a label that will be displayed, a URL to which that item should be linked, and an optional third value visible, which is a boolean value indicating whether or not that menu item should be displayed. This is used here when defining the **Login** and **Logout** menu items. We only want the **Login** menu item to be displayed as a clickable link if the user is not already logged in. And conversely, we would only want the **Logout** menu link to be displayed if the user is already logged in. The use of the visible element in the array allows us to display these links dynamically based on whether the user is logged in or not. The use of Yii::app()->user->isGuest is for this. This returns true if the user is not logged in and false if the user is logged in. I am sure that you have already noticed that the **Login** option turns into a **Logout** option in our application's main menu whenever you are logged in, and vice versa.

Let's update our menu to provide the users with a way to navigate to our specific TrackStar functionality. First off, we don't want anonymous users to be able to access any real functionality except the login. So we need to make sure that the login page is more or less the home page for anonymous users. Also, the main home page for logged-in users should just be a listing of their projects. We'll achieve this by making the following changes:

1. Changing our default home URL for the application to be the project listing page rather than just `site/index`, as it is now.

2. Changing the default action within our default controller `SiteController` to be the login action. In this way, any anonymous user that visits the top-level URL `http://localhost/trackstar/` will be redirected to the login page.

3. Altering our `actionLogin()` method to redirect the user to the project listing page if they are already logged in.

4. Changing the **Home** menu item to read **Projects**, and changing the URL to be the project listing page.

These are simple changes that we need to make. Starting at the top, we can change the home URL application property in our main application `config.php` file. Open up `protected/config/main.php` and add the following `name=>value` pair to the returned array:

```
'homeUrl'=>'/trackstar/project',
```

This is all that is needed to make that change.

For the next change, open up `protected/controllers/SiteController.php` and add the following to the top of the controller class:

```
public $defaultAction = 'login';
```

This sets the default action to be login. Now if you visit your top-level URL `http://localhost/trackstar/` for the application, you should be taken to the login page. The only issue with this is that you will continue to be taken to the login page from this top-level URL regardless of whether you are already logged in or not. Let's fix this by implementing step 3 of the previous list. Change the `actionLogin()` method within `SiteController` to include the following code at the beginning of the method:

```
public function actionLogin()
{

    if(!Yii::app()->user->isGuest)
        {
            $this->redirect(Yii::app()->homeUrl);
        }
```

This will redirect all the logged-in users to the application `homeUrl`, which we just previously set to be the project listing page.

Finally let's alter the input array to our `CMenu` widget, to change the specification for the **Home** menu item. Alter that block of code in the `main.php` layout file and replace the line `array('label'=>'Home', 'url'=>array('/site/index')),` with the following:

```
array('label'=>'Projects', 'url'=>array('/project')),
```

With this replacement, all of our previously outlined changes are in place. If we now visit the TrackStar application as an anonymous user, we are directed to the login page. If we click on the **Projects** link, we are still directed to the login page. We can still access the **About** and **Contact** pages, which is fine for an anonymous user. If we log in, we are directed to the project listing page. Now if we click on the **Projects** link, we are allowed to see the project listings.

Creating a breadcrumb navigation

Turning back to our `main.php` layout file, the three lines of code that follow our menu widget define another Zii extension widget called `CBreadcrumbs`:

```
<?php $this->widget('zii.widgets.CBreadcrumbs', array(
    'links'=>$this->breadcrumbs,
)); ?><!-- breadcrumbs -->
```

This is another Zii widget that can be used to display a list of links indicating the position of the current page, relative to the other pages in the whole website. For example, a linked navigation list of the format **Projects >> Project 1 > > Edit** indicates that the user is viewing an edit page for project number one. This is helpful for the user to find their way back to where they started, which is a listing of all the projects, as well as easily see where they are in the website-page hierarchy. This is why it is referred to as a **breadcrumb**. Many websites implement this type of UI navigational component in their design.

To use this widget, we need to configure its `links` property, which specifies the links that are to be displayed. The expected value for this property is an array that defines the `breadcrumb` path from a starting point, down to the specific page being viewed. Using our previous example, we could specify the `links` array as such:

```
array(
    'Projects'=>array('project/index'),
    'Project 1'=>array('project/view','id'=>1),
    'Edit',
    )
```

The breadcrumbs widget, by default, adds the very top-level **Home** link automatically, based on the application configuration setting homeUrl. So what would be generated from the previous code snippet would be a breadcrumb like the following:

Home >> Projects >> Project 1 >> Edit

Since we explicitly set our application $homeUrl property to be the project listings page, our first two links are the same in this case. The code in the layout file sets the link property to be the $breadcrumbs property of the controller class that is rendering the view. You can see this explicitly being set in the several view files that were autogenerated for us when we created our controller files using the Gii code generation tool. For example, if you take a look at protected/views/project/update.php, you will see the following code snippet at the very top of that file:

```
$this->breadcrumbs=array(
  'Projects'=>array('index'),
  $model->name=>array('view','id'=>$model->id),
  'Update',
);
```

And if we navigate to that page in the website, we will see the following navigational breadcrumb generated just below the main navigation:

Home » Projects » Test Project One » Update

Specifying the content being decorated by the layout

The next line in the layout file shows where the content of the view file that is being decorated by this layout file is placed:

```
<?php echo $content; ?>
```

This was discussed earlier in the chapter. When you use $this->render() in a controller class to display a certain view file, the use of a layout file is implied. Part of what this method does is to place all of the content in the specific view file being rendered into a special variable called $content, which is then made available to the layout file. So if we take our project update view file as an example again, the contents of $content would be the rendered content contained in the file protected/views/project/update.php.

Defining the footer

Just as with the *header* area, it is often the case that websites are designed to have consistent *footer* content repeated across many pages. The final few lines of our `main.php` layout file define a consistent `footer` for every page:

```
<div id="footer">
    Copyright &copy; <?php echo date('Y'); ?> by My Company.<br/>
    All Rights Reserved.<br/>
    <?php echo Yii::powered(); ?>
</div><!-- footer -->
```

Nothing special going on here, but we should go ahead and update it to reflect our specific website. We can leave the **Powered by Yii Framework.** line in there to help promote this great framework. We can simply change `My Company` in the previous code snippet to `TrackStar` and we're done. Refreshing the pages in the website will now reveal our footer as depicted in the following screenshot:

Copyright © 2012 by TrackStar.
All Rights Reserved.
Powered by Yii Framework.

Nesting the layouts

Though it is true that the original layout we have been seeing on our pages is utilizing the file `protected/layouts/main.php`, this is not the whole story. When our initial application was created, all of the controllers were created to extend from the base controller located at `protected/components/Controller.php`. If we take a peek into this file, we see that there is a layout property explicitly defined. But it does not specify the main layout file. Rather it specifies `column1` as the default layout file for all the child classes. You may have already noticed that when the new application was created, there were a few layout files generated for us as well, all in the `protected/views/layouts/` directory:

- `column1.php`
- `column2.php`
- `main.php`

So unless explicitly overridden in a child class, our controllers are defining `column1.php` as the primary layout file and not `main.php`.

So why did we spend all that time going through `main.php`, you ask? Well it turns out that the `column1.php` layout file is itself decorated by the `main.php` layout file. So not only can normal view files be decorated by layout files, but layout files themselves can be decorated by other layout files forming a hierarchy of nested layout files. This allows for great flexibility in design and also greatly minimizes the need for any repeated markup in the view files. Let's take a closer look at `column1.php` to see how this is achieved.

The contents of that file are as follows:

```php
<?php $this->beginContent('//layouts/main'); ?>
<div id="content">
  <?php echo $content; ?>
</div><!-- content -->
<?php $this->endContent(); ?>
```

Here we see the use of a couple of methods that we have not seen before. The base controller methods `beginContent()` and `endContent()` are being used to decorate the enclosed content with the specified view. The view being specified here is our main layout page `'//layouts/main'`. The `beginContent()` method actually makes use of the built-in Yii widget `CContentDecorator`, whose primary purpose is to allow for nested layouts. So whatever content is between the calls `beginContent()` and `endContent()` will be decorated with the view specified in the call `beginContent()`. If nothing is specified, it will use the default layout specified at the controller level, or if not specified at the controller level, at the application level.

> In the preceding code snippet, we see the view file being specified with double slashes '//'. In this case, the view will be searched for under the application's view path rather than in the currently active modules view path. This forces it to use the main application view path rather than the module's view path. Modules are the subject of the next chapter.

The rest works just as a normal layout file. All of the markup in the specific view file will be contained in the variable `$content` when this `column1.php` layout file is rendered, and then the other markup contained in this layout file will be contained again in the variable `$content` made available for the final rendering of the main parent layout file `main.php`.

Let's walk through an example. Take the rendering of the login view as an example, that is the following code in the `SiteController::actionLogin()` method:

```php
$this->render('login');
```

Behind the scenes the following steps are being performed:

1. Render all of the content in the specific view file /protected/views/site/login.php, and make that content available via the variable $content to the layout file specified in the controller, which in this case is column1.php.

2. Since column1.php is itself being decorated by the layout main.php, the content between the beingContent() and endContent() calls is again rendered and made available to the main.php file, again via the $content variable.

3. The layout file main.php is rendered and returned back to the user, incorporating both the content from the specific view file for the login page as well as the "nested" layout file column1.php.

Another layout file that was autogenerated when we initially created the application is column2.php. You probably won't be surprised to discover that this file lays out a two-column design. We can see this used in the project pages where we have a little submenu **Operations** widget displayed along the right-hand side. The contents of this layout are as follows, and we can see that the same approach is being used to achieve the nested layout as well:

```php
<?php $this->beginContent('//layouts/main'); ?>
<div class="span-19">
  <div id="content">
    <?php echo $content; ?>
  </div><!-- content -->
</div>
<div class="span-5 last">
  <div id="sidebar">
  <?php
    $this->beginWidget('zii.widgets.CPortlet', array(
      'title'=>'Operations',
    ));
    $this->widget('zii.widgets.CMenu', array(
      'items'=>$this->menu,
      'htmlOptions'=>array('class'=>'operations'),
    ));
    $this->endWidget();
  ?>
  </div><!-- sidebar -->
</div>
<?php $this->endContent(); ?>
```

Creating themes

Themes provide a systematic way of customizing the design layout of a web application. One of the many benefits of an MVC architecture is the separation of the presentation from the rest of the "backend" stuff. Themes make great use of this separation by allowing you to easily and dramatically change the overall look and feel of a web application during runtime. Yii allows for an extremely easy application of themes to provide greater flexibility in your web application design.

Building themes in Yii

In Yii, each theme is represented as a directory consisting of view files, layout files, and relevant resource files, such as images, CSS files, and JavaScript files. The name of a theme is the same as its directory name. By default, all themes reside under the same directory WebRoot/themes. Of course, as is the case with all other application settings, this default directory can be configured to be a different one. To do so, simply alter the basePath properties and the baseUrl properties of the themeManager application component.

Contents under a theme directory should be organized in the same way as those under the application base path. So all the view files are located under a views/ directory, layout view files under views/layouts/, and system view files under views/system/. For example, if we have created a new theme called custom and want to replace the update view of our ProjectController with a new view under this theme, we need to create a new update.php view file and save it in our application project as themes/custom/views/project/update.php.

Creating a theme

Let's take this for a spin to give our TrackStar application a little facelift. We need to name our new theme and create a directory under the Webroot/themes directory with this same name. We'll exercise our extreme creativity and call our new theme newtheme.

Create a new directory to hold this new theme that is located at Webroot/themes/newtheme. Then under this newly created directory, create two other new directories called css/ and views/. The former is not required by the theming system but helps us keep our CSS organized. The latter is required if we are going to make any alterations to our default view files, which we are. Since we are going to change the main.php layout file just a little, we need yet another directory under this newly created views/ directory called layouts/ (remember that the directory structure needs to mirror that in the default Webroot/protected/views/ directory).

Now let's make some changes. Since our view file markup is already referencing the css class and id names currently defined in the `Webroot/css/main.css` file, the fastest path to a new face of the application is to use this as a starting point and make changes to it as needed. Of course this is not a requirement, as we could recreate every single view file of our application in the new theme. However to keep things simple, we'll create our new theme by making a few changes to the `main.css` file that was autogenerated for us when we created the application, as well as the primary layout file `main.php`.

To begin with, let's make a copy of these two files and place them in our new theme directory. Copy the file `Webroot/css/main.css` to a new location `Webroot/themes/newtheme/css/main.css`, and also copy the file `Webroot/protected/views/layouts/main.php` to a new location `Webroot/themes/newtheme/views/layouts/main.php`.

Now we can open up the newly copied version of the `main.css` file, remove the contents, and add in the necessary styles for our new theme. For the purpose of our example, we will use the CSS available from the downloadable code for this chapter, or the standalone file available at `https://gist.github.com/3779729`.

You may have noticed that some of these changes are referencing the image files that do not yet exist in our project. We have added an `images/background.gif` image reference in the body declaration, a new `images/bg2.gif` image is referenced in the `#mainmenu` ID declaration, and a new `images/header.jpg` image in the `#header` ID declaration. These are available in the downloadable source code. We'll place these new images into an image directory within the `css/` directory, namely `Webroot/themes/newtheme/css/images/`.

After these changes are in place, we need to make a couple of small adjustments to our `main.php` layout file in this new theme. For one, we need to alter the markup in the `<head>` element to properly reference our new `main.css` file. Currently the `main.css` file is being pulled in via this line:

```
<link rel="stylesheet" type="text/css" href="<?php echo Yii::app()-
>request->baseUrl; ?>/css/main.css" />
```

This references the application request `baseUrl` property to construct the relative path to the CSS file. However, we want to use our new `main.css` file located in our new theme. For this, we can lean on the theme manager application component defined by default to use the Yii built-in `CThemeManager.php` class. We access the theme manager in the same way that we access other application components. So rather than using the request base URL, we should use the base URL defined by the theme manager, which knows what theme the application is using at any given time. Alter the previously mentioned code in `/themes/newtheme/views/layouts/main.php`, as follows:

```
<link rel="stylesheet" type="text/css" href="<?php echo Yii::app()-
>theme->baseUrl; ?>/css/main.css" />
```

Once we configure our application to use our new theme (something we have not yet done), this `baseUrl` will resolve to the relative path to where our theme directory resides.

The other small change that we need to make is to remove the display of the application title from the header. Since we altered our CSS to use a new image file to provide our header and logo information, we don't need to display the application name in this section. So in `/themes/newtheme/views/layouts/main.php` again, we simply need to change the following code:

```
<div id="header">
  <div id="logo"><?php echo CHtml::encode(Yii::app()->name); ?></div>
</div><!-- header -->
```

Alter the previous code as follows:

```
<div id="header"></div><!-- header image is embedded into the #header
declaration in main.css -->
```

We have put in a comment to remind us where our header image is defined.

Now once we configure the application to use our new theme, it will first look for a `main.php` layout in the themes directory and use that file if it exists.

Configuring the application to use a theme

Okay, with our `newtheme` theme that we now created and have in place, we need to tell the application to use this theme. Doing so is very easy. Just alter the main application's `theme` property setting by changing the main application configuration file. By now we will have become old pros at doing this. Simply add the following `name=>value` pair to the returned array in the `/protected/config/main.php` file:

```
'theme'=>'newtheme',
```

Once this is saved, our application is now using our newly created theme and has a brand new face. When we take a look at the login page, which is also our default home page if not logged in, we now see what is depicted in the following screenshot:

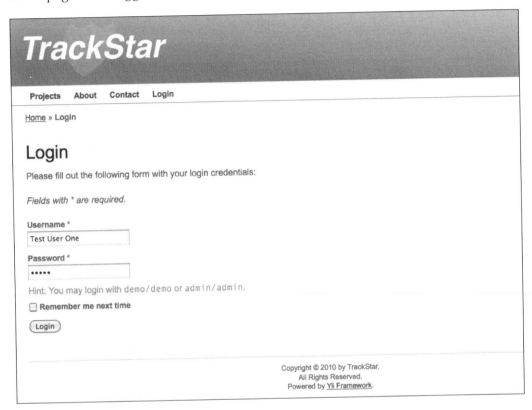

This, of course, is not a huge change. We have kept the changes fairly minimal, but they do illustrate the process of creating a new theme. The application will first look for view files in this new theme and use them if they exist, otherwise it will pull them from the default location. You see how easy it is to give the application a new look and feel. You could create a new theme for each season or based on your different moods, and then change the application to fit the season or mood quickly and easily, as desired.

Translating the site to other languages

Before we close this chapter, we are going to talk about internationalization (i18n) and localization (l10n) in Yii. **Internationalization** refers to the process of designing software applications in such a manner that they can be adapted to various languages without having to make underlying engineering changes. **Localization** refers to the process of adapting internationalized software applications for a specific geographic location or language, by adding locale-dependent formatting and translating text. Yii provides support for these in the following ways:

- It provides the locale data for nearly every language and region
- It provides services to assist in the translation of text message strings and files
- It provides locale-dependent date and time formatting
- It provides locale-dependent number formatting

Defining locale and language

Locale refers to a set of parameters that define the user's language, country, and any other user-interface preferences that may be relevant to a user's location. It is typically identified by a composite ID consisting of a language identifier and a region identifier. For example, a locale ID of en_us stands for the English language in the region of the United States. For consistency, all locale IDs in Yii are standardized to the format of either LanguageID or LanguageID_RegionID in lowercase (for example, en or en_us).

In Yii, locale data is represented as an instance of the CLocale class or a child class thereof. It provides locale-specific information including currency and numeric symbols for currency, number, date, and time formats, and date-related names such as months, days of the week, and others. Given a locale ID, one can get the corresponding CLocale instance by either using the static method CLocale::getInstance($localeID) or using the application. The following example code creates a new instance based on the en_us locale identifier using the application component:

```
Yii::app()->getLocale('en_us');
```

Yii comes with locale data for nearly every language and region. The data comes from the Common Locale Data Repository (http://cldr.unicode.org/), and is stored in files that are named according to their respective locale ID, and located in the Yii framework directory framework/i18n/data/. So in the previous example of creating a new CLocale instance, the data used to populate the attributes came from the file framework/i18n/data/en_us.php. If you look under this directory, you will see datafiles for many languages and regions.

Going back to our example, if we wanted to get the names of the months in English that is specific to the US region, we could execute the following code:

```
$locale = Yii::app()->getLocale('en_us');
print_r($locale->monthNames);
```

The output of which would produce the following:

Array ([1] => January [2] => February [3] => March [4] => April [5] => May [6] => June [7] => July [8] => August [9] => September [10] => October [11] => November [12] => December)

If we wanted the same month names for the Italian language, we could do the same but create a different CLocale instance:

```
$locale = Yii::app()->getLocale('it');
print_r($locale->monthNames);
```

Now our output would produce the following:

Array ([1] => gennaio [2] => febbraio [3] => marzo [4] => aprile [5] => maggio [6] => giugno [7] => luglio [8] => agosto [9] => settembre [10] => ottobre [11] => novembre [12] => dicembre)

The first instance is based on the data file framework/i18n/data/en_us.php and the latter on framework/i18n/data/it.php. If desired, the application's localeDataPath property can be configured in order to specify a custom directory in which you can add your custom locale data files.

Performing language translation

Perhaps the most desired feature of i18n is language translation. As mentioned previously, Yii provides both message translation and view file translation. The former translates a single text message to a desired language, and the latter translates an entire file to the desired language.

A translation request consists of the object that is to be translated (either a string of text or a file), the source language that the object is in, and the target language to which the object is to be translated. A Yii application makes a distinction between its target language and its source language. The **target** language is the language (or locale) that we are targeting for the user, whereas the **source** language refers to the language in which the application files are written. So far, our TrackStar application has been written in English and is also targeted for users of the English language. Our target and source languages thus far have been the same. The internationalization features of Yii, which include translation, are only applicable when these two languages are different.

Performing message translation

Message translation is performed by calling the following application method:

```
Yii::t(string $category, string $message, array $params=array ( ),
string $source=NULL, string $language=NULL)
```

This method translates the message from the source language to the target language.

When translating a message, the category must be specified to allow a message to be translated differently under different categories (contexts). The category Yii is reserved for the messages used by the Yii framework core code.

Messages can also contain parameter placeholders that will be replaced with the actual parameter values upon calling Yii::t(). The following example depicts the translation of an error message. This message translation request would replace the {errorCode} placeholder in the original message with the actual $errorCode value:

```
Yii::t('category', 'The error: "{errorCode}" was encountered during
the last request.',    array('{errorCode}'=>$errorCode));
```

The translated messages are stored in a repository called **message source**. A message source is represented as an instance of CMessageSource or a child class thereof. When Yii::t() is invoked, it will look for the message in the message source and return its translated version if it is found.

Yii comes with the following types of message sources:

- **CPhpMessageSource**: This is the default message source. The message translations are stored as key-value pairs in a PHP array. The original message is the key and the translated message is the value. Each array represents the translations for a particular category of messages, and is stored in a separate PHP script file whose name is the category name. The PHP translation files for the same language are stored under the same directory named as the locale ID. And all these directories are located under the directory specified by `basePath`.

- **CGettextMessageSource**: The message translations are stored as `GNU Gettext` files.

- **CDbMessageSource**: The message translations are stored in database tables.

A message source is loaded as an application component. Yii predeclares an application component named `messages` to store the messages that are used in a user application. By default, the type of this message source is `CPhpMessageSource` and the base path for storing the PHP translation files is `protected/messages`.

An example will go a long way to help bring all of this together. Let's translate the form field labels on our **Login** form into a fictitious language that we'll call `Reversish`. **Reversish** is written by taking an English word or phrase and writing it in reverse. So here are the Reversish translations of our login form field labels:

English	Reversish
Username	Emanresu
Password	Drowssap
Remember me next time	Emit txen em rebmemer

We'll use the default `CPhpMessageSource` implementation to house our message translations. So the first thing we need to do is create a PHP file containing our translations. We'll make the locale ID `rev`, and we'll just call the category `default` for now. We need to create a new file under the messages base directory that follows the format `/localeID/CategoryName.php`. So we need to create a new file located at `/protected/messages/rev/default.php` and then add the following translation array to this file:

```php
<?php
return array(
    'Username' => 'Emanresu',
    'Password' => 'Drowssap',
    'Remember me next time' => 'Emit txen em rebmemer',
);
```

Next we need to set the application target language to be Reversish. We can do this in the application configuration file so that it will impact the entire site. Simply add the following `name=>value` pair to the returned array in the `/protected/config/main.php` file:

```
'language'=>'rev',
```

Now the last thing we need to do is to make our calls to `Yii::t()` so that our login form field labels are sent through the translation. These form field labels are defined in the `LoginForm::attributeLabels()` method. Replace that entire method with the following code:

```
/**
  * Declares attribute labels.
  */
 public function attributeLabels()
 {
   return array(
     'rememberMe'=>Yii::t('default','Remember me next time'),
     'username'=>Yii::t('default', 'Username'),
     'password'=>Yii::t('default', 'Password'),
   );
 }
```

Now if we visit our **Login** form again, we see a new Reversish version as depicted in the following screenshot:

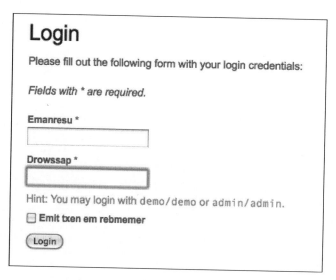

Performing file translation

Yii also provides the ability to use different files based on the target locale ID setting of the application. File translation is accomplished by calling the application method `CApplication::findLocalizedFile()`. This method takes in the path to a file and will look for that file with the same name, but under a directory that has been named with the same name as the target locale ID. The target locale ID is specified either as an explicit input to the method or as what is specified in the application configuration.

Let's try this out. All we really need to do is create the appropriate translation file. We'll stick with translating the login form. So we create a new view file `/protected/views/site/rev/login.php` and then add our translated content. Again, this is too long to list in its entirety, but you can view this in the downloadable code files or the standalone content at `https://gist.github.com/3779850`.

We are already setting the target language for the application in the main configuration file, and the call to get the localized file will be taken care of for us behind the scenes when calling `render('login')`. So with this file in place, our login form now looks as shown in the following screenshot:

Summary

In this chapter, we have seen how a Yii application allows you to quickly and easily polish up the design. We were introduced to the concept of layout files, and walked through how to use these in an application to lay out content and design that needs to be implemented in a similar manner across many different web pages. This also introduced us to the CMenu and CBreadcrumbs built-in widgets that provide very easy to use UI navigational constructs on each page.

We then introduced the idea of a theme within web applications and how you can create them in Yii. We saw that themes allow you to easily put a new face on an existing web application, and allow you to redesign your application without rebuilding any of the functionality or "backend".

Finally, we looked at changing the face of the application through the lens of i18n and language translation. We learned how to set the target locale of the application to enable localization settings and language translations.

We have made a few references in this and past chapters to "modules", but have yet to dive into what exactly these are within a Yii application. That is going to be the focus of the next chapter.

11
Using Yii Modules

So far we have added a lot of functionality to our TrackStar application. And if you recall back to *Chapter 7, User Access Control*, we introduced user access controls to restrict certain functionalities based on a user role hierarchy. This was very helpful in restricting access to some of the administrative functions on a per project basis. For example, within a specific project, you may not want to allow all the members of the team to delete the project. We used a role based access control implementation to assign users to specific roles within a project, and then allowed/restricted access to the functionality based on these roles.

However, what we have not yet addressed are the administrative needs of the application as a whole. Web applications such as TrackStar often require very special users who have the ability to have full access to administer everything. One example is the ability to manage all the CRUD operations for every single user of the system, regardless of the project. A *full administrator* of our application should be able to log in and remove or update any user, any project, any issue, moderate all comments, and so on. Also, it is often the case that we build extra features that apply to the whole application, such as the ability to leave site-wide system messages to all the users, manage e-mail campaigns, turn on/off certain application features, manage the roles and permissions hierarchy itself, change the site theme, and others. Because the functionality exposed to the administrator can differ greatly from the functionality exposed to normal users, it is often a good idea to keep these features very separate from the rest of the application. We will be accomplishing this separation by building all of our administrative functionality in what is called a **module** in Yii.

Feature planning

In this chapter we will focus on the following granular development tasks:

- Creating a new module to house administrative functionality
- Creating the ability for administrators to add system-wide messages for application users, to view on the projects listing page
- Applying a new theme to the module
- Creating a new database table to hold the system message data
- Generating all CRUD functionality for our system messages
- Restricting access to all functionality within the new module to admin users
- Displaying new system messages on the projects listing page

Working with modules

A **module** in Yii is very much like an entire mini-application contained within a larger application. It has a very similar structure, containing models, views, controllers, and other supporting components. However, modules cannot be deployed themselves as standalone applications; they must reside within an application.

Modules are very useful in helping to architect your application in a modular fashion. Large applications can often be segmented into discrete application features that could be built separately using modules. Site features such as adding a user forum or user blogs, or site-administrator functionality, are some examples that could be segmented from the main site features, allowing them to be developed separately and having them be easily reusable in future projects. We are going to use a module to create a distinct place in our application to house our administrative functionality.

Creating a module

Creating a new module is a snap when using our good friend Gii. With our URL changes in place, the tool is now accessible via `http://localhost/trackstar/gii`. Navigate there and select the **Module Generator** option in the left-hand side menu. You will be presented with the following screenshot:

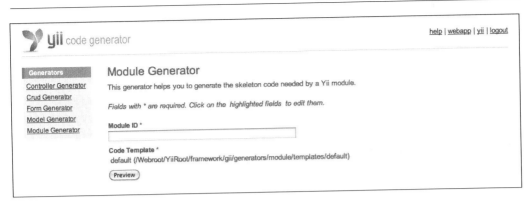

We need to provide a unique name for the module. Since we are creating an admin module, we'll be super creative and give it the name `admin`. Type this in the **Module ID** field and click on the **Preview** button. As shown in the following screenshot, it will present you with all of the files that it intends to generate, allowing you to preview each file prior to creating them:

Code File	Generate ☐
modules/admin/AdminModule.php	new ☑
modules/admin/components	new ☑
modules/admin/controllers/DefaultController.php	new ☑
modules/admin/messages	new ☑
modules/admin/models	new ☑
modules/admin/views/default/index.php	new ☑
modules/admin/views/layouts	new ☑

Preview Generate

Click on the **Generate** button to have it create all of these files. You will need to ensure that your /protected folder is writable by the web server process for it to autocreate the necessary directories and files. The following screenshot shows the successful generation of a module:

```
Preview

The module has been generated successfully.

To access the module, you need to modify the application configuration as follows:

<?php
return array(
    'modules'=>array(
        'admin',
    ),
    ......
);
```

```
Generating code using template "/Webroot/YiiRoot/framework/gii/generators
    generated modules/admin/AdminModule.php
    generated modules/admin/components
    generated modules/admin/controllers/DefaultController.php
    generated modules/admin/messages
    generated modules/admin/models
    generated modules/admin/views/default/index.php
    generated modules/admin/views/layouts
done!
```

Let's take a closer look at what the module generator created for us. A module in Yii is organized as a directory, the name of which is the same as the unique name of the module. By default, all module directories reside under protected/modules. The structure of each module directory is very similar to that of our main application. What this command has done for us is to create the skeleton of the directory structure for the admin module. Since this was our first module, the top-level directory protected/modules was created, and then an admin/ directory was created underneath it. The following screenshot shows all of the directories and files that were created when we executed the module command:

```
admin/
    AdminModule.php             the module class file
    components/                 containing reusable user components
    controllers/                containing controller class files
        DefaultController.php   the default controller class file
    messages/                   stores message translations specific to the module
    models/                     containing model class files
    views/                      containing controller view and layout files
        default/                containing view files for DefaultController
            index.php           the index view file
        layouts/                containing layout view files
```

A module must have a `module` class that extends either directly or from a child of `CWebModule`. The module class name is created by combining the module ID (that is, the name we supplied when we created the module `admin`) and the string `Module`. The first letter of the module ID is also capitalized. So in our case, our admin module class file is named `AdminModule.php`. The module class serves as the central place for storing information that is shared within the module code. For example, we can use the `params` property of `CWebModule` to store module-specific parameters, and use its `components` property to share application components at the module level. This module class serves a similar role to the module as the application class does to the entire application. So `CWebModule` is to our module what `CWebApplication` is to our application.

Using a module

Just as the successful creation message indicated, before we can use our new module, we need to configure the `modules` property of the main application to include it for use. We did this before when we added the `gii` module to our application, which allowed us to access the Gii code generation tool. We make this change in the main configuration file `protected/config/main.php`. The following highlighted code indicates the necessary change:

```
'modules'=>array(
    'gii'=>array(
        'class'=>'system.gii.GiiModule',
        'password'=>'iamadmin',
    ),
    'admin',
),
```

After saving this change, our new `admin` module is wired up for use. We can take a look at the simple index page that was created for us by visiting `http://localhost/trackstar/admin/default/index`. The request-routing structure for accessing the pages in our module is just like that for our main application pages, except that we need to include the `moduleID` directory in the route as well. Our routes will be of the general form `/moduleID/controllerID/actionID`. So the URL request `/admin/default/index` is requesting the `admin` module's default controller's index method. When we visit this page, we see something similar to the following screenshot:

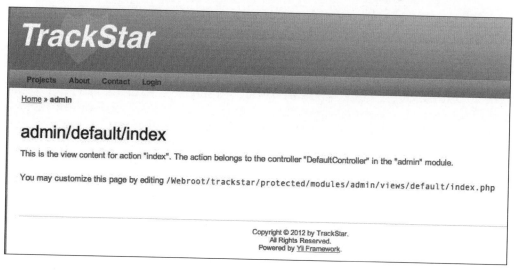

Module layout

One thing we will notice is that the theme we created in the previous chapter, `newtheme`, is also being applied to our module. The reason for this is that our module controller classes are extending `protected/components/Controller.php`, which specifies its layout as `$layout='//layouts/column1'`. The key is the double slashes in front of this definition. This specifies that we use the main application path rather than the specific module path for finding the layout file. So we are getting the same layout file applied to our module as we are to the rest of our application. If we make this a single slash rather than double, we would see our `admin` module having no layout applied to it at all. Go ahead and give it a try. The reason for this is that now, with just the single slash, that is, `$layout='/layouts/column1'`, it is looking for layout files within the module rather than the parent application. Please go ahead and make this change, and keep the single slash definition as we proceed.

You can configure almost everything separately in a module, including the default path for layout files. The default layout path for web modules is /protected/modules/[moduleID]/views/layouts, where [moduleID] in our case is admin. We can see that there are no files under this directory, so there is no default layout to be applied to the module.

Since we have a theme specified, there is slightly more to the story in our case. We can also manage all of our module view files, including the module layout view files, within this theme. If we were to do that, we'd need to add to our theme directory structure to accommodate our new module. The directory structure is very much as expected. It is of a general form /themes/[themeName]/views/[moduleID]/layouts/ for the layout files and /themes/[themeName]/views/[moduleID]/[controllerID]/ for the controller view files.

To help clarify this, let's walk through Yii's decision making process when it is trying to decide what view files to use for our new admin module. As mentioned earlier, if we specify the layout view file with double slashes preceding it ("//"), it will look to the parent application to find the layout file. But let's look at the case where we use a single slash and ask it to find the appropriate layout file within the module. In the single slash scenario, here is what is happening when $this->render('index') is issued in the DefaultController.php file within our admin module:

1. Since render() is being called, as opposed to renderPartial(), it is going to attempt to decorate the specified index.php view file with a layout file. And since our application is currently configured to use a theme called newtheme, it is going to first look for layout files under this theme directory. Our new module's DefaultController class extends our application component Controller.php, which has column1 specified as its $layout property. This property is not overridden, so it is also the layout file for DefaultController. Finally, since this is all happening within the admin module, Yii first looks for the following layout file:

    /themes/newtheme/views/admin/layouts/column1.php

    (Note the inclusion of the moduleID in this directory structure.)

2. This file does not exist, so it reverts to looking in the default location for the module. As previously mentioned, the default layout directory is specific to each module. So in this case it will attempt to locate the following layout file:

    /protected/modules/admin/views/layouts/column1.php

3. This file also does not exist, so it will be unable to apply a layout. It will now simply attempt to render the specified `index.php` view file without a layout. However, again since we have specified the specific `newtheme` theme for this application, it will first look for the following view file:

   `/themes/newtheme/views/admin/default/index.php`

4. This file also does not exist, so it will look again for this controller (`DefaultController.php`) in the default location within this module (`AdminModule`), namely `/protected/modules/admin/views/default/index.php`.

This explains why the page `http://localhost/trackstar/admin/default/index` is rendered without any layout (again, in the case where we are using a single slash to prefix the layout file declaration `$layout='/layouts/column1'`). To keep things completely separate and simple for now, let's manage our view files in the default location for our module rather than under the `newtheme` theme. Also, let's apply to our `admin` module the same design as our original application had, that is, how the application looked before we applied the new theme. In this way, our `admin` pages will have a very different look from our normal application pages, which will help remind us that we are in the special admin section, but we won't have to spend any time coming up with a new design.

Applying a layout

First let's set a default layout value for our module. We set our module-wide configuration settings in the `init()` method within our module class `/protected/modules/AdminModule.php`. So open up that file and add the following highlighted code:

```
class AdminModule extends CWebModule
{
  public function init()
  {
    // this method is called when the module is being created
    // you may place code here to customize the module or the
application

    // import the module-level models and components
    $this->setImport(array(
      'admin.models.*',
      'admin.components.*',
    ));

    $this->layout = 'main';

  }
```

In this way, if we have not specified a layout file at a more granular level, such as in a controller class, all of the module views will be decorated by the layout file `main.php` located in the default layout directory for our module, namely `/protected/modules/admin/views/layouts/`.

Now of course, we need to create this file. Make a copy of the two layout files `/protected/views/layouts/main.php` and `/protected/views/layouts/column1.php` from the main application, and place them both in the `/protected/modules/admin/views/layouts/` directory. After you have copied these files over to the new location, we need to make a few small changes to both of them.

First let's alter `column1.php`. Remove the explicit reference to `//layouts/main` in the call `beginContent()`:

```
<?php $this->beginContent(); ?>
<div id="content">
  <?php echo $content; ?>
</div><!-- content -->
<?php $this->endContent(); ?>
```

Not specifying an input file when calling `beginContent()` will result in it using the default layout for our module, which we just set to be our newly copied `main.php` file.

Now let's make a few changes to our `main.php` layout file. We are going to add **Admin Console** to our application header text to emphasize that we are in a separate part of the application. We will also alter our menu items to have a link to the **Admin** home page, as well as a link to go back to the main site. We can remove the **About** and **Contact** links from this menu as we don't need to repeat those options in our **Admin** section. The additions to the file are highlighted as follows:

```
...
<div class="container" id="page">

  <div id="header">
    <div id="logo"><?php echo CHtml::encode(Yii::app()->name) . "
Admin Console"; ?></div>
  </div><!-- header -->

  <div id="mainmenu">
    <?php $this->widget('zii.widgets.CMenu',array(
      'items'=>array(
        array('label'=>'Back To Main Site', 'url'=>array('/project')),
        array('label'=>'Admin', 'url'=>array('/admin/default/index')),
        array('label'=>'Login', 'url'=>array('/site/login'),
  'visible'=>Yii::app()->user->isGuest),
```

```
        array('label'=>'Logout ('.Yii::app()->user->name.')',
    'url'=>array('/site/logout'), 'visible'=>!Yii::app()->user->isGuest)
        ),
     )); ?>
   </div><!-- mainmenu -->
```

We can leave the rest of the file unchanged. Now if we visit our admin module page http://localhost/trackstar/admin/default/index, we see something like the following screenshot:

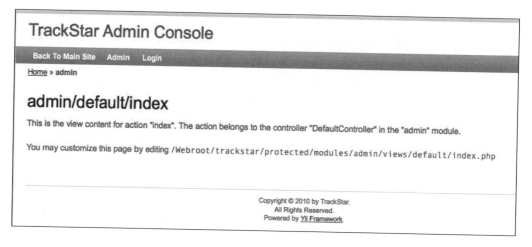

And if we click on the **Back To Main Site** link, we see that we are taken back to the newly themed version of our main application.

Restricting admin access

One problem you may have already noticed is that anyone, including guest users, can access our new admin module. We are building this admin module to expose application functionality that should only be accessible to users with administrative access. So we need to address this issue.

Luckily, we have already implemented an RBAC access model in our application, back in *Chapter 7, User Access Control*. All we need to do now is extend it to include a new role for administrators and have new permissions available for that role.

If you recall from *Chapter 7, User Access Control* , we used a Yii `console` command to implement our RBAC structure. We need to add to that. So open up the file /`protected/commands/shell/RbacCommand.php` containing that `console` command, and add the following code where we created the `owner` role:

```
//create a general task-level permission for admins
$this->_authManager->createTask("adminManagement", "access to the
application administration functionality");
//create the site admin role, and add the appropriate permissions
$role=$this->_authManager->createRole("admin");
$role->addChild("owner");
$role->addChild("reader");
$role->addChild("member");
$role->addChild("adminManagement");
//ensure we have one admin in the system (force it to be user id #1)
$this->_authManager->assign("admin",1);
```

This creates a new task called `adminManagement` and a new role called `admin`. It then adds the `owner`, `reader`, and `member` roles along with the `adminManagement` task as children, so that the `admin` role inherits permissions from all of these. Finally, it assigns the `admin` role to the first user in our system to ensure that we have at least one admin to access our admin module.

Now we have to rerun our command to update the database with these changes. To do so, just run the `yiic` command-line tool with the `rbac` command:

```
% cd Webroot/trackstar/protected
% ./yiic rbac
```

> With this additional role being added, we should also update the text in the message that is displayed when prompted, to continue to indicate that a fourth role will be created. We will leave this as an exercise for the reader. This change has been made in the downloadable code files for your reference.

With these changes to our RBAC model in place, we can add an access check to the `AdminModule::beforeControllerAction()` method so that nothing within the `admin` module will be executed unless the user is in the `admin` role:

```
public function beforeControllerAction($controller, $action)
{
  if(parent::beforeControllerAction($controller, $action))
  {
     // this method is called before any module controller action is
performed
```

```
       // you may place customized code here
       if( !Yii::app()->user->checkAccess("admin") )
           {
           throw new CHttpException(403,Yii::t('application','You are
   not authorized to perform this action.'));
           }
       return true;
   }
   else
     return false;
}
```

With this in place, if a user who has not been assigned the admin role now attempts to visit any page within the **Admin** module, they will receive an HTTP 403 authorization error page. For example, if you are not logged in and you attempt to visit the **Admin** page, you will receive the following result:

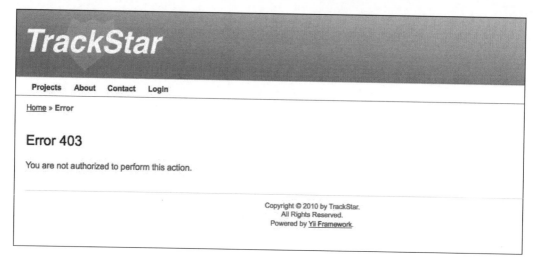

And the same holds true for any user that has not been assigned to the admin role.

Now we can conditionally add a link to the **Admin** section of the site to our main application menu. In this way, users with administrative access won't have to remember a cumbersome URL to navigate to the **Admin** console. As a reminder, our main application menu is located in our application's theme default application layout file /themes/newtheme/views/layouts/main.php. Open up that file and add the following highlighted code to the menu section:

```
<div id="mainmenu">
  <?php $this->widget('zii.widgets.CMenu',array(
    'items'=>array(
```

```
        array('label'=>'Projects', 'url'=>array('/project')),
        array('label'=>'About', 'url'=>array('/site/page',
'view'=>'about')),
        array('label'=>'Contact', 'url'=>array('/site/contact')),
        array('label'=>'Admin', 'url'=>array('/admin/default/index'),
'visible'=>Yii::app()->user->checkAccess("admin")),
        array('label'=>'Login', 'url'=>array('/site/login'),
'visible'=>Yii::app()->user->isGuest),
        array('label'=>'Logout ('.Yii::app()->user->name.')',
'url'=>array('/site/logout'), 'visible'=>!Yii::app()->user->isGuest)
    ),
  )); ?>
</div><!-- mainmenu -->
```

Now upon logging into the application as a user with `admin` access (we set this to be `user id = 1`, "**User One**" in our case), we will see a new link in our top navigation that will take us to our newly added **Admin** section of the site.

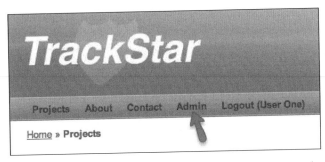

Adding a system-wide message

A **module** can be thought of as a mini-application itself, and adding functionality to a module is really the same process as adding functionality to the main application. Let's add some new functionality just for administrators; we will add the ability to manage system-wide messages displayed to users when they first log in to the application.

Creating the database table

As is often the case with brand new functionality, we need a place to house our data. We need to create a new table to store our system-wide messages. For the purpose of our examples, we can keep this very simple. Here is the definition for our table:

```
CREATE TABLE `tbl_sys_message`
(
    `id` INTEGER NOT NULL PRIMARY KEY AUTO_INCREMENT,
    `message` TEXT NOT NULL,
    `create_time` DATETIME,
    `create_user_id` INTEGER,
    `update_time` DATETIME,
    `update_user_id` INTEGER
)
```

We'll of course create a new database migration to manage our changes when adding this new table.

```
% cd Webroot/trackstar/protected
% ./yiic migrate create_system_messages_table
```

These commands create a new migration file under the `protected/migrations/` directory. The contents of this file can be obtained from the downloadable code or the standalone code snippet that is available at `https://gist.github.com/3785282`. (We did not include the class name; remember that the name of your file and corresponding class will have a different timestamp prefix.)

Once this file is in place, we can run our migration to add this new table:

```
% cd Webroot/trackstar/protected
% ./yiic migrate
```

Creating our model and CRUD scaffolding

Now that we have our table created, our next step is to generate the `model` class
using our favorite tool, the Gii code generator. We'll first use the **Model Generator**
option to create the `model` class and the **Crud Generator** option to create our basic
scaffolding to quickly interact with this model. Go ahead and navigate to the Gii tool
form for creating a new model (`http://localhost/trackstar/gii/model`). This
time, since we are doing this within the context of a module, we need to explicitly
specify the model path. Fill out the form with the values depicted in the following
screenshot (though of course your **Code Template** path value should be specific to
your local setup):

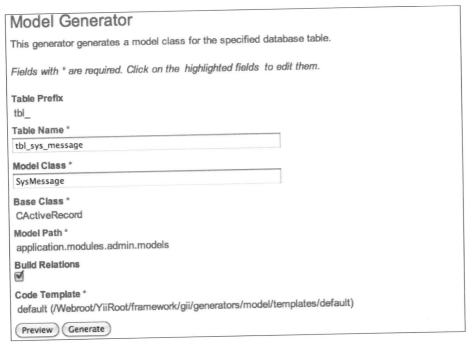

Note that we changed the **Model Path** textbox to `application.modules.admin.`
`models`. Go ahead and generate the **Model Class** value by clicking on the
Generate button.

Now we can create the CRUD scaffolding in much the same way. Again, the only real difference between what we have done previously and what we are doing now is our specification that the location of the model class is in the admin module. After choosing the **Crud Generator** option from the Gii tool, fill out the **Model Class** and **Controller ID** form fields as shown in the following screenshot:

Crud Generator

This generator generates a controller and views that implement CRUD operations for the specified data model.

*Fields with * are required. Click on the highlighted fields to edit them.*

Model Class *

application.modules.admin.models.SysMessage

Controller ID *

admin/sysMessage

Base Controller Class *
Controller

Code Template *
default (/Webroot/YiiRoot/framework/gii/generators/crud/templates/default)

This alerts the tool to the fact that our model class is under the admin module, and that our controller class as well as all other files related to this code generation should be placed within the admin module as well.

Complete the creation by first clicking on the **Preview** button and then on **Generate**. The following screenshot shows a list of all of the files that are created by this action:

Code File
modules/admin/controllers/SysMessageController.php
modules/admin/views/sysMessage/_form.php
modules/admin/views/sysMessage/_search.php
modules/admin/views/sysMessage/_view.php
modules/admin/views/sysMessage/admin.php
modules/admin/views/sysMessage/create.php
modules/admin/views/sysMessage/index.php
modules/admin/views/sysMessage/update.php
modules/admin/views/sysMessage/view.php

Adding a link to our new functionality

Let's add a new menu item within the main `admin` module navigation that links to our newly created message functionality. Open up the file `/protected/modules/admin/views/layouts/main.php` that contains the main menu navigation for our module, and add the following `array` item to the menu widget:

```
array('label'=>'System Messages', 'url'=>array('/admin/sysMessage/
index')),
```

If we take a look at our page for creating a new system message at `http://localhost/trackstar/admin/sysMessage/create`, we see the following:

The autocreated controller and view files for our new system message functionality were created to use the two-column layout file from the main application. If you take a look inside the `SysMessageController.php` class file, you will see the layout defined as such:

```
public $layout='//layouts/column2';
```

Notice the double slashes in front. So we can see that our newly added admin functionality is not using our `admin` module layout files. We could alter the `controller` class to use our existing, single-column layout file in the `admin` module, or we can add a two-column layout file to our module layout files. The latter is going to be slightly easier and will also look better, as all of the view files are created to have their submenu items (that is the links to all the CRUD functionality) be displayed in a second right-hand column. We also need to alter our newly created model class and corresponding form to remove some unneeded form fields. The following is all that we have to do:

1. Copy the two-column layout from our main application over to our module, that is, copy `/protected/views/layouts/column2.php` over to `/protected/modules/admin/views/layouts/column2.php`.

2. Remove `//layouts/main` as the input to the `beginContent()` method call on the first line, in the newly copied `column2.php` file.

3. Alter the `SysMessage` model class to extend `TrackstarActiveRecord`. (If you recall, this adds the code to automatically update our `create_time/user` and `update_time/user` properties.)

4. Alter the `SysMessageController` controller class to use the new `column2.php` layout file from within the module directory and not the one from the main application. The autogenerated code has specified `$layout='//layouts/column2'`, but we need this to simply be `$layout='/layouts/column2'`.

5. Since we are extending `TrackstarActiveRecord`, we can remove the unnecessary fields from our autogenerated, sys-messages creation form and remove their associated rules from the model class. For example, remove the following form fields from the `modules/admin/views/sysMessage/_form.php`:

```
<div class="row">
    <?php echo $form->labelEx($model,'create_time'); ?>
    <?php echo $form->textField($model,'create_time'); ?>
    <?php echo $form->error($model,'create_time'); ?>
</div>

<div class="row">
    <?php echo $form->labelEx($model,'create_user_id'); ?>
    <?php echo $form->textField($model,'create_user_id'); ?>
    <?php echo $form->error($model,'create_user_id'); ?>
</div>

<div class="row">
    <?php echo $form->labelEx($model,'update_time'); ?>
    <?php echo $form->textField($model,'update_time'); ?>
```

```
<?php echo $form->error($model,'update_time'); ?>
</div>

<div class="row">
  <?php echo $form->labelEx($model,'update_user_id'); ?>
  <?php echo $form->textField($model,'update_user_id'); ?>
  <?php echo $form->error($model,'update_user_id'); ?>
</div>
```

6. Then change these two rules from the `SysMessage::rules()` method:

```
array('create_user, update_user', 'numerical',
'integerOnly'=>true), and array('create_time, update_time',
'safe'),
```

It is important to only specify the rules for those fields that the user can input. Any fields that have rules defined can be set in a bulk manner from a POST or GET request, and leaving in rules for fields you do not want users to have access to can lead to security issues.

One last change we should make is to update our simple access rules to reflect the requirement that only the users in the `admin` role can access our action methods. This is mostly for illustrative purposes since we already took care of the access using our RBAC model approach in the `AdminModule::beforeControlerAction` method itself. We could actually just remove the `accessRules()` method entirely. However, let's update them to reflect the requirement so you can see how that would work using the access rule approach. In the `SysMessageController::accessRules()` method, change the entire content to the following:

```
public function accessRules()
{
  return array(
    array('allow',  // allow only users in the 'admin' role access to
our actions
       'actions'=>array('index','view', 'create', 'update', 'admin',
'delete'),
       'roles'=>array('admin'),
    ),
    array('deny',  // deny all users
      'users'=>array('*'),
    ),
  );
}
```

Okay, with all of this in place, if we now access our new message input form by visiting `http://localhost/trackstar/admin/sysMessage/create`, we are presented with something similar to the following screenshot:

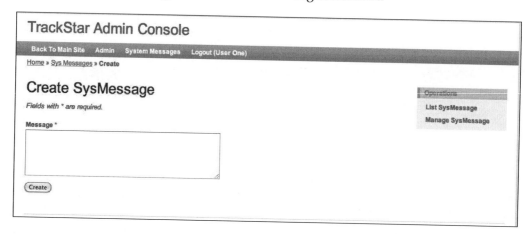

Fill out this form with the message `Hello Users! This is your admin speaking...` and click on **Create**. The application will redirect you to the details listing page for this newly created message, as shown in the following screenshot:

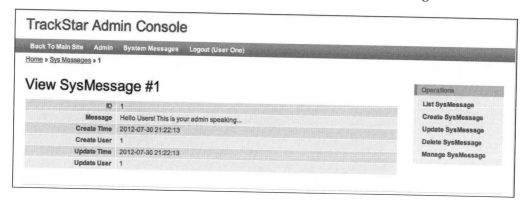

Displaying the message to users

Now that we have a message in our system, let's display it to the user on the application home page.

Importing the new model class for application-wide access

In order to access the newly created model from anywhere in our application, we need to import it as part of the application configuration. Alter `protected/config/main.php` to include the new `admin module models` folder:

```
// autoloading model and component classes
'import'=>array(
  'application.models.*',
  'application.components.*',
  'application.modules.admin.models.*',
),
```

Selecting the most recently updated message

We'll restrict the display to just one message, and we'll choose the most recently updated message based on the `update_time` column in the table. Since we want to add this to the main projects listing page, we need to alter the `ProjectController::actionIndex()` method. Alter that method by adding the following highlighted code:

```
public function actionIndex()
  {
      $dataProvider=new CActiveDataProvider('Project');

      Yii::app()->clientScript->registerLinkTag(
          'alternate',
          'application/rss+xml',
          $this->createUrl('comment/feed'));

      //get the latest system message to display based on the update_
time column
      $sysMessage = SysMessage::model()->find(array(
        'order'=>'t.update_time DESC',
      ));
      if($sysMessage !== null)
        $message = $sysMessage->message;
      else
          $message = null;

      $this->render('index',array(
        'dataProvider'=>$dataProvider,
        'sysMessage'=>$message,
      ));
  }
```

Now we need to alter our view file to display this new bit of content. Add the following code to `views/project/index.php`, just above the `<h1>Projects</h1>` header text:

```php
<?php if($sysMessage !== null):?>
    <div class="sys-message">
        <?php echo $sysMessage; ?>
    </div>
<?php endif; ?>
```

Now when we visit our projects listing page (that is our application's homepage), we can see it displayed as shown in the following screenshot:

Adding a little design tweak

Okay, this does what we wanted it to do, but this message does not really stand out to the user very well. Let's change that by adding a little snippet to our main CSS file (`/themes/newtheme/css/main.css`):

```css
div.sys-message
{
  padding:.8em;
  margin-bottom:1em;
  border:3px solid #ddd;
  background:#9EEFFF;
  color:#FF330A;
  border-color:#00849E;
}
```

With this in place, our message now really stands out on the page. The following screenshot shows the message with these changes in place:

One might argue that this design tweak went a little too far. Users might get a headache if they have to stare at those message colors all day. Rather than toning down the colors, let's use a little JavaScript to fade the message out after 5 seconds. Since we will be displaying the message every time the user visits this **Home** page, it might be nice to prevent them from having to stare at it for too long.

We'll make things easy on ourselves and take advantage of the fact that Yii comes shipped with the powerful JavaScript framework jQuery. **jQuery** is an open source, JavaScript library that simplifies the interaction between the HTML **Document Object Model** (the **DOM**) and JavaScript. It is outside the scope of this book to dive into the details of jQuery. It is well worth visiting its documentation to become a little more acquainted with its features. Since Yii comes shipped with jQuery, you can simply register jQuery code in the view files, and Yii will take care of including the core jQuery library for you.

We'll also use the application helper component `CClientScript` to register our jQuery JavaScript code for us in the resulting web page. It will make sure that it has been placed in the appropriate place, and has been properly tagged and formatted.

So let's alter what we previously added to include a snippet of JavaScript that will fade out the message. Replace what we just added to `views/project/index.php` with the following:

```php
<?php if($sysMessage != null):?>
    <div class="sys-message">
        <?php echo $sysMessage; ?>
    </div>
<?php
   Yii::app()->clientScript->registerScript(
      'fadeAndHideEffect',
      '$(".sys-message").animate({opacity: 1.0}, 5000).
fadeOut("slow");'
   );
endif; ?>
```

Now if we reload our main projects listing page, we see the message fade out after 5 seconds. For more information on cool jQuery effects that you can easily add to your pages, take a look at the JQuery API documentation available at `http://api.jquery.com/category/effects/`.

Finally, to convince yourself that everything is working as expected, you can add another system-wide message. Since this newer message will have a more recent `update_time` property, it will be the one to display on the projects listing page.

Summary

In this chapter, we have introduced the concept of a Yii module, and demonstrated its practicality by using one to create an administrative section of the site. We demonstrated how to create a new module, how to change the layout and theme of a module, how to add application functionality within the module, and even how to take advantage of an existing RBAC model, to apply authorization access controls to functionality within a module. We also demonstrated how to use jQuery to add a dash of UI flare to our application.

With the addition of this administrative interface, we now have all of the major pieces of the application in place. Though the application is incredibly simple, we feel it is time to get it ready for production. The next chapter will focus on preparing our application for production deployment.

12
Production Readiness

Even though our application lacks a significant amount of feature functionality, our (albeit imaginary) deadlines are approaching and our (also imaginary) client is getting anxious about getting the application into a production environment. Even though it may be some time before our application actually sees the light of day in production, it is time to get the application "production ready". In this, our final chapter of development, we are going to do just that.

Feature planning

In order to achieve the goal of preparing our application for a production environment, we are going to focus on the following granular tasks:

- Implement Yii's application logging framework to ensure we are logging information about critical production errors and events
- Implement Yii's application error handling framework to ensure we properly handle errors in production and understand how this works differently in a production environment rather than in a development environment
- Implement application data caching to help improve performance

Logging

Logging is a topic that should arguably have been covered before this late stage in the application development. Informational, warning, and severe error messages are invaluable when it comes to troubleshooting in software applications, and most certainly for those in a production environment being used by real users.

As developers, we are all familiar with this story. You have met all of the functional requirements of the application you are building. All of the unit and functional tests are passing. The application has been approved by QA, and everyone feels great about it being ready for production. But as soon as it goes in and is under real production load, with real users interacting with it, it behaves unexpectedly. A good logging strategy could make the difference between a swift resolution and rolling back weeks or even months of hard work.

Yii provides flexible and extensible logging capabilities. The data logged can be classified according to log levels and message categories. Using level and category filters, log messages can be further routed to different destinations, such as written to files on disc, stored in a database, sent to administrators as emails, or displayed in browser windows.

Message logging

Our application has actually been logging many informational messages upon each request the entire time. When the initial application was created it was configured to be in *debug* mode and while in this mode, the Yii framework itself logs information messages. We can't actually see these messages because, by default, they are being logged to memory. So, they are around only for the lifetime of the request.

Whether or not the application is in this debug mode is controlled by the following line in the root `index.php` file:

```
defined('YII_DEBUG') or define('YII_DEBUG',true);
```

To see what is being logged, let's whip up a quick little action method in our `SiteController` class to display the messages:

```
public function actionShowLog()
{
   echo "Logged Messages:<br><br>";
CVarDumper::dump(Yii::getLogger()->getLogs());
}
```

Here we are using Yii's `CVarDumper` helper class, which is an improved version of `var_dump` or `print_r`, due to its ability to properly handle recursive reference objects.

If we invoke this action by making the request `http://localhost/trackstar/site/showLog`, we see something similar to the following screenshot:

> Logged Messages:
>
> array ('0' => array ('0' => 'Loading \"log\" application component in /Webroot/trackstar/index.php (13)' '1' => 'trace' '2' => 'system.CModule' '3' => 1348712301.5371) '1' => array ('0' => 'Loading \"request\" application component in /Webroot/trackstar/index.php (13)' '1' => 'trace' '2' => 'system.CModule' '3' => 1348712301.5384) '2' => array ('0' => 'Loading \"urlManager\" application component in /Webroot/trackstar/index.php (13)' '1' => 'trace' '2' => 'system.CModule' '3' => 1348712301.5399))

If we comment out our global application debug variable, defined in `index.php`, and refresh the page, we'll notice an empty array; that is, nothing was logged. This is because this system-level debugging information level logging is accomplished by calling `Yii::trace`, which only logs these messages if the application is in this special debug mode.

We can log messages in a Yii application using one of two static application methods:

- `Yii::log($message, $level, $category);`
- `Yii::trace($message, $category);`

As mentioned, the main difference between these two methods is that `Yii::trace` logs the message only when the application is in debug mode.

Categories and levels

When logging a message using `Yii::log()`, we need to specify its category and level. **Category** is a string and is used to provide extra context to the message being logged. This string can be anything you like, but a convention that many use is a string in the format of xxx.yyy.zzz, which resembles the path alias. For example, if a message is logged in our application's `SiteController` class, we may choose to use the category `application.controllers.SiteController`.

In addition to specifying the category, when using `Yii::log`, we can also specify a level for the message. The level can be thought of as the severity of the message. You can define your own levels, but typically they take on one of the following values:

- **Trace**: This level is commonly used for tracing the execution flow of the application during development.
- **Info**: This is for logging general information. This is the default level if none is specified.

- **Profile**: This is to be used with the performance profile feature, which is described later in this chapter.

- **Warning**: This is for warning messages.

- **Error**: This is for fatal error messages.

Adding a login message log

As an example, let's add some logging to our user login method. We'll provide some basic debugging information at the beginning of the method to indicate that the method is being executed. We'll then log an informational message upon a successful login, as well as a warning message if the login fails. Alter our `SiteController::actionLogin()` method as the following highlighted code suggests (the entire method is present in the downloadable code or you can download the standalone method from `https://gist.github.com/3791860`).

```php
public function actionLogin()
{
    Yii::trace("The actionLogin() method is being requested",
"application.controllers.SiteController");
    ...


    // collect user input data
    if(isset($_POST['LoginForm']))
    {

        ...
    if($model->validate() && $model->login())
        {
            Yii::log("Successful login of user: " . Yii::app()->user->id,
"info", "application.controllers.SiteController");
            $this->redirect(Yii::app()->user->returnUrl);
        }
        else
        {
            Yii::log("Failed login attempt", "warning", "application.
controllers.SiteController");
        }


    }
    ...
}
```

If we now successfully log in (or perform a failed attempt) and visit our page to view the logs, we don't see them (if you commented out the debug mode declaration, make sure you have put the application back in debug mode for this exercise). Again, the reason is that, by default, the logging implementation in Yii simply stores the messages in memory. They disappear when the request completes. This is not terribly useful. We need to route them to a more persistent storage area so we can view them outside of the request in which they are generated.

Message routing

As we mentioned earlier, by default, messages logged using `Yii::log` or `Yii::trace` are kept in memory. Typically, these messages are more useful if they are displayed in browser windows, saved to some persistent storage (such as in a file), in a database, or sent as an email. Yii's *message routing* allows for the log messages to be routed to different destinations.

In Yii, message routing is managed by a `CLogRouter` application component. It allows you to define a list of destinations to which the log messages should be routed.

In order to take advantage of this message routing, we need to configure the `CLogRouter` application component in our `protected/config/main.php` configuration file. We do this by setting its routes property with the desired log message destinations.

If we open up the main configuration file, we see that some configuration has already been provided (again, courtesy of using the `yiic webapp` command to initially create our application). The following is already defined in our configuration:

```
'log'=>array
  'class'=>'CLogRouter',
  'routes'=>array(
    array(
      'class'=>'CFileLogRoute',
      'levels'=>'error, warning',
    ),
    // uncomment the following to show log messages on web pages
    /*
    array(
      'class'=>'CWebLogRoute',
    ),
    */
  ),
),
```

The log application component is configured to use the framework class CLogRouter. Certainly, you could also create and use a custom child class of this if you have logging requirements not fully met by the base framework implementation; but in our case, this will work just fine.

What follows the class definition in the previous configuration is the definition of the routes property. In this case, there is just one route specified. This one is using the Yii framework message routing class, CFileLogRoute. The CFileLogRoute message routing class uses the filesystem to save the messages. By default, messages are logged in a file under the application runtime directory, /protected/runtime/ application.log. In fact, if you have been following along with us and have your own application, you can take a peek at this file and will see several messages that have been logged by the framework. The levels specification dictates that only messages whose log level is either error or warning will be routed to this file. The part of the configuration in the previous code that is commented out specifies another route, CWebLogRoute. If used, this will route the message to be displayed on the currently requested web page. The following is a list of message routes currently available in Version 1.1 of Yii:

- CDbLogRoute: Saves messages in a database table
- CEmailLogRoute: Sends messages to specified e-mail addresses
- CFileLogRoute: Saves messages in a file under the application's runtime directory or any other directory of your choice
- CWebLogRoute: Displays messages at the end of the current web page
- CProfileLogRoute: Displays profiling messages at the end of the current web page

The logging that we added to our SiteController::actionLogin() method used Yii::trace for one message and then used Yii::log for two more. When using Yii::trace the log level is automatically set to trace. When using the Yii::log we specified an info log level if the login was successful, but a warning level if the login attempt failed. Let's alter our log routing configuration to write the trace and info level messages to a new, separate file called infoMessages.log in the same directory as our application.log file. Also, let's configure it to write the warning messages to the browser. To do that, we will make the following changes (highlighted) to the configuration:

```
'log'=>array(
  'class'=>'CLogRouter',
  'routes'=>array(
    array(
      'class'=>'CFileLogRoute',
      'levels'=>'error',
```

```
    ),
    array(
      'class'=>'CFileLogRoute',
      'levels'=>'info, trace',
      'logFile'=>'infoMessages.log',
    ),
     array(
      'class'=>'CWebLogRoute',
      'levels'=>'warning',
    ),
```

Now, after saving these changes, let's try out the different scenarios. First, try a successful login. Doing so will write our two login messages out to our new / `protected/runtime/infoMessages.log` file, one for the trace and the other one logging the successful login. After successfully logging in, viewing that file reveals the following (the full listing was truncated to save a few trees):

```
. . . . .
2012/06/15 00:31:52 [trace] [application.controllers.SiteController]
The actionLogin() method is being requested
2012/06/15 00:31:52 [trace] [system.web.CModule] Loading "user"
application component
2012/06/15 00:31:52 [trace] [system.web.CModule] Loading "session"
application component
2012/06/15 00:31:52 [trace] [system.web.CModule] Loading "db"

application component
2012/06/15 00:31:52 [trace] [system.db.CDbConnection] Opening DB
connection
. . . . .
2012/06/15 00:31:52 [info] [application.controllers.SiteController]
Successful login of user: 1

. . . . .
```

As you can see, there is a lot more in there than just our two messages! But our two did show up; they are in bold in the previous listing. Now that we are routing all trace messages to this new file, all framework trace messages are showing up here as well. This is actually very informative and really helps you get a picture of the lifecycle of a request as it makes its way through the framework. There is a lot going on under the covers. We would obviously turn off this verbose level of logging when moving this application to production. In non-debug mode, we would only see our single info level message. But this level of detail can be very informative when trying to track down bugs and just figuring out what the application is doing. It is very comforting to know it is here when/if ever needed.

Now let's try the failed login attempt scenario. If we now log back out and try our login again, but this time specify incorrect credentials to force a failed login, we see our **warning** level display along the bottom of the returned web page just as we configured it to do. The following screenshot shows this warning being displayed:

Application Log

Timestamp	Level	Category	Message
22:48:11.544615	warning	application.controllers.SiteController	Failed login attempt in /Webroot/trackstar/protected/controllers/SiteController.php in /Webroot/trackstar/index.php (13)

When using the `CFileLogRouter` message router, the log files are stored under the `logPath` property and the filename is specified by the `logFile` method. Another great feature of this log router is automatic logfile rotation. If the size of the logfile is greater than the value set in the `maxFileSize` property (in kilobytes) a rotation is performed, which renames the current log file by suffixing the filename with `.1`. All existing logfiles are moved backwards one place, that is, `.2` to `.3`, `.1` to `.2`. The property `maxLogFiles` can be used to specify how many files are to be kept.

> If you use `die;` or `exit;` in your application to terminate the execution, log messages may not be properly written to their intended destinations. If you need to explicitly terminate the execution of your Yii applications, use `Yii::app()->end()`. This provides the application an opportunity to write out log messages successfully. Also, the `CLogger` component has an `$autoDump` property that, if set to `true`, will allow the writing of log messages to their destinations in real time (that is, as `->log()` is called). This should only be used for debugging purposes due to its potential performance impact, but can be a very valuable debugging option.

Handling errors

Properly handling the errors that invariably occur in software applications is of utmost importance. This, again, is a topic that arguably should have been covered prior to coding our application, rather than at this late stage. Luckily, though, since we have been leaning on tools within the Yii framework to autogenerate much of our core application skeleton, our application is already taking advantage of some of Yii's error handling features.

Yii provides a complete error handling framework based on PHP 5 exceptions, a built-in mechanism for handling exceptional circumstances in the program through centralized points. When the main Yii application component is created to handle an incoming user request, it registers its `CApplication::handleError()` method to handle PHP warnings and notices, and it registers its `CApplication::handleException()` method to handle uncaught PHP exceptions. Consequently, if a PHP warning/notice or an uncaught exception occurs during the application execution, one of the error handlers will take over the control and start the necessary error handling procedure.

> The registration of error handlers is done in the application's constructor by calling the PHP functions `set_exception_handler` and `set_error_handler`. If you prefer not to have Yii handle these types of errors and exceptions, you may override this default behavior by defining the global constants `YII_ENABLE_ERROR_HANDLER` and `YII_ENABLE_EXCEPTION_HANDLER` to be false in the main `index.php` entry script.

By default, the application will use the framework class `CErrorHandler` as the application component tasked with handling PHP errors and uncaught exceptions. Part of the task of this built-in application component is displaying these errors using appropriate view files based on whether or not the application is running in *debug* mode or in *production* mode. This allows you to customize your error messages for these different environments. It makes sense to display much more verbose error information in a development environment to help troubleshoot problems. But allowing users of a production application to view this same information could compromise security. Also, if you have implemented your site in multiple languages, `CErrorHandler` also selects the preferred language for displaying the error.

You raise exceptions in Yii in the same way you would normally raise a PHP exception. One uses the following general syntax to raise an exception when needed:

```
throw new ExceptionClass('ExceptionMessage');
```

The two exception classes Yii provides are:

- `CException`
- `CHttpException`

`CException` is a generic exception class. `CHttpException` represents an HTTP error and also carries a `statusCode` property to represent the HTTP status code. Errors are displayed differently in the browser, depending on the exception class that is thrown.

Displaying errors

As was previously mentioned, when the CErrorHandler application component is handling an error, it makes a decision as to which view file to use when displaying the error. If the error is meant to be displayed to end users, as is the case when using CHttpException, the default behavior is to use a view named errorXXX, where XXX represents the HTTP status code (for example, 400, 404, or 500). If the error is an internal one and should only be displayed to developers, it will use a view named Exception. When the application is in debug mode, a complete call stack as well as the error line in the source file will be displayed.

However, when the application is running in production mode, all errors will be displayed using the errorXXX view files. This is because the call stack of an error may contain sensitive information that should not be displayed to just any end user.

When the application is in production mode, developers should rely on the error logs to provide more information about an error. A message of level error will always be logged when an error occurs. If the error is caused by a PHP warning or notice, the message will be logged with the category php. If the error is caused by an uncaught exception, the category will be exception.ExceptionClassName, where the exception class name is one of, or a child class of, either CHttpException or CException. One can thus take advantage of the logging features discussed in the previous section to monitor errors that occur within a production application. Of course, if fatal PHP errors occur you will still need to check your error log defined by your PHP configuration settings instead of Yii's error log.

By default, CErrorHandler searches for the location of the corresponding view file in the following order:

- WebRoot/themes/ThemeName/views/system: The system view directory under the currently active theme

- WebRoot/protected/views/system: The default system view directory for an application

- YiiRoot/framework/views: The standard system view directory provided by the Yii framework

You can customize the error display by creating custom error view files under the system view directory of the application or theme.

Yii also allows you to define a specific controller action method to handle the display of the error. This is actually how our application is configured. We'll see this as we go through a couple of examples.

Some of the code that was generated for us as a by-product of using the Gii Crud Generator tool to create our CRUD scaffolding is already taking advantage of Yii's error handling. One such example is the `ProjectController::loadModel()` method. That method is defined as follows:

```
public function loadModel($id)
    {
     $model=Project::model()->findByPk($id);
     if($model===null)
        throw new CHttpException(404,'The requested page does not
exist.');
        return $model;
    }
```

We see that it is attempting to load the appropriate project model AR instance based on the input `id` querystring parameter. If it is unable to locate the requested project, it throws a `CHttpException` as a way to let the user know that the page they are requesting, in this case the project details page, does not exist. We can test this in our browser by explicitly requesting a project that we know does not exist. Since we know our application does not have a project associated with an `id` of 99, a request for `http://localhost/trackstar/project/view/id/99` will result in the following page being returned:

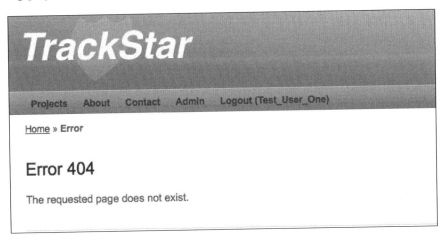

This is nice, because the page looks like any other page in our application, with the same theme, header, footer, and so on.

This is actually not the default behavior for rendering this type of error page. Our initial application was configured to use a specific controller action for the handling of such errors. We mentioned this was another option as to how to handle errors in an application. If we take a peek into our main configuration file, /protected/config/main.php, we see the following application component declaration:

```
'errorHandler'=>array(
   // use 'site/error' action to display errors
    'errorAction'=>'site/error',
),
```

This configures our error handler application component to use the SiteController::actionError() method to handle all of the exceptions intended to be displayed to users. If we take a look at that action method, we notice that it is rendering the protected/views/site/error.php view file. This is just a normal controller view file, so it will also render any relevant application layout files and will apply the appropriate theme. This way, we are able to provide the user with a very friendly experience when certain errors happen.

To see what the default behavior is, without this added configuration, let's temporarily comment out the previous lines of configuration code (in protected/config/main.php) and request the nonexistent project again. Now we see the following page:

Page Not Found

The requested page does not exist.

The requested URL was not found on this server. If you entered the URL manually please check your spelling and try again. If you think this is a server error, please contact the webmaster.

Since we have not explicitly defined any custom error pages following the convention outlined earlier, this is the framework/views/error404.php file in the Yii framework itself.

Go ahead and revert these changes to the configuration file to have the error handling use the SiteController::actionError() method once again.

Now let's see how this compares to throwing a CException class, rather than the HTTP exception class. Let's comment out the current line of code throwing the HTTP exception and add a new line to throw this other exception class. Make the highlighted changes to the protected/controllers/ProjectController.php file:

```
public function loadModel($id)
   {
      $model=Project::model()->findByPk($id);
```

```
    if($model===null)
        //throw new CHttpException(404,'The requested page does not
exist.');
        throw new CException('This is an example of throwing a
CException');
    return $model;
}
```

Now if we make our request for a nonexistent project, we see a very different result. This time we see a system generated error page with a full stack trace error info dump along with the specific source file where the error occurred:

CException

This is an example of throwing a CException

/Webroot/trackstar/protected/controllers/ProjectController.php(215)

```
203
204
205     /**
206      * Returns the data model based on the primary key given in the GET variable.
207      * If the data model is not found, an HTTP exception will be raised.
208      * @param integer the ID of the model to be loaded
209      */
210     public function loadModel($id)
211     {
212         $model=Project::model()->findByPk($id);
213         if($model===null)
214             //throw new CHttpException(404,'The requested page does not exist.');
215             throw new CException('This is an example of throwing a CException');
216         return $model;
217     }
218
219     /**
220      * Performs the AJAX validation.
221      * @param CModel the model to be validated
222      */
223     protected function performAjaxValidation($model)
224     {
225         if(isset($_POST['ajax']) && $_POST['ajax']==='project-form')
226         {
227             echo CActiveForm::validate($model);
```

Stack Trace

```
#0  ☐ /Webroot/trackstar/protected/controllers/ProjectController.php(30): ProjectController->loadModel("99")
```

It displays the fact that a CException class was thrown along with the description **This is an example of throwing a CException**, the source file, specific line in the file where the error occurred, and then the full stack trace.

So, throwing this different exception class, along with the fact the application is in debug mode, has a different result. This is the type of information we would like to display to help troubleshoot the problem, but only as long as our application is running in a private development environment. Let's temporarily comment out the debug setting in the root `index.php` file in order to see how this would display when in "production" mode:

```
// remove the following line when in production mode
//defined('YII_DEBUG') or define('YII_DEBUG',true);
```

With this commented out, if we refresh our request for our nonexistent project, we see that the exception is displayed as an end user friendly HTTP 500 error, as depicted in the following screenshot:

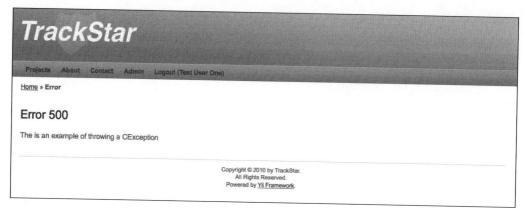

So we see that none of our sensitive code or stack trace information is displayed when in the "production" mode.

Caching

Caching data is a great method for helping to improve the performance of a production web application. If there is specific content that is not expected to change upon every request, using a cache to store and serve this content can decrease the time it takes to retrieve and process that data.

Yii provides some nice features when it comes to caching. To take advantage of Yii's caching features, you begin with configuring a cache application component. Such a component is one of several child classes extending CCache, the base class for cache classes with different cache storage implementations.

Yii provides many specific cache component class implementations that store the data utilizing different approaches. The following is a list of the current cache implementations that Yii provides as of Version 1.1.12:

- CMemCache: Uses the PHP memcache extension.

- CApcCache: Uses the PHP APC extension.

- CXCache: Uses PHP XCache extension.

- CEAcceleratorCache: Uses the PHP EAccelerator extension.

- CDbCache: Uses a database table to store cached data. By default, it will create and use a SQLite3 database under the runtime directory. You can explicitly specify a database for it to use by setting its connectionID property.

- CZendDataCache: Uses Zend Data Cache as the underlying caching medium.

- CFileCache: Uses files to store cached data. This is particularly suitable to cache a large chunk of data (such as pages).

- CDummyCache: Presents the consistent cache interface, but does not actually perform any caching. The reason for this implementation is that if you are faced with a situation where your development environment does not have cache support, you can still execute and test your code that will need to use cache once available. This allows you to continue to code to a consistent interface, and when the time comes to actually implement a real caching component you will not need to change the code written to write or retrieve data from cache.

- CWinCache: CWinCache implements a cache application component based on WinCache. For more information visit http://www.iis.net/expand/wincacheforphp.

All of these components extend from the same base class, CCache, and expose a consistent API. This means that you can change the implementation of the application component in order to use a different caching strategy without having to change any of the code that is using the cache.

Cache configuration

As was mentioned, using cache in Yii typically involves choosing one of these implementations and then configuring the application component for use in the /protected/config/main.php file. The specifics of the configuration will, of course, depend on the specific cache implementation. For example, if one were to use the memcached implementation, that is CMemCache, which is a distributed memory object caching system that allows you to specify multiple host servers as your cache servers, configuring it to use two servers might look something like the following:

```
array(
    ......
    'components'=>array(
        ......
        'cache'=>array(
            'class'=>'system.caching.CMemCache',
            'servers'=>array(
                array('host'=>'server1', 'port'=>12345, 'weight'=>60),
                array('host'=>'server2', 'port'=>12345, 'weight'=>40),
            ),
        ),
    ),
);
```

To keep things relatively simple for the reader following along with the TrackStar development, we'll use the filesystem implementation CFileCache as we go through some examples. This should be readily available on any development environment that allows read and write access to files from the filesystem.

> If for some reason this is not an option for you but you still want to follow along with the code examples, simply use the CDummyCache option. As mentioned, it won't actually store any data in the cache, but you can still write code against its API and change the implementation at a later time.

CFileCache provides a file-based caching mechanism. When using this implementation, each data value being cached is stored in a separate file. By default, these files are stored under the protected/runtime/cache/ directory, but one can easily change this by setting the cachePath property when configuring the component. For our purposes this default is fine, so we simply need to add the following to the components array in our /protected/config/main.php configuration file, as such:

```
// application components
  'components'=>array(
```

```
...
'cache'=>array(
        'class'=>'system.caching.CFileCache',
    ),
    ...
),
```

With this in place, we can access this new application component anywhere in our running application via `Yii::app()->cache`.

Using a file-based cache

Let's try out this new component. Remember that system message we added as part of our administrative functionality in the previous chapter? Rather than retrieving it from the database upon every request, let's store the value initially returned from the database in our cache for a limited amount of time so that not every request has to retrieve the data from the database.

Let's add a new public method to our `SysMessage` (`/protected/modules/admin/models/SysMessage.php`) AR model class to handle the retrieval of the latest system messages. Let's make this new method both `public` and `static` so that other parts of the application can easily use this method to access the latest system message without having to explicitly create an instance of `SysMessage`.

Add our method to the `SysMessage` class as follows:

```
/**
 * Retrieves the most recent system message.
 * @return SysMessage the AR instance representing the latest system
message.
 */

public static function getLatest()
{

  //see if it is in the cache, if so, just return it
  if( ($cache=Yii::app()->cache)!==null)
  {
    $key='TrackStar.ProjectListing.SystemMessage';
    if(($sysMessage=$cache->get($key))!==false)
      return $sysMessage;
  }
  //The system message was either not found in the cache, or
  //there is no cache component defined for the application
  //retrieve the system message from the database
```

```
$sysMessage = SysMessage::model()->find(array(
    'order'=>'t.update_time DESC',
));
if($sysMessage != null)
{
    //a valid message was found. Store it in cache for future
retrievals
    if(isset($key))
        $cache->set($key,$sysMessage,300);
        return $sysMessage;
}
else
    return null;
}
```

We'll cover the details in just a minute. First, let's change our application to use this new method to verify whether caching is working. We still need to change the `Project Controller::actionIndex()` method to use this newly created method. This is easy. Just replace the code that was generating the system message from the database, with a call to this new method. That is, in `ProjectController::actionIndex()`, simply change the following code:

```
$sysMessage = SysMessage::model()->find(array('order'=>'t.update_time
DESC',));
```

To the following:

```
$sysMessage = SysMessage::getLatest();
```

Now the system message being displayed on the projects listing page should be taking advantage of the file cache. We can check the cache directory to verify.

If we do a directory listing for the default location being used for file caching, `protected/runtime/cache/`, we do indeed see that a couple of files were created. Both of them rather strangely named (yours may be slightly different) `18baacd81490 0e9b36b3b2e546513ce8.bin` and `2d0efd21cf59ad6eb310a0d70b25a854.bin`.

One holds our system message data and the other is from our configuration of `CUrlManager` from previous chapters. By default, `CUrlManager` will use the cache component to cache the parsed URL rules. You can set the `cacheId` parameter of `CUrlManager` to `false` to disable caching for this component.

If we open up the `18baacd814900e9b36b3b2e546513ce8.bin` file as text, we can see the following:

```
a:2:{i:0;O:10:"SysMessage":12:{s:18:" :" CActiveRecord _ _md";N;s:19:"
:" CActiveRecord _ _new";b:0;s:26:" :" CActiveRecord _ _attributes"
;a:6:{s:2:"id";s:1:"2";s:7:"message";s:56:"This is a second message
from your system administrator!";s:11:"create_time";s:19:"2012-07-31
21:25:33";s:14:"create_user_id";s:1:"1";s:11:"update_
time";s:19:"2012-07-31 21:25:33";s:14:"update_user_id";s:1:"1";}
s:23:" :"18CActiveRecord _18_related";a:0:{}s:17:" :" CActiveRecord
_ _c";N;s:18:" 18:" CActiveRecord _ _:" _pk";s:1:"2";s:21:"
:" CActiveRecord _ _alias";s:1:"t";s:15:" :" CModel _ _
errors";a:0:{}s:19:" :" CModel _ _validators";N;s:17:" :" CModel
_ _scenario";s:6:"update";s:14:" :" CComponent _ _e";N;s:14:" :"
CComponent _ _m";N;}i:1;N;}
```

This is the serialized cached value of our most recently updated SysMessage AR class instance, which is exactly what we would expect to be there. So, we see that the caching is actually working.

Now let's revisit the code for our new `SysMessage::getLatest()` method in a bit more detail. The first thing the code is doing is checking to see if the requested data is already in the cache, and if so returning that value:

```
//see if it is in the cache, if so, just return it
if( ($cache=Yii::app()->cache)!==null)
{
    $key='TrackStar.ProjectListing.SystemMessage';
    if(($sysMessage=$cache->get($key))!==false)
      return $sysMessage;
}
```

As we mentioned, we configured the cache application component to be available anywhere in the application via `Yii::app()->cache`. So, it first checks to see if there even is such a component defined. If so, it attempts to look up the data in the cache via the `$cache->get($key)` method. This does more or less what you would expect. It attempts to retrieve a value from the cache based on the specified key. The key is a unique string identifier that is used to map to each piece of data stored in the cache. In our system message example, we only need to display one message at a time and therefore can have a fairly simple key identify the single system message to display. The key can be any string value as long as it remains unique for each piece of data we want to cache. In this case we have chosen the descriptive string `TrackStar.ProjectListing.SystemMessage` as the key used when storing and retrieving our cached system message.

When this code is executed for the very first time, there will not yet be any data associated with this key value in the cache. Therefore, a call to `$cache->get()` for this key will return `false`. So, our method will continue to the next bit of code, which simply attempts to retrieve the appropriate system message from the database, using the AR class:

```
$sysMessage = SysMessage::model()->find(array(
    'order'=>'t.update_time DESC',
));
```

We then proceed with the following code that first checks if we did get anything back from the database. If we did, it stores it in the cache before returning the value; otherwise, `null` is returned:

```
if($sysMessage != null)
{
    if(isset($key))
        $cache->set($key,$sysMessage->message,300);
        return $sysMessage->message;
}
else
    return null;
```

If a valid system message was returned, we use the `$cache->set()` method to store the data into the cache. This method has the following general form:

```
set($key,$value,$duration=0,$dependency=null)
```

When placing a piece of data into the cache, one must specify a unique key as well as the data to be stored. The key is a unique string value, as discussed previously, and the value is whatever data is desired to be cached. This can be in any format as long as it can be serialized. The duration parameter specifies an optional **time-to-live** (**TTL**) requirement. This can be used to ensure that the cached value is refreshed after some period of time. The default is `0`, which means it will never expire. (Actually, internally, Yii translates a value of `<=0` for the duration to expire in one year. So, not exactly *never*, but definitely a long time.)

We call the `set()` method in the following manner:

```
$cache->set($key,$sysMessage->message,300);
```

We set the key to be what we had defined it before, `TrackStar.ProjectListing.SystemMessage`; the data being stored is the message attribute of our returned `SystemMessage` AR class, that is the message column of our `tbl_sys_message` table; and then we set the duration to be `300` seconds. This way, the data in the cache will expire every 5 minutes, at which time the database is queried again for the most recent system message. We did not specify a dependency when we set the data. We'll discuss this optional parameter next.

Cache dependencies

The dependency parameter allows for an alternative and much more sophisticated approach to deciding whether or not the stored data in the cache should be refreshed. Rather than declaring a simple time period for the expiration of cached data, your caching strategy may require that the data become invalid based on things such as the specific user making the request, the general mode, state of the application, or whether a file on the file system has been recently updated. This parameter allows you to specify such cache validation rules.

The dependency is an instance of `CCacheDependency` or its child class. Yii makes available the following specific cache dependencies:

- `CFileCacheDependency`: The data in the cache will be invalid if the specified file's last modification time has changed since the previous cache lookup.

- `CDirectoryCacheDependency`: Similar to the previous one for the file cache dependency, but this checks all the files and subdirectories within a given specified directory.

- `CDbCacheDependency`: The data in the cache will be invalid if the query result of a specified SQL statement is changed since the previous cache lookup.

- `CGlobalStateCacheDependency`: The data in the cache will be invalid if the value of the specified global state is changed. A global state is a variable that is persistent across multiple requests and multiple sessions in an application. It is defined via `CApplication::setGlobalState()`.

- `CChainedCacheDependency`: This allows you to chain together multiple dependencies. The data in the cache will become invalid if any of the dependencies on the chain are changed.

- `CExpressionDependency`: The data in the cache will be invalid if the result of the specified PHP expression is changed.

To provide a concrete example, let's use a dependency to expire the data in the cache whenever a change to the `tbl_sys_message` database table is made. Rather than arbitrarily expiring our cached system message after five minutes, we'll expire it exactly when we need to, that is, when there has been a change to the `update_time` column for one of the system messages in the table. We'll use the `CDbCacheDependency` implementation to achieve this, since it is designed to invalidate cached data based on a change in the results of a SQL query.

We alter our call to the `set()` method to set the duration time to `0` so that it won't expire based on time but pass in a new dependency instance with our specified SQL statement, as such:

```
$cache->set($key, $sysMessage, 0, new CDbCacheDependency('SELECT
MAX(update_time) FROM tbl_sys_message'));
```

Changing the duration TTL time to `0` is not at all a prerequisite of using a dependency. We could have just as easily left the duration in as `300` seconds. This would just stipulate another rule to render the data in the cache invalid. The data would only be valid in the cache for a maximum of 5 minutes, but would also be regenerated prior to this time limit if there is a newer message, that is, a later `update_time` value in the table.

With this in place, the cache will only expire when the results of the query statement are changed. This example is a little contrived, since we were originally caching the data to avoid a database call altogether. Now we have configured it to execute a database query every time we attempt to retrieve data from the cache. However, if the cached data was a much more complex data set that involved much more overhead to retrieve and process, a simple SQL statement for cache validity could make a lot of sense. The specific caching implementation, the data stored, the expiration time, as well as any other data validation in the form of these dependencies, will all depend on the specific requirements of the application being built. It is good to know that Yii has many options available to help meet our varied requirements.

Query caching

The query caching approach of caching a database result is so often needed in database driven applications that Yii provides an even easier implementation for this, called **query caching**. As its name implies, query caching stores the results of a database query in cache and saves the query execution time on subsequent requests as these are served directly from cache. In order to enable a query, you need to ensure the `queryCacheID` property of the `CDbConnection` property refers to the `ID` attribute of a valid cache component. It refers to `'cache'` by default, which is what we already have configured from the preceding cache example.

To use query caching, we simply call the `cache()` method of `CDbConnection`. This method takes in a duration, to specify the number of seconds the query is to remain in cache. If the duration is set to `0`, caching is disabled. You can also specify a `CCacheDependency` instance as a second argument, and specify how many subsequent queries should be cached as a third argument. This third argument defaults to `1`, which means that only the next SQL query will be cached.

So, let's change our previous cache implementation to use this cool query caching feature. Using the query caching, our implementation of the `SysMessage::getLatest()` method is greatly simplified. All we need to do is the following:

```
//use the query caching approach
$dependency = new CDbCacheDependency('SELECT MAX(update_time) FROM
tbl_sys_message');
$sysMessage = SysMessage::model()->cache(1800, $dependency)-
>find(array(
    'order'=>'t.update_time DESC',
));
return $sysMessage;
```

Here we have the same basic approach as before, but we don't have to deal with the explicit checking and setting of the cached values. We called the `cache()` method to indicate we want to cache the result for 30 minutes or, by specifying the dependency, refresh the value before that time if a more recent message becomes available.

Fragment caching

The previous examples demonstrate the use of data caching. This is where we take a single piece of data and store it in the cache. There are other approaches available in Yii to store fragments of pages generated by a portion of a view script or even the entire page itself.

Fragment caching refers to caching a fragment of a page. We can take advantage of fragment caching inside view scripts. To do so, we use the `CController::beginCache()` and `CController::endCache()` methods. These two methods are used to mark the beginning and the end of the rendered page content that should be stored in cache. Just as is the case when using a data caching approach, we need a unique key to identify the content being cached. In general, the syntax for using fragment caching inside a view script is as follows:

```
...some HTML content...
<?php
if($this->beginCache($id))
{
```

```
// ...content you want to cache here
$this->endCache();
}
?>
...other HTML content...
```

The method `beginCache()` returns `false` when there is a cached version available, and the cached content will be automatically inserted at that place; otherwise, the content inside the if-statement will be executed and will be cached when `endCache()` is invoked.

Declaring fragment caching options

When calling `beginCache()`, we can supply an array as the second parameter consisting of caching options to customize the fragment caching. As a matter of fact, the `beginCache()` and `endCache()` methods are a convenient wrapper of the `COutputCache` filter/widget. Therefore, the caching options can be initial values for any properties of the `COutputCache` class.

Arguably one of the most common options specified when caching data is the duration, which specifies how long the content can remain valid in the cache. It is similar to the `duration` parameter we used when caching our system messages. You can specify the `duration` parameter when calling `beginCache()` as follows:

```
$this->beginCache($key, array('duration'=>3600))
```

The default setting for this fragment caching approach is different than that for the data caching. If we do not set the duration it defaults to 60 seconds, meaning the cached content will be invalidated after 60 seconds. There are many other options you can set when using fragment caching. For more information, refer to the API documentation for `COutputCache` as well as the fragment caching section of the Yii definitive guide, available on the Yii framework site: http://www.yiiframework.com/doc/guide/1.1/en/caching.fragment

Using fragment cache

Let's implement this in our TrackStar application. We'll again focus on the project listings page. As you may recall, towards the bottom of the project listings page there is a list of the comments that users have left on the issues associated with each project. This list just indicates who left a comment on which issue. Rather than regenerating this list upon each request, let's use fragment caching to cache this list for, say, two minutes. The application can tolerate this data being slightly stale, and two minutes is really not that long to have to wait for an updated comment list.

To do this, we make our changes to the listing view file, `protected/views/` `project/index.php`. We'll wrap the call to our entire recent comments portlet inside this fragment caching approach, as such:

```php
<?php
$key = "TrackStar.ProjectListing.RecentComments";
if($this->beginCache($key, array('duration'=>120))) {
    $this->beginWidget('zii.widgets.CPortlet', array(
      'title'=>'Recent Comments',
    ));
    $this->widget('RecentCommentsWidget');
    $this->endWidget();
    $this->endCache();
}
?>
```

With this in place, if we visit the project listings page for the first time, our comments list will be stored in the cache. If we then quickly (by quickly, we mean before two minutes have elapsed) add a new comment to one of the issues within a project, and then toggle back to the project listings page, we won't immediately see the newly added comment. But if we keep refreshing the page, once the content in the cache expires (a maximum of two minutes in this case), the data will be refreshed and our new comment will be displayed in the listing.

> You could also simply add an `echo time();` PHP statement to the previously cached content to see if it is working as expected. If the content is properly caching, the time display will not update until the cache is refreshed. When using the file cache, remember to ensure that your `/protected/runtime/` directory is writable by the web server process, as this is where the cache content is stored by default.

We could avoid this situation by declaring a cache dependency, rather than a fixed duration. Fragment caching also supports cache dependencies. So, we could change the `beginCache()` method call, seen previously, to the following:

```php
if($this->beginCache($key, array('dependency'=>array(
        'class'=>'system.caching.dependencies.CDbCacheDependency',
        'sql'=>'SELECT MAX(update_time) FROM tbl_comment')))) {
```

Here we have used the `CDbCacheDependency` method to cache the content until an update is made to our comments table.

Page caching

In addition to fragment caching, Yii offers options to cache the results of the entire page request. The page caching approach is similar to the fragment caching approach. However, because the content of an entire page is often generated by applying additional layouts to a view, we can't simply call beginCache() and endCache() in the layout file. The reason is that the layout is applied within the call to the CController::render() method after the content view is evaluated. So, we would always miss the opportunity to retrieve the content from the cache.

Therefore, to cache a whole page, we should entirely skip the execution of the action generating the page content. To accomplish this, we can use the COutputCache class as an action filter in our controller class.

As an example, let's use the page caching approach to cache the page results for every project detail page. The project detail pages in TrackStar are rendered by requesting URLs of the format http://localhost/trackstar/project/view/id/[id], where [id] is the specific project ID we are requesting the details of. What we want to do is set up a page caching filter that will cache the entire contents of this page separately for every ID requested. We need to incorporate the project ID into the key value when we cache the content. That is, we don't want to make a request for the details of project #1 and have the application return a cached result for project #2. The COutputCache filter allows us to do just that.

Open up protected/controllers/ProjectController.php and alter the existing filters() method as such:

```
public function filters()
{
  return array(
    'accessControl', // perform access control for CRUD operations
    array(
            'COutputCache + view',  //cache the entire output from the
  actionView() method for 2 minutes
            'duration'=>120,
            'varyByParam'=>array('id'),
        ),
  );
}
```

This filter configuration utilizes the `COutputCache` filter to cache the entire output generated by the application from a call to `ProjectController::actionView()`. The `+ view` parameter added just after the `COutputCache` declaration, as you may recall, is the standard way we include specific action methods to which a filter should apply. The duration parameter specifies a TTL of 120 seconds (two minutes), after which the page content will be regenerated.

The `varyByParam` configuration is a really great option that we alluded to before. Rather than putting the responsibility on you, the developer, to come up with a unique key strategy for the content being cached, this feature allows the variation to be handled automatically. For example, in this case, by specifying a list of names that correspond to GET parameters in the input request. Since we are caching the page content of requests for projects by `project_id`, it makes perfect sense to use this ID as part of the unique key generation for caching the content. By specifying `'varyByParam'=>array('id')`, `COutputCache` does this for us based on the input querystring parameter `id`. There are more options available to achieve this type of autocontent variation strategy when using `COutputCache` to cache our data. As of Yii 1.1.12, the following variation features are available:

- **varyByRoute**: By setting this option to `true`, the specific request route will be incorporated into the unique identifier for the cached data. Therefore, you can use the combination of the requested controller and action to distinguish cached content.

- **varyBySession**: By setting this option to `true`, a unique session ID is used to distinguish the content in the cache. Each user session may see different content, but all of this content can still be served from the cache.

- **varyByParam**: As discussed earlier, this uses the input GET querystring parameters to distinguish the content in the cache.

- **varyByExpression**: By setting this option to a PHP expression, we can use the result of this expression to distinguish the content in the cache.

So, with the above filter configured in our `ProjectController` class, each request for a specific project details page is stored in the cache for two minutes before being regenerated and again stored in the cache. You can test this out by first viewing a specific project, then updating that project in some way. Your updates will not be immediately displayed if done within the cache duration time of two minutes.

Caching entire page results is a great way to improve site performance, however it certainly does not make sense for every page in every application to be cached. Even in our example, caching the entire page for the project details page does not allow us to correctly use our pagination implementation for our issues listing. We used this as a quick example of how to implement page caching, but it is not always the right approach in every case. A combination of these three approaches, data, fragment, and page caching, allows you to adjust your caching strategy to meet your application requirements. We have really just scratched the surface of all caching options available within Yii. Hopefully this has whet your appetite to further investigate the full caching landscape available.

General performance tuning tips

As you are preparing your application for production, there are a few other things to take into consideration. The following sections briefly outline some other areas of consideration when working to tweak the performance of a Yii-based web application.

Using APC

Enabling the PHP APC extension is perhaps the easiest way to improve the overall performance of an application. The extension caches and optimizes PHP intermediate code and avoids the time spent in parsing PHP scripts for every incoming request.

It also provides a very fast storage mechanism for cached content. With APC enabled, you can use the CApcCache implementation for caching content, fragments, and pages.

Disabling the debug mode

We discussed the debug mode earlier in the chapter, but it won't hurt to hear it again. Disabling debug mode is another easy way to improve performance and security. A Yii application runs in debug mode if the constant YII_DEBUG is defined as true in the main index.php entry script. Many components, including those down in the framework itself, incur extra overhead when running in the debug mode.

Also, as was mentioned way back in *Chapter 2, Getting Started*, when we first created a Yii application, most of your Yii application files do not need to be, nor should they be, in the publically accessible web directory. A Yii application has just one entry script, which is often the only file that needs to be placed in the web directory. Other PHP scripts, including all of the Yii framework files, should be protected. This is why the default name of the primary application directory is called protected/. To avoid security issues, it is recommended to keep it from being publicly accessible.

Using yiilite.php

When the PHP APC extension is enabled, one can replace yii.php with a different Yii bootstrap file named yiilite.php. This can help to further boost the performance of a Yii-powered application. The file yiilite.php comes with every Yii release. It is the result of merging some commonly used Yii class files. Both comments and trace statements are stripped from the merged file. Therefore, using yiilite.php would reduce the number of files being included and avoid execution of trace statements.

> Note that using yiilite.php without APC may actually reduce performance. This is because yiilite.php contains some classes that are not necessarily used in every request and would take extra parsing time. It is also observed that using yiilite.php is slower with some server configurations; even when APC is turned on. The best way to judge whether to use yiilite.php or not is to run a benchmark using the "Hello World" demo that is included in the code bundle.

Using caching techniques

As we described and demonstrated in this chapter, Yii provides many caching solutions that may improve the performance of a web application significantly. If the generation of some data takes a long time, we can use the data caching approach to reduce the data generation frequency; if a portion of page remains relatively static, we can use the fragment caching approach to reduce its rendering frequency; if a whole page remains relative static, we can use the page caching approach to save the rendering cost for the whole page.

Enabling schema caching

If the application is using **Active Record (AR)**, you can turn on the schema caching in a production environment to save the time of parsing database schema. This can be done by configuring the CDbConnection::schemaCachingDuration property to be a value greater than zero.

Besides these application-level caching techniques, we can also use server-side caching solutions to boost the application's performance. The enabling of APC caching that we described here, belongs to this category. There are other server-side techniques, such as Zend Optimizer, eAccelerator, and Squid, just to name a few.

These, for the most part, just provide some good practice guidelines as you work to prepare your Yii application for production or troubleshoot an existing application for bottlenecks. General application performance tuning is much more of an art than a science, and there are many, many factors outside of the Yii framework that play into the overall performance. Yii has been built with performance in mind since its inception and continues to outperform many other PHP-based application development frameworks by a long shot (see `http://www.yiiframework.com/performance/` for more details). Of course, every single web application will need to be tweaked to enhance the performance, but making Yii the development framework of choice certainly puts your application on a great performance footing from the onset.

For further details, see the *Performance Tuning* section of the Yii definitive guide at `http://www.yiiframework.com/doc/guide/1.1/en/topics.performance`.

Summary

In this chapter, we have turned our attention to making changes to our application in order to help improve its maintainability and performance in a production environment. We first covered application logging strategies available in Yii, and how to log and route messages based on varying severity levels and categories. We then turned our focus to error handling and how Yii exploits the underlying exception implementation in PHP 5 to provide a flexible and robust error handling framework. We then learned about some different caching strategies available in Yii. We learned about the caching of application data and content at varying levels of granularity. Data caching for specific variables or individual pieces of data, fragment caching for content areas within pages, and full page caching to cache the entire rendered output of a page request. Finally, we provided a list of good practices to follow when working to improve the performance of a Yii-powered web application.

Congratulations! We should pat ourselves on the back. We have created an entire web application from conception to production readiness. Of course we should pat Yii on the back as well, as it helped ease and quicken the process at every turn. Our TrackStar application is already pretty great; but as is the case with all such projects, there is always room for enhancement and improvement. A nice foundation has been laid on which to build, and now that you have the power of Yii on your side you could very quickly turn this into a much more useable and feature-rich application. Also a great many of the examples covered will translate well to other types of web applications you may be building. I hope you now feel confident using Yii and will enjoy the benefits of doing so on your future projects. Happy developing!

Index

using 298, 299
functional tests 50

G

Generate button 28
getHelp() method 170
getTypeOptions() method 93
getUserOptions() method 105
Gii
  about 26
  configuring 61
  used, to create Project AR class 62-65
Gii code creation tool
  using, to create model class 126
Gii code generator 265
Gii tool 189
goodbye.php 36
Graphical User Interface (GUI) 168

H

hasFlash() method 183
Hello World! program
  about 26
  controller, creating 26
  Gii, configuring 26-30
  hello.php view, customizing 30
  request routing, reviewing 31
high-level tasks 225
home page
  last login time, displaying 149, 150

I

identity states 148
importArray() method 215
index.php file 218
init() method 204, 258
installing
  about 20
  database 22
  packages, URL 20
  steps 20, 21
  Yii 19-21
  Zend Framework 212, 213
interactive shell
  using 49

Internationalization 244
IPs parameter 158
Issue AR class 193
Issue::attributeLabels() method 91
IssueController::actionAdmin()
    method 118-120
IssueController::actionCreate() method 105
IssueController::actionIndex()
    method 118-120
IssueController::actionView() method 193,
    194, 202
IssueController class 155
IssueController::filters() method 119
IssueController::loadModel() method 202
issue CRUD operations
  creating 85
  issues, listing 108
  new issue, creating 87, 88
  project controller, altering 108, 109
  project view file, altering 109-111
  using 86
issue detail view
  changing 114-116
Issue::getStatusText() method 116
Issue::getTypeText() method 116
Issue model class
  creating 85
Issue::relations() method 116, 190
Issue::rules() method 91
Issue::search() method 120
Issue::search() model class method 121
isUserInRole() method 179

J

jQuery 273

L

labelEx() method 91
language translation
  performing 245, 246
last login time
  displaying, on home page 149, 150
last_login_time attribute 134
last_login_time field 148
layout
  about 226

O

Object Relational Mapping. *See* **ORM**
objects
  building 81-84
one-to-many relationship 190
ORM 16, 85
owner and requester fields
  data, generating 105-107
  dropdowns choices, setting 102-105
  fixing 95
  project context, enforcing 95
owner and requester names
  displaying 116
  relational AR, using 116, 117

P

pages
  linking 35
  new page, linking to 35, 36
params property 255
partial views 194
password confirmation field
  adding 136-138
performance tuning, tips
  APC, using 302
  caching techniques, using 303
  debug mode, disabling 302
  schema caching, enabling 303, 304
  yiilite.php, using 303
per-project basis
  roles, adding to users 171
PHP Data Objects (PDO) extension
  URL 46
PHPUnit
  installing 52
  URL 52
pid querystring parameter 122
portlets
  about 198
  URL, for info 187
postFilter() method 96
preFilter() method 96
production environment
  preparing, granular tasks 275
Project AR class 175

  creating, Gii used 62-65
project context
  about 95
  filter, adding 96
  filtered actions, specifying 97
  filter logic, adding 98, 99
  filters, defining 96
  project details page, altering 101
  project ID, adding 100
project controller
  new action method, adding 179, 180
ProjectController::actionAdduser()
    method 185
ProjectController::actionIndex()
    method 222, 271, 292
ProjectController::actionView()
    method 223
ProjectController class 177, 179
ProjectController classes 155
ProjectController::loadModel() method 285
project details page
  widget, adding to 207, 208
project issues
  managing 79
project members
  about 41, 154
  using 41
project model class
  altering 177
project owner 41, 154
project reader 154
projects
  CRUD operations, enabling 65
  deleting 74
  form field validation 69-73
  in admin role, managing 74-76
  new project, creating 68, 69
  operations, enabling for projects 65
  reading 73
  scaffolding, creating 65, 66
  table, creating 56, 57
  updating 74
projects, TrackStar
  about 40, 41
  issues 41
project table
  creating 56

ProjectUserForm 176

Q

query caching 296

R

RBAC
  about 153, 160
  authorization hierarchy, creating 166, 167
  authorization manager, configuring 162
  business rules, adding 173
  console application command,
      writing 167-170
  database tables, creating 162-165
  new action method, adding to project
      controller 179, 180
  new form model class, adding 178, 179
  new project AR methods, implementing
      174, 175
  new view file, adding to display
      form 181, 183
  project model class, altering 177
  roles adding to users, on per-project
      basis 171, 172
  users, adding to projects 176, 177
  users, assigning to roles 170
rbac command 261
Really Simple Syndication (RSS) 212
RecentComments widget 206
RecentCommentsWidget::getData()
      method 205
registerLinkTag() method 223
relational AR queries, Yii 200-203
relations() method 104
render() method 194, 227, 257
renderPartial() method 194, 257
Reversish 247
Role Based Access Control. *See* RBAC
roles
  adding, to users on per-project basis 171
roles parameter 158
routing rules
  configuring 218, 219
r querystring variable 14
RSS feed 211

RSS feed link
  adding 222, 223
rules() method 69, 134, 139
rules() public function 70
run() method 204

S

safeDown() method 59, 84
safeUp() method 59, 84
save() method 139
scaffolding code
  altering 192
  comments, adding 193, 194
  form, displaying 194-198
schema
  designing 80
  entity-relationship 81
  many-to-many relationship 81
scopes() method 200
send() method 215
shell command 261
simple access control filter 153
SiteController 15
SiteController::actionError() method 286
SiteController::actionLogin() method 143,
      180, 280
SiteController class action method 160
software development life cycle (SDLC) 39
source language 246
statistical queries 190
status and type text
  displaying 112
  text display, adding to form 113
SysMessageController::accessRules()
      method 269
SysMessage::getLatest() method 293
system-wide message
  CRUD scaffolding, creating 265, 266
  database table, creating for 264
  managing 263
  model class, creating 265, 266

T

table
  creating, for comments 188-191

Thank you for buying
Web Application Development with Yii and PHP
Second Edition

About Packt Publishing

Packt, pronounced 'packed', published its first book "*Mastering phpMyAdmin for Effective MySQL Management*" in April 2004 and subsequently continued to specialize in publishing highly focused books on specific technologies and solutions.

Our books and publications share the experiences of your fellow IT professionals in adapting and customizing today's systems, applications, and frameworks. Our solution based books give you the knowledge and power to customize the software and technologies you're using to get the job done. Packt books are more specific and less general than the IT books you have seen in the past. Our unique business model allows us to bring you more focused information, giving you more of what you need to know, and less of what you don't.

Packt is a modern, yet unique publishing company, which focuses on producing quality, cutting-edge books for communities of developers, administrators, and newbies alike. For more information, please visit our website: www.packtpub.com.

About Packt Open Source

In 2010, Packt launched two new brands, Packt Open Source and Packt Enterprise, in order to continue its focus on specialization. This book is part of the Packt Open Source brand, home to books published on software built around Open Source licences, and offering information to anybody from advanced developers to budding web designers. The Open Source brand also runs Packt's Open Source Royalty Scheme, by which Packt gives a royalty to each Open Source project about whose software a book is sold.

Writing for Packt

We welcome all inquiries from people who are interested in authoring. Book proposals should be sent to author@packtpub.com. If your book idea is still at an early stage and you would like to discuss it first before writing a formal book proposal, contact us; one of our commissioning editors will get in touch with you.

We're not just looking for published authors; if you have strong technical skills but no writing experience, our experienced editors can help you develop a writing career, or simply get some additional reward for your expertise.

Yii 1.1 Application Development Cookbook

ISBN: 978-1-84951-548-1 Paperback: 392 pages

Over 80 recipes to help you master using the Yii PHP framework

1. Learn to use Yii more efficiently through plentiful Yii recipes on diverse topics

2. Make the most efficient use of your controller and views and reuse them

3. Automate error tracking and understand the Yii log and stack trace

4. Full of practically useful solutions and concepts that you can use in your application, with clearly explained code and all the necessary screenshots

WordPress 3 Complete

ISBN: 978-1-84951-410-1 Paperback: 344 pages

Create your own complete website or blog from search with WordPress

1. Learn everything you need for creating your own feature-rich website or blog from scratch

2. Clear and practical explanations of all aspects of WordPress

3. In-depth coverage of installation, themes, plugins, and syndication

4. Explore WordPress as a fully functional content management system

5. Clear, easy-to-follow, concise; rich with examples and screenshots

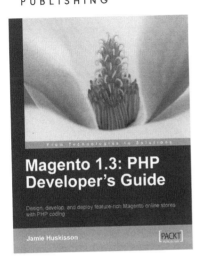
Magento 1.3: PHP Developer's Guide

ISBN: 978-1-84719-742-9   Paperback: 260 pages

Design, develop, and deploy feature-rich Magento online stores with PHP coding

1. Extend and customize the Magento e-commerce system using PHP code

2. Set up your own data profile to import or export data in Magento

3. Build applications that interface with the customer, product, and order data using Magento's Core API

4. Packed with examples for effective Magento Development

Zend Framework 1.8 Web Application Development

ISBN: 978-1-84719-422-0   Paperback: 380 pages

Design, develop, and deploy feature-rich PHP web applications with this MVC framework

1. Create powerful web applications by leveraging the power of this Model-View-Controller-based framework

2. Learn by doing – create a "real-life" storefront application

3. Covers access control, performance optimization, and testing

4. Best practices, as well as debugging and designing discussion

Please check **www.PacktPub.com** for information on our titles

Made in the USA
San Bernardino, CA
11 January 2013